D0875259

# Bloom's Modern Critical Interpretations

The Adventures of
  Huckleberry Finn
The Age of Innocence
Alice's Adventures in
  Wonderland
All Quiet on the
  Western Front
Animal Farm
Antony and Cleopatra
The Awakening
The Ballad of the Sad
  Café
Beloved
Beowulf
Black Boy
The Bluest Eye
Brave New World
The Canterbury Tales
Cat on a Hot Tin
  Roof
Catch-22
The Catcher in the
  Rye
The Chronicles of
  Narnia
The Color Purple
Crime and
  Punishment
The Crucible
Cry, the Beloved
  Country
Darkness at Noon
Death of a Salesman
The Death of Artemio
  Cruz
The Diary of Anne
  Frank
Don Quixote
Emerson's Essays
Emma
Fahrenheit 451
A Farewell to Arms
Frankenstein
F. Scott Fitzgerald's
  Short Stories
The Glass Menagerie

The Grapes of Wrath
Great Expectations
The Great Gatsby
Gulliver's Travels
Hamlet
Heart of Darkness
The House on Mango
  Street
I Know Why the
  Caged Bird Sings
The Iliad
Invisible Man
Jane Eyre
John Steinbeck's Short
  Stories
The Joy Luck Club
J.D. Salinger's Short
  Stories
Julius Caesar
The Jungle
King Lear
Long Day's Journey
  into Night
Lord of the Flies
The Lord of the
  Rings
Love in the Time of
  Cholera
Macbeth
The Man Without
  Qualities
Mark Twain's Short
  Stories
The Merchant of
  Venice
The Metamorphosis
A Midsummer Night's
  Dream
Miss Lonelyhearts
Moby-Dick
My Ántonia
Native Son
Night
1984
The Odyssey
Oedipus Rex

The Old Man and the
  Sea
On the Road
One Flew over the
  Cuckoo's Nest
One Hundred Years of
  Solitude
Othello
Persuasion
Portnoy's Complaint
Pride and Prejudice
Ragtime
The Red Badge of
  Courage
Romeo and Juliet
The Rubáiyát of Omar
  Khayyám
The Scarlet Letter
A Separate Peace
Silas Marner
Slaughterhouse-Five
Song of Solomon
The Sound and the
  Fury
The Stranger
A Streetcar Named
  Desire
Sula
The Sun Also Rises
The Tale of Genji
A Tale of Two Cities
"The Tell-Tale Heart"
  and Other Stories
The Tempest
Their Eyes Were
  Watching God
Things Fall Apart
The Things They
  Carried
To Kill a Mockingbird
Ulysses
Waiting for Godot
The Waste Land
Wuthering Heights
Young Goodman
  Brown

*Bloom's Modern Critical Interpretations*

Aldous Huxley's
# *Brave New World*
*New Edition*

*Edited and with an introduction by*
## Harold Bloom
Sterling Professor of the Humanities
Yale University

BLOOM'S
LITERARY CRITICISM
*An Infobase Learning Company*

Bloom's Literary Criticism
An imprint of Infobase Learning
132 West 31st Street
New York NY 10001

**Library of Congress Cataloging-in-Publication Data**
    Aldous Huxley's Brave new world / edited and with an introduction by Harold Bloom. — New ed.
        p. cm. — (Bloom's modern critical interpretations)
    Includes bibliographical references and index.
    ISBN 978-1-60413-579-4 (alk. paper)
    1. Huxley, Aldous, 1894–1963. Brave new world.  2. Dystopias in literature.
    I. Bloom, Harold.  II. Title: Brave new world.
    PR6015.U9B6724 2011
    823'.912—dc22
                                            2011014751

Bloom's Literary Criticism books are available at special discounts when purchased in bulk quantities for businesses, associations, institutions, or sales promotions. Please call our Special Sales Department in New York at (212)967-8800 or (800)322-8755.

You can find Bloom's Literary Criticism on the World Wide Web at
http://www.infobaselearning.com

Contributing editor: Pamela Loos
Cover design by Takeshi Takahashi
Composition by IBT Global, Troy NY
Cover printed by Yurchak Printing, Landisville, PA
Book printed and bound by Yurchak Printing, Landisville, PA
Date printed: July 2011
Printed in the United States of America

10 9 8 7 6 5 4 3 2 1

This book is printed on acid-free paper.

All links and Web addresses were checked and verified to be correct at the time of publication. Because of the dynamic nature of the Web, some addresses and links may have changed since publication and may no longer be valid.

# Contents

Editor's Note     vii

Introduction     1
    *Harold Bloom*

*Brave New World*     3
    *Philip Thody*

From Savages to Men Like Gods     17
    *Peter Edgerly Firchow*

Sweet Scents and Stench: Traces of Post/Modernism
    in Aldous Huxley's *Brave New World*     37
    *Hans J. Rindisbacher*

Power of Images/Images of Power in
    *Brave New World* and *Nineteen Eighty-Four*     53
    *Mario Varricchio*

Oedipus in Dystopia: Freud and Lawrence
    in Aldous Huxley's *Brave New World*     73
    *Brad Buchanan*

Aldous Huxley's Americanization of
    the *Brave New World* Typescript     95
    *Jerome Meckier*

Huxley's Feelies: The Cinema of
    Sensation in *Brave New World*     125
    *Laura Frost*

"When the Indian Was in Vogue":
   D. H. Lawrence, Aldous Huxley,
   and Ethnological Tourism in the Southwest                153
   *Carey Snyder*

Chronology              185

Contributors            187

Bibliography            189

Acknowledgments              193

Index              195

# Editor's Note

My introduction attests to the enduring relevance of *Brave New World*, despite its more threadbare aspects. Philip Thody opens the volume with a look at Huxley's political and social ambiguities. Peter Edgerly Firchow then casts the novel as a critique and revision of futurism, H.G. Wells style.

Hans J. Rindisbacher detects elements of modernism and postmodernism in Huxley's strategies of representation and contextualizes the novel within "olfactory literary history." Mario Varricchio then explores the work's cinematic underpinnings.

Brad Buchanan traces the shadows of Freud and Lawrence cast on the novel, after which Jerome Meckier delves into the changes Huxley made to the American publication.

Laura Frost returns us to the sensations of the cinema and Huxley's "feelies." The volume concludes with Carey Snyder's discussion of Huxley and Lawrence's appropriations of Native American and southwestern cultural identities.

HAROLD BLOOM

# Introduction

In his "Foreword" to a 1946 edition of *Brave New World* (1931), Aldous Huxley expressed a certain regret that he had written the book when he was an amused, skeptical aesthete rather than the transcendental visionary he had since become. Fifteen years had brought about a world in which there were "only nationalistic radicals of the right and nationalistic radicals of the left," and Huxley surveyed a Europe in ruins after the completion of the Second World War. Huxley himself had found refuge in what he always was to call "the Perennial Philosophy," the religion that is "the conscious and intelligent pursuit of man's Final End, the unitive knowledge of the immanent Tao or Logos, the transcendent godhead or Brahman." As he sadly remarked, he had given his protagonist, the Savage, only two alternatives: to go on living in the Brave New World whose God is Ford (Henry), or to retreat to a primitive Indian village, more human in some ways, but just as lunatic in others. The poor Savage whips himself into the spiritual frenzy that culminates with his hanging himself. Despite Huxley's literary remorse, it seems to me just as well that the book does not end with the Savage saving himself through a mystical contemplation that murmurs "That are Thou" to the Ground of All Being.

A half century after Huxley's "Foreword," *Brave New World* is at once a bit threadbare, considered strictly as a novel, and more relevant than ever in the era of genetic engineering, virtual reality, and the computer hypertext. Cyberpunk science fiction has nothing to match Huxley's outrageous inventions, and his sexual prophecies have been largely fulfilled. Whether the Third Wave of a Gingrichian future will differ much from Huxley's *Brave New*

1

*World* seems dubious to me. A new technology founded almost entirely upon information rather than production, at least for the elite, allies Mustapha Mond and Newt Gingrich, whose orphanages doubtless can be geared to the bringing up of Huxley's "Bokanovsky groups." Even Huxley's intimation that "marriage licenses will be sold like dog licenses, good for a period of twelve months," was being seriously considered in California not so long ago. It is true that Huxley expected (and feared) too much from the "peaceful" uses of atomic energy, but that is one of his few failures in secular prophecy. The God of the Christian Coalition may not exactly be Our Ford, but he certainly is the God whose worship assures the world without end of Big Business.

Rereading *Brave New World* for the first time in several decades, I find myself most beguiled by the Savage's passion for Shakespeare, who provides the novel with much more than its title. Huxley, with his own passion for Shakespeare, would not have conceded that Shakespeare could have provided the Savage with an alternative to a choice between an insane utopia and a barbaric lunacy. Doubtless, no one ever has been saved by reading Shakespeare, or by watching him performed, but Shakespeare, more than any other writer, offers a possible wisdom, as well as an education in irony and the powers of language. Huxley wanted his Savage to be a victim or scapegoat, quite possibly for reasons that Huxley himself never understood. *Brave New World*, like Huxley's earlier and better novels *Antic Hay* and *Point Counter Point*, is still a vision of T.S. Eliot's *The Waste Land*, of a world without authentic belief and spiritual values. The author of *Heaven and Hell* and the anthologist of *The Perennial Philosophy* is latent in *Brave New World*, whose Savage dies in order to help persuade Huxley himself that he needs a reconciliation with the mystical Ground of All Being.

PHILIP THODY

# Brave New World

One of the many resemblances between Aldous Huxley and his grand-father lies in the interest which both men took in the question of human fertility. For Thomas Henry, it seems—rather surprisingly—to have been a personal problem as well as a concern natural in a biologist, for in 1858 he wrote to his friend Dr Dyster that he wished 'a revised version of the Genus Homo would come out, at any rate as far as the female part of it is concerned—one half of them seem to me doomed to incessant misery so long as they are capable of childbirth'.[1] Unlike T. H. Huxley, who eventually fathered eight children, Aldous had only one son, and his concern with the problem was of a more general nature. It nevertheless recurs with obsessive force in almost all his books, and it is remarkable how early he appreciated the gravity of what is now mankind's gravest problem. In 1925 he was already commenting that any of his grandchildren who wanted to 'get away from it all' would have to take their holidays in Central Asia, and in 1956 he expressed the same idea in dramatically statistical terms when he wrote in an essay entitled *The Desert*, that 'solitude is receding at the rate of four and a half kilometres per annum'. Long before ecology, conservation and environmental studies had become fashionable concerns, he made Lord Edward Tantamount in *Point Counter Point* speak of the 'natural, cosmic revolution' which would make man bankrupt if he continued to plunder the planet, and

From *Aldous Huxley: A Biographical Introduction*, pp. 48–60, 133–34. Copyright © 1973 by Philip Thody.

3

in *Do What You Will* he goes so far as to argue that mankind has already passed the point of no return. Since the productivity of the machine has permitted the creation of twice the number of people than can be supported by a return of the primitive agricultural methods advocated by Gandhi, the purest idealism could have the most disastrous consequences. Tamberlaine's butcheries would be 'insignificant indeed compared with the massacres so earnestly advocated by our mild and graminivorous Mahatma', and the combination between natural fertility and human ingenuity has sprung a trap more devilish than disease itself.[2]

It is this concern over the fact that there are now too many people for civilization to remain human that provides the first of the many strands transforming *Brave New World* into something much deeper than a purely satirical account of the dehumanizing effect which science, in 1932, seemed likely to have on society. In creating a culture where human growth is deliberately stunted in the embryo in order that 'ninety-six identical twins' can work 'ninety-six identical machines', the science of *Brave New World* has merely responded to a problem created by the Ford whom Huxley found he so much admired when faced with the teeming poverty of India. Babies who come out of test-tubes naturally do so in exactly the numbers, size and type required to keep society stable, and Huxley's picture of a world wholly under human control appears at first sight to be the success story of all time. It is only on reflection that one realizes that the problems of human society have been solved in *Brave New World* in the only way that so deeply pessimistic a thinker as Huxley can really envisage: by the removal from human life of those qualities which make man different from the animals. Nobody is allowed to have children of their own, and the words 'mother' and 'father' have become the ultimate in unmentionable obscenity. People are indeed prevented from 'breeding themselves into subhuman misery'.[3] But at the same time, they are refused any opportunity to plan their own lives, educate their own children, possess or transmit their own property, change their role, rank or employment in society, or even live permanently with another person of their own choice. Both physical and mental unhappiness have disappeared. But so too have art, religion, freedom, philosophy and poetry. The risks inseparable from man's ability to breed, to fight, to think up new ways of organizing his society, of persecuting his fellows or blowing himself to pieces, the dangers inherent in life as it naturally exists on a biological level or as man has made it through his invention of society, have been judged too great. 'Anything for a quiet life' is the basic and consciously formulated slogan of this society in which the idea of 'repressive tolerance' is put into practice with quite remarkable success. People are not only bred and conditioned to love their slavery. Airy public expression of discontent is quietly put down by a police force which vaporizes the rioters with a 'euphoric, narcotic, pleasantly hallucinant' drug called soma.

There are, nevertheless, some important differences between Huxley's picture of the affluent society and the views which Herbert Marcuse and others were to put forward some thirty years after the publication of *Brave New World*. Whereas the theoreticians of the new left invariably presuppose, in their denunciation of a consumer-orientated society, that freedom and equality have been deliberately destroyed by some kind of nefarious conspiracy on the part of international capitalism and the shareholders of Marks and Spencers, Huxley's critique has no political overtones. It is the impersonal pressure of population and industry, it is man's success in his most laudable activities of eliminating disease and relieving poverty—making two blades of grass grow where only one grew before—that have made him put himself in this inhuman situation. *Brave New World* is unique in Huxley's work by its complete lack of moral indignation and its absolute ethical neutrality. Nobody is to blame, and there are no villains. Moreover, when one looks at the picture of human experience presented in Huxley's other novels, as well as in historical works—such as *Grey Eminence* or *The Devils of Loudun*, the arguments put forward in defence of this benevolently administered world seem neither wholly ironic nor totally unconvincing.

It is indeed in its relationship with Huxley's work and his general personality that much of the peculiar excellence and particular fascination of *Brave New World* are to be found. Its individual themes, of course, are not new. They are announced at various points in the early novels, had been developed by other thinkers in the immediate post-war period, and are in many cases more consistent with the avowedly satirical nature of the work than with its ambiguous portrait of how human beings solve their problems by ceasing to be human. Mr Scogan, in *Crome Yellow*, evokes a future in which 'an impersonal generation will take the place of Nature's hideous system'. 'In vast state incubators', he continues, 'rows upon rows of gravid bottles will supply the world with the population it requires. The family system will disappear; society, sapped at its very base, will have to find new foundations; and Eros, beautifully and irresponsibly free, will flit like a gay butterfly from flower to flower through a sunlit world', and every one of his predictions is made to come true in *Brave New World*. Francis Chellifer, in *Those Barren Leaves*, arguing that stability can be achieved only in a society where the ideal working man is 'eight times as strong as the present day workman, with only a sixteenth of his mental capacity', defends the use of what Huxley later calls dysgenics to avoid the problems of natural intelligence, and thus anticipates the rigid caste system created in AF 632.[4] The portrait in *Brave New World* of a society wholly dominated by applied science had also been anticipated

outside Huxley's own work by Bertrand Russell, one of the models for Mr
Scogan, in a book he had published in 1931 entitled *The Scientific Outlook*.
Like Huxley, Russell had insisted on the incompatibility between a rationally
organized society and any form of art or literature, and argued that the general public would, in such a society, be forbidden access to works like *Hamlet*
and *Othello* 'on the grounds that they glorify private murder'. He had also
observed how Pavlov's experiments could be extended to create conditioned
reflexes in human beings, and the character training in Huxley's brave new
world mirrors Russell's diagnosis of how behaviourism could prevent 'lower-
caste people wasting the Community's time on books'.[5] The first sight which
the Deltas have of print and pictures is accompanied by violent noises and
a mild electric shock, and just as Pavlov, by consistently ringing a bell every
time he gave the dog its dinner, managed to make the animal salivate by the
bell alone, so the administrators in *Brave New World* ensure that the vulner-
ability of the human mind can be put to some practical purpose. Indeed, so
much of *Brave New World* resembles *The Scientific Outlook* that one wonders
at times if Huxley put any original ideas into his book.

This charge of plagiarism, however, does not apply either to Huxley's
knowledge of science or to the relationship between *Brave New World* and
the deeper levels of his personality. In 1963, writing in the *Memorial Volume* which he edited after his brother's death, Sir Julian Huxley went out
of his way to discount rumours that Aldous's knowledge of biology always
came to him at second hand. 'Most people seem to imagine', he wrote, 'that
Aldous came to me for help over the biological facts and ideas he utilized so
brilliantly in *Brave New World* and elsewhere in his novels and essays. This
was not so. He picked them all up from his miscellaneous reading and from
occasional discussions with me and a few other biologists, from which we
profited as much as he.'[6] Moreover, what one might call the main philosophical theme in *Brave New World* is a very personal element in the novel, and
its emotional impact stems from the fact that Huxley, perhaps without fully
realizing what he was doing, made use of the apparently impersonal *genre* of
a science fiction fantasy to express a deeply felt personal dilemma. 'A world
in which ideas did not exist would be a happy world', he wrote in 1954 in his
preface to Krishnamurti's *The First and Last Freedom*, and the remark is strikingly similar to the views which the Director of Hatcheries and Conditioning puts forward in the opening chapter of *Brave New World*: 'Particulars, as
everyone knows, make for virtue and happiness; generalities are intellectually
necessary evils. Not philosophers, but fret-sawyers and stamp collectors compose the backbone of society.'[7] The dilemma with which Mustapha Mond
confronts the Savage when he has to justify the absence from the brave new
world of Shakespeare, the Bible, all imaginative literature and all disinterested

scientific inquiry is a real one, and the answer proposed in *Brave New World* loses its irony when placed in the context both of Huxley's early work and of his later, mystical development. Since only unhappy people produce literature, and unhappiness itself is so intense, certain and widespread, might it not be a good idea to accept that literature will disappear if suffering is abolished? Since human life requires such misery if the specifically human activities of art and science are to continue, might it not be preferable to end the requirement whereby man must live an animal existence on human terms? Why not, by removing the human element, move him nearer to the animals, and thus destroy the unhappiness which has so far been the unjustifiably high price which he has had to pay for being human?

This kind of question is not one which literature normally asks. Not only is it too naïve, but the problem of inserting it into a convincing account of how people actually behave is quite insuperable. In *Point Counter Point*, for example, as in *Les Chemins de la Liberté*, *The Brothers Karamazov* or *Last Exit to Brooklyn*, the very suggestion that people could be happy if they tried is as ridiculous as the idea that they might all suddenly levitate or start to play cricket. The suggestion could only be seriously developed in a work benefiting from the science fiction convention that all things logically possible are also technically feasible. Huxley's exploitation of science fiction as a medium for the expression of ideas provides, in this respect, perhaps the final step in the acquisition for this *genre* of its literary *lettres de noblesse*. It was not only for its concision, social relevance, dramatic qualities, scientific ingenuity and technical expertise that *Brave New World* deserved the signal honour of bridging the two cultures gap by receiving an enthusiastic review from Joseph Needham in F. R. Leavis's *Scrutiny* while at the same time being described as 'a very great book' by Charlotte Haldane in *Nature*. Huxley had also, in his shortest novel since *Crome Yellow*, cast the personal dilemma which runs through his whole work into the highly general medium of a novel about the future. What he asked, over and above the question about the incompatibility between art and happiness, was whether human life could be lived on human terms, or whether the biological accident which gave man his unique status as, a suffering, thinking and imaginative being should in some way be rectified. 'So you claim', remarks the World Controller when the Savage insists on contracting out of the 'brave new world' of which he has heard so much, 'the right to grow old and impotent; the right to have syphilis and cancer; the right to have too little to eat; the right to be lousy; the right to live in constant apprehension of what may happen tomorrow; the right to catch typhoid; the right to be tortured by unspeakable pains of every kind?' When the Savage takes a deep breath and says 'I do', the World Controller's ironic 'You're welcome to it' seems to be Huxley's own comment on such obvious lunacy.

It is true that there were, in *Nature* rather than in *Scrutiny*, doubts as to whether the question was altogether fairly put, and whether the complex emotional impulses inspiring *Brave New World* did not spoil what ought to have been an objective analysis of social and scientific problems. Thus Mrs Haldane did not limit herself to anticipating the pill and querying the degree of prescience which Huxley had shown in equipping his young ladies with 'so primitive a garment as a Malthusian belt stuffed with contraceptives when a periodic injection of suitable hormones would afford ample protection'.[8] She also commented, in terms which her husband later regarded as revenge for the satirical portrait given of him under the character of Shearwater in *Antic Hay*, upon the dual personality which, in her view, spoilt the balance in all Huxley's novels. 'Dr. Jekyll and Mr. Hyde', she wrote, 'are nothing to Dr. Huxley and Mr. Arnold. Mr. Arnold is always doing it. He did it in *Point Counter Point*; he does it in *Brave New World*. Dr. Huxley, who knows and cares about biology and music, science and art, is again ousted by this double of his, this morbid, masochistic, medieval Christian,' and she saw the ending of the novel, in which the Savage commits suicide, as exemplifying the triumph of the Arnold over the Huxley spirit. Yet the Huxleys were no less afflicted than the Arnolds with the metaphysical concerns which Mrs Haldane clearly regarded as the function of science to dispel, and Joseph Needham went so far as to argue that it was precisely Huxley's awareness of how limited the purely scientific attitude could be which made the book so uniquely valuable. What gave the biologist a 'sardonic smile as he reads it', he declared in his review of *Brave New World* in *Scrutiny*, 'is the fact that he knows that *the biology is perfectly right*'. 'Successful experiments are even now being made', he continued, 'in the cultivation of embryos of small mammals *in vitro*, and one of the most horrible of Mr. Huxley's predictions, the production of low-grade workers of precisely identical genetic constitution from one egg, is perfectly possible.'[9] Moreover, he continued, Huxley's novel was invaluable as a description of the kind of society likely to be produced by scientists blind to any values whose existence could not be proved by laboratory experiment. It was, in short, an object lesson for the logical positivists who followed the early Wittgenstein in rejecting statements about ethics, aesthetics and religion as 'meaningless', and a particular warning to scientists of what might happen to them as well as to other people if their more enthusiastic disciples won.

This denunciation of the effect which scientific intolerance could have on society is undoubtedly one of the more conscious and deliberate aspects of *Brave New World*. When Huxley made Francis Chellifer, in *Those Barren Leaves*, remark that his father's Wordsworthian statements about nature were 'as meaningless as so many hiccoughs', he was already treating the cruder interpretations of the *Tractatus Logico-Philosophicus* in a half satirical light, and there is no ambiguity whatsoever about Huxley's later defence of art and literature against the new philistinism of applied science. The same is true of his attack on Freudianism, and here again the themes of *Brave New World* can be traced back to his earlier novels and short stories. Thus in *The Farcical History of Richard Greenow*, the friend who tries to psychoanalyse Richard by the free association technique favoured by the earlier Freudians receives the answer 'bosom' in response to the stimulus 'aunt' (Richard remembers playing with toy soldiers while sitting on his aunt's lap) and that of Wilkinson in response to the stimulus 'God' (there floats into Richard's inward eye 'the face of a boy he had known at school and at Oxford, one Godfrey Wilkinson, called God for short'). The amateur analyst consequently infers that Richard's troubles lie in the fact that he 'had had, as a child, a great Freudian passion for his aunt; and that later on, he had had another passion, almost religious in its fervour, for someone called Wilkinson', and his complete failure to understand what is really happening to his friend foreshadows the criticism that Huxley made much later on, in 1963, in an essay called *Human Potentialities*. There, he wrote of Freud as the man 'who never mentioned any part of the human body except the mouth, the anus and the urethra',[10] and his basic objection really changed little in the forty years separating *The Farcical History* from *Human Potentialities*. The Freudians are wrong because they take into account only one aspect of human physiology, and base their conclusions upon only one kind of evidence: that which emanates from the supposed working of the unconscious in a primarily sexual context. In *Brave New World* it is more the implied ethical teachings of Freudianism that attract his scorn, the rejection of complex and mature emotions in favour of instant gratification and the pleasure principle. His disapproval is, in fact, almost Victorian in its moral intensity, thus revealing yet another apparently contradictory strand in the complex personality of a writer whose work was regarded by *The Times*, in 1963, as having been 'devoted in the main to the violent demolition of Victorian and Edwardian values'.[11]

Thus in *Brave New World* it is the declared aim of the authorities to translate into the sexual behaviour of adults the total irresponsibility and immaturity which supposedly characterize a child's attitude to its own body. 'When the individual feels, the community reels' is the slogan which explains why promiscuous sex is so actively encouraged, and Huxley's insistence upon this theme was another aspect of the novel which, while boosting its sales and encouraging the Australian authorities to act as his publicity agents by banning the book,[12] attracted praise from Joseph Needham, who wrote in *Scrutiny*,

Whether consciously or not Mr. Huxley has incorporated the views of many psychologists, e.g. Dr. Money Kryle. In an extremely interesting paper Dr. Kryle has suggested that social discontent, which has always been the driving force in social change, is a manifestation of the Oedipus complex of the members of society, and cannot be removed by economic means. With decrease of sexual taboos, these psychologists suggest, there would be a decrease in frustration and hence of that aggression which finds its outlet in religion, socialism or the more violent forms of demand for social change.

Huxley did not, in fact, need to get this idea from Dr Kryle. One of the principal themes in his own early novels is that it is much better to make love than war, and much less harmless to be a lecher than an idealist. The critical presentation of sexuality in *Brave New World* is consequently more of an indication of the general direction which his own ideas were taking than the sign of yet another intellectual debt, and his next two major works, *Eyeless in Gaza* and *Ends and Means*, mark a revulsion both against sexuality and against the total rejection of all conventional values which had characterized the early novels. The founder of the civilization described in *Brave New World* always chose to call himself, 'whenever he spoke of psychological matters, "our Freud" rather than "our Ford"', and it is doubtless as a tribute to the attitude he thus epitomized that all opportunities are taken to prevent emotional tensions building up to the point where they threaten the stability of society. The family, together with all its attendant conflicts, has been replaced by the breeding bottle and the state nursery. At the same time, the universal availability of contraceptives, together with the inculcation, in early childhood, of the duty to be promiscuous, has fulfilled Miss Triplow's prediction in *Those Barren Leaves* and 'made chastity superfluous'. All the adult emotions traditionally associated with sex—love, fidelity, a sense of responsibility, the recognition of another person as supremely and uniquely valuable—have been abolished. All that remains is a search for purely physical pleasure, with T. S. Eliot's 'pneumatic' providing the only adjective of commendation available to describe a woman's charms. If the contraceptives should fail to work, the flood-lit abortion centre in Chelsea provides a ready alternative; and the 'Pregnancy advisory centres' so liberally advertised in the London of 1972 provide yet another example of how some of Huxley's prophecies are being fulfilled more quickly than he expected.

The Freudian idea that we should avoid repressions and frustrations, that the way to happiness lies in the satisfaction of those primitive, instinctual, sexual drives which previous societies have been compelled to inhibit, is thus criticized first and foremost for the effect that it has on people's emotional life. Although he does not specifically mention it, one of the 'established spiritual values' whose importance Huxley rediscovered at the end of *Jesting Pilate* was a belief in monogamy and what one is almost tempted to call romantic love. In *Brave New World* Bernard Marx would like to spend the day alone with his loved one Lenina, walking by themselves in the Lake District, and this almost Wordsworthian attitude to nature, presented in *Those Barren Leaves* in an essentially comical light, is another sign of how Huxley's attitudes were changing. In *Brave New World*, however, the constant reduction of adult human beings to childlike animals is also associated with the deliberate destruction of all intellectual curiosity, and it is difficult to tell whether it is the stunting of the emotions or the prostitution of the mind which Huxley finds most abhorrent. In 'After Ford (or Freud) 632', the only criteria by which society judges itself are those of stability and efficiency. Free, disinterested, open-ended research consequently regarded as being just as dangerous as art, literature or religion, for the essential characteristic of true scientific inquiry is that no one can know whither it might lead. Each member of society is permitted to know only so much as is immediately relevant to the tasks he has to perform, and even those alpha-plus intellectuals whose pre- and post-natal conditioning has left them with enough intelligence to think for themselves are not allowed to explore any new ideas.

Huxley's realization that the systematic application of technology could lead to a situation where science itself is considered highly dangerous is yet another indication of the fundamental similarity between his attitudes and those of his grandfather. If there was anything to which Thomas Henry Huxley unremittingly devoted his enormous energy, it was the propagation to all members of society of the methods and ideals of scientific inquiry. It was consequently as much by respect for family tradition as through personal taste that Aldous Huxley made this destruction of science by its own hand into an important theme in the actual plot of *Brave New World*, and in this he was quite consciously using a novel about the future to comment on current development in his and our society. The plot revolves round the discovery, by Bernard Marx and Lenina Crowne, of the existence in one of the 'savage reservations' in South America, of Linda, a woman from their own civilization who had been lost some twenty years earlier during an outing very similar to their own. By an unfortunate and almost incredible accident, Linda's excursion among the Pueblo Indians had coincided with her getting pregnant by her lover—now Director of World Hatcheries. By an ironic reversal of traditional standards, it is the very fact that she has had a baby which has prevented her from appealing to her own civilization for help, and she has been forced to bring up her son alone. When he had asked questions—'How did the world begin?', 'What are chemicals?'—Linda had been totally unable to reply. The only book she had ever heard of was her own work manual on *The Chemical and Bacteriological Conditioning of the Embryo, Practical Instructions for Beta Workers* and all she knew of chemicals was that they came out of bottles. It is by the quality of the human beings it produces that a civilization can be judged, and it is in the character of Linda that we see what the inhabitants of *Brave New World* are really like and what our own culture might become if the pressures for wholly vocational education are allowed to triumph. They have lost all their adaptability, all their ability and willingness to understand other people, all sense of wonder and curiosity, and all power to withstand, in loneliness and isolation, the human experiences of being persecuted or facing death. In his early novels, Huxley seemed to many critics to have followed his grandfather's iconoclastic example and destroyed any Victorian values still left standing after Thomas Henry had so convincingly demolished their religious foundations. In *Brave New World* it is not only the implied insistence on the importance of marriage and pre-marital chastity which suggests that he is going back to what was best in both the agnostic and the Protestant traditions of Victorian England. Education, he implies, must involve more than a vigorous intellectual training in the arts and sciences. Children must also learn to bear misfortune with courage, and to postpone their pleasures until they can face up to their responsibilities. Sexual permissiveness, intellectual conformism and social stability may perhaps lead to a more efficient and comfortable society than has ever existed in the past. But on no account must they be preferred to the ideals of responsibility and self-reliance which have so far characterized the essentially Protestant tradition of Western democracy.

Matthew and even Thomas Arnold would, in this respect, have felt just as much sympathy as Thomas Henry Huxley for the character depicted with most approval in *Brave New World*. Helmholtz Watson, whose lectures on Advanced Emotional Engineering are much admired both by his students and the Authorities, decides to opt out of the comfortable world of an alpha-plus literary intellectual and chooses instead to undergo the rigours of life on an isolated island. There, he will at least have the opportunity of thinking his own thoughts, even though the fact that he does so in conditions of intellectual quarantine will effectively prevent him from influencing what goes on elsewhere. What is equally significant, however, is that the character who more convincingly represents Huxley himself, Bernard Marx, finally lacks the strength of character needed to support loneliness and exile. Like Philip Quarles, Bernard Marx is an alpha-plus intellectual with a physical defect. The rumour runs that 'somebody made a mistake when he was still in the bottle—thought he was a gamma and put alcohol into his blood surrogate', and Bernard consequently suffers from the same feelings of personal inadequacy which characterize all Huxley's autobiographical figures. By tastes and instinct, he resembles the inner-directed man of the Protestant tradition. Yet because of his physical defect, he lacks the psychological qualities which would enable him to fight successfully against the outer-directed, managerial society in which he lives. The self-confidence emanating from the public careers of the earlier generation of Arnolds and Huxleys has disappeared. What takes its place, in *Brave New World*, is not only a fuller realization of how physiological accidents can destroy moral stamina. There is also a more disturbing awareness of how ambiguous certain kinds of moral behaviour can be, and of how preferable an attitude of critical detachment might consequently become. It is never long, in *Brave New World*, before what appears to be a straightforward attack on contemporary trends takes on more ambiguous overtones and what W. H. G. Armytage, in *Yesterday's Tomorrows*, classifies as the product of a 'disenchanted mechanophobe' reveals more disturbing if more interesting implications.

In the eighteenth century, and especially in the *Contes* of Voltaire or Diderot, the role of the outsider in fiction was fairly easily defined. It was to provide, by the introduction of the common sense supposedly prevailing elsewhere, a criticism of the nonsensical principles on which modern, European civilization was based. There is also an outsider in *Brave New World*, Linda's son John, who is rescued from the savage reservation and brought to London by Bernard Marx, and it is his reactions to the marvellous world which he has heard about from his mother which provide the main story line in the novel. By a happy accident, his reading has not been limited to *The Chemical and Bacteriological Conditioning of the Embryo, Practical Instructions for Beta Workers*. He has also read one of the forbidden works of AF 632, *The Complete Works of William Shakespeare*, and it is by the standards of Shakespearian tragedy and romance that he judges the society which finds him so delicious and stimulating a novelty. Lenina Crowne seems to him the most beautiful and perfect creature he has ever seen, and he falls madly and devotedly in love with her. But instead of going to bed with her straight away as the other young men of her acquaintance have all been conditioned to do in such circumstances, the Savage behaves very oddly. He insists on her fitting in not only with *Romeo and Juliet* but with the even more extraordinary concepts he has absorbed from the fertility rites and initiation ceremonies of the Pueblo Indians. When she cannot understand what he is talking about—and she is quite incapable of imagining that anyone else's frame of reference could possibly be different from hers—John seeks refuge in an isolated and abandoned air-lighthouse on the Hog's Back. There, revolted by the spectacle of a society from which all effort, skill, and sympathy and patience have been removed, he tries to go back to nature and live by his own efforts. Less rationally, he also tries to whip his body into an acceptance of the chastity which the memories of Lenina's charms make into an impossible ideal, but in AF 632, any deviation from the norm, and especially one with such intriguing sexual overtones, attracts crowds of spectators. Lenina is among them, and tries to come and talk to John. But the Savage, already 'frantically, without knowing it', wishing that the blows he is giving his own body were raining down on Lenina, strikes at her with his whip. She stumbles and falls, and as he strikes again and again 'at his own rebellious flesh, or at that plump incarnation of turpitude writhing in the heather at his feet', events get out of hand in a way that gives Huxley's attempt to revive the moral values of nineteenth-century England some disquieting overtones. The crowd of spectators 'drawn by the fascination of the horror of pain and, from within, impelled by that habit of cooperation, that desire for unanimity and atonement, which their conditioning had so ineradicably implanted in them', begin to imitate his gestures. Soon, John's search for purity has turned into a sado-masochistic sexual orgy; and the outsider who, in an age more certain of its values, would have represented triumphant sanity, hangs himself in despair.

Another possible if less dramatic sign of the ambiguous attitude which Huxley encourages his reader to adopt towards the society described in *Brave New World* is the extremely humane provision made for those who wish to explore heterodox ideas. When Helmholtz Watson goes off to think his own thoughts, write his own books and perhaps even invent his own God, no one will be allowed to interfere with him. He will, to use Isaiah Berlin's distinction in *Two Concepts of Liberty*, be endowed with all the negative freedom that a man can desire. What he will not have, however, is what Isaiah Berlin calls positive freedom: the opportunity to try to impose his own will on the outside world. The 'repressive tolerance' of consumer orientated society is indeed fully consistent both with certain forms of intellectual freedom and with the behaviour of those individuals who feel that their first duty is towards themselves. What it does not and cannot allow is any changes in its own fundamental patterns. Huxley seems almost to be recommending the *Brave New World* solution as the correct one when he writes, in the opening chapter of *The Perennial Philosophy*, of the way in which 'provision was and still is made by every civilized society for giving thinkers a measure of protection from the ordinary stresses and strains of social life. The hermitage, the monastery, the college, the academy and the research laboratory; the begging bowl, the endowment, the patronage, and the grant of tax-payers' money—such are the principal devices that have been used by actives to conserve that rare bird, the religious, philosophical or scientific contemplative.'[13] Whereas Thomas Henry Huxley—like his other grandson Julian—was a man of action as well as an intellectual, a teacher and administrator as well as an author who helped to change man's concept of his nature, Aldous Huxley limited himself for most of his life to sitting in a room and writing books. Each of the devices he mentions in *The Perennial Philosophy* is characterized by the assumption that the thinker will be neither expected nor allowed to emerge from his ivory tower and play a role in the society that subsidizes his production of ideas, and the islands to which the authorities of *Brave New World* exile their deviant intellectuals would have suited Huxley down to the ground. It was nevertheless in the years immediately following the publication of what still remains his most successful work that Huxley ceased to be what he himself later described as an 'amused, Pyrrhonic aesthete'[14] who stood aside from the world and laughed. For all their gloom and violence, the thirties were still to some extent a time of hope, and the very acuteness of the crisis through which Western society was passing created a future that still seemed to be relatively open. Huxley was one of the many intellectuals and writers who then tried to play an active part in politics and avoid the horrors which, for those who read it in the forties, made *Brave New World* seem even more like a paradise.

## NOTES

1. Quoted by Ronald Clark, *op. cit.*, p. 74. Mr Clark has very generously supplemented his remark by the information that the letter was written on 18 August 1858—that is to say before T. H. Huxley's family grew to seven children between 1858 and 1865.

2. AR 63; AA 77; Lord Tantamount (according to Ronald Clark, *op. cit.*, based upon John Scott Haldane, J. B. S. Haldane's father). PCP 25, 80; comment on Gandhi DWYW 68.

3. *Island*, p. 84. See also p. 59 in same book: 'By 1930, any clear-sighted observer could have seen that for three quarters of the human race, freedom and happiness were almost out of the question'; see also the chapter on population in *Brave New World Revisited*, CW 1964, pp. 11–23.

4. CY 28, 130; BL 91; in *Brave New World Revisited*, Huxley writes (p. 11): 'I forget the exact date of the events recorded in *Brave New World*; but it was somewhere in the sixth or seventh century AF (After Ford).'

5. Bertrand Russell, *The Scientific Outlook*, Allen and Unwin, 1931, p. 221. I am indebted to Peter Bowering's study of Huxley's novels for having drawn my attention to this parallel.

6. MV 22.

7. Krishnamurti—quoted by Atkins, *op. cit.*, p. 183; BNW 16.

8. *Nature*, 23 April 1932, pp. 597–8.

9. Joseph Needham—*Scrutiny*, Vol. 1, no. 1, May 1933, pp. 76–9.

10. Published as the closing essay in a collection edited by Julian Huxley under the title *The Humanist Frame*, Allen and Unwin, 1961. Farcical History—see *Limbo*, pp. 66–8.

11. *The Times*, 25.11.63. Other critics to notice the Victorian side of Huxley's personality include the reviewer in the TLS for 12.8.55 who wrote in his account of GG that Huxley had remained 'curiously Victorian'; Frank Swinnerton, who notes a letter describing Huxley's 'Victorian giggle' (*Figures in the Foreground*, Hutchinson,

1963, p. 188); Laurence Brander, *op. cit.*, p. 191, who attributes the fact that Huxley was 'disappointed' in LSD to the 'recurring concern about social responsibility' stemming from his 'inability to get away from himself and his Victorian forebears'; and Clark, *op. cit.*, p. 220, who calls him 'the last of the Victorians'.

12. See *The Times*, 18.1.33. The ban was lifted on 29.3.37. In 1947, one of my uncles reproved me for reading PCP and recommended Jeffrey Farnol as a healthier alternative.

13. PP 25. The remark is most appropriate to the financial support given to Arts Faculties in British Universities.

14. Foreword to the 1946 edition of BNW. See Penguin Classics, 1955, p. 8.

PETER EDGERLY FIRCHOW

# *From Savages to Men Like Gods*

It is communism based, not on poverty but on riches, not on humility but
on pride, not on sacrifice but on complete fulfilment in the flesh of all
strong desire, not in Heaven but in earth. We will be Sons of God who
walk here on earth, not bent on getting and having, because we know we
inherit all things. We will be aristocrats, and as wise as the serpent in deal-
ing with the mob. For the mob shall not crush us nor starve us nor cry us
to death. We will deal cunningly with the mob, the greedy soul, we will
gradually bring it to subjection.

From *The Letters of D. H. Lawrence*

The European talks of progress because by the aid of a few scientific
discoveries he has established a society which has mistaken comfort for
civilization.

Benjamin Disraeli

H. G. Wells's future has finally caught up with him and, by an irony that
he would have been among the first to appreciate, it has forgotten him. Not
altogether selflessly, but with an astonishing literary energy and determination he toiled half a century, drawing up blueprints of a future filled with
gadgets and—to use Orwell's phrase—enlightened sunbathers. What a pity
that he did not live to see the Costa Brava swarming with tanned nudity and

---

From *The End of Utopia: A Study of Aldous Huxley's* Brave New World, pp. 57–76, 134–36.
Copyright © 1984 by Associated University Presses.

17

transistor radio sets. For a whole generation of readers growing up between 1900 and 1930, this little, fat, and jolly man, half prophet and half huckster, became identified with the shape of things to come. The very mention of the future, J. B. S. Haldane noted in 1924, necessarily evoked his name. Only Jules Verne rivaled him as a writer of scientific romances, and Verne's future was already fading into reality by the time Wells reached the peak of his popular success in the early twenties.

Not surprisingly, therefore, Wells was a favorite target for those who did not share his confidence in the future or in science. As Mark Hillegas has suggested in his interesting study of Wells's literary enemies, *The Future as Nightmare*, to be against utopia and to be against Wells were, during the first half of this century, very nearly synonymous. To this rule Aldous Huxley was no exception. Nor did Huxley take any special pains to hide the fact that in *Brave New World* he was, among other things, blasting Wells. On the contrary, Wells is one of only two contemporary writers to be mentioned by name in the novel—thinly disguised as "Dr. Wells"—the other being Shaw. In at least one letter dating from the period during which he was working on the novel, Huxley openly avowed his aim to expose the "horror of the Wellsian Utopia" (L. 348), and some thirty years later he even named Wells's *Men Like Gods* (1923) as the inspiration for a parody that later "got out of hand and turned into something quite different from what I intended."[1]

Somewhere behind Our Ford and Our Freud, then, lurks Our Wells. He bears rather the same relation to *Brave New World* that Leibniz does to *Candide*, for—rightly or wrongly—Huxley identified Wells, as he wrote in a letter to T. S. Eliot, with "Wellsian Progress" (L. 380), with the doctrine that man can live by technology alone and with the presumption that men could come to be like unto gods. Wells, in Huxley's view, had merely shifted the tense of Pangloss's best-of-all-possible-worlds from the present into the future. For the skeptical Huxley, as for the skeptical Voltaire, the real world was a fallen one.

Ironically, the apple that Wells proffered modern man was a Huxleyan growth. Before becoming a novelist and a Fabian socialist, Wells had been a biologist, trained for a brief time by the great T. H. Huxley himself. Wells had imbibed natural selection at the fountainhead, but natural selection, as Darwin's bulldog knew, had at least left Nature red in tooth and claw in place of the vanished divinity, whereas artificial selection, in the form now proposed by Wells, left only man. Perhaps this is why Wells appears in *Brave New World* as a doctor, rather than in any other guise. What the grandfather had given, the grandson now hoped to take away. Poetic, or at least novelistic, justice would be done.

Wells was deeply offended by *Brave New World*, interpreting the attack personally and blustering about Huxley's "betrayal" of the future. Even as late as 1940, it still rankled sufficiently for him to go out of his way, in *The New World Order*, to denounce that "Bible of the impotent genteel, Huxley's *Brave New World*," and in the same year he told Klaus Mann that he thought Huxley was a "fool." Wells believed that he had been misrepresented by this "disagreeable fantasy."[2] His resentment, one must in all fairness admit, was not altogether unjustified. Anyone who has the stamina to read through the mass of Wells's scientific fantasies will soon discover that he was not always a facile optimist, especially in his earlier books. In *The Time Machine* (1895), for instance, one of the best known of them all, he draws a remarkable portrait of man's eventual degeneration and extinction. Nor was the early Wells unaware of the dangers of science. The pursuit of scientific knowledge for its own sake and without reference to a system of moral values leads to disaster in *The Island of Dr. Moreau* (1896) and in *The Invisible Man* (1897). And in two other, related works, *A Story of the Days to Come* (1899) and *When the Sleeper Wakes* (1899), he demonstrates in detail how worlds controlled by technical ingenuity and moral ineptitude can go dangerously awry. Even in *Men Like Gods* and *A Modern Utopia* (1905), Wells warns against states which, no matter how ideal in other respects, prefer uniformity to individuality. As his own unconventional life amply testifies, he was all for individual freedom. "I am neither a pessimist nor an optimist at bottom," he declared in 1934, and one is rather tempted to agree with that verdict.[3]

But to yield wholly to this temptation would be wrong. The early Wells is quite a different creature from the middle Wells, and even the warnings of the early period are more warnings against capitalist science than against science as such. Until the last two years of his life when he took it all back and asked for an epitaph reading "God damn you all: I told you so,"[4] Wells had always been enough of a socialist and meliorist to believe that democracy, reason, and science would in the long run triumph over selfishness and willful ignorance. Like a kind of socialist Christ, the Sleeper at the end of *When the Sleeper Wakes* takes upon himself the injustices of this world and, sacrificing his own life, destroys the forces of oligarchy and ushers in the age of scientific socialism. The relish with which Wells contemplates the coming of this secular paradise is perhaps best conveyed by the conclusion of *A Story of the Days to Come*, where a dying oligarch goes to seek help from a young doctor. "Why should we save you in particular?" the doctor asks. "You see—from one point of view—people with imaginations and passions like yours have to go—they have to go."

"Go?"

"Die out. It's an eddy."

He was a young man with a serene face. He smiled at Bindon. "We get on with research, you know; we give advice when people have the sense to ask for it. And we bide our time."

"Bide your time?"

"We hardly know enough yet to take over the management, you know."

"You needn't be anxious. Science is young yet. It's got to keep on growing for a few generations. . . . Some day—some day, men will live in a different way." He looked at Bindon and meditated. "There'll be a lot of dying out before that day can come."[5]

When this sort of doctor finally succeeds, he becomes, one suspects, either a ranking member of the scientific-socialistic samurai of *A Modern Utopia*, or else a Fordian Dr. Wells. Or worse.

What Huxley questioned in Wells's future worlds was not the good intentions, but the bad conclusions. Was it really possible for all men to be equal, as Wells and the socialists seemed to maintain? If, by means of genetic control and artificial selection, as in *Men Like Gods*, "every individual is capable of playing the superior part, who will consent," Huxley asked in *Proper Studies*, "or be content to do the dirty work and obey? The inhabitants of Mr. Wells's numerous utopias solve the problem by ruling and being ruled, doing high-brow and low-brow work, in turns . . . an admirable state of affairs if it could be arranged . . . though personally, I find my faith too weak." If men could be bred into gods, Huxley argued, they would also quarrel like gods, with a consequent and ineluctable *Götterdämmerung*. All order is hierarchical order. Cut the great chain of being and you cut yourself adrift. "States function as smoothly as they do," Huxley concludes, "because the greater part of the population is not very intelligent, dreads responsibility, and desires nothing better than to be told what to do. . . . A state with a population consisting of nothing but these superior people could not hope to last for a year" (281–82).

The dream of universal equality is, in Huxley's view, just that: a dream. When you try to put the dream into practice, you get—what? A nightmare. This, in sum, is the meaning of the so-called Cyprus Experiment in *Brave New World*, in which a population of twenty-two thousand Alpha-plus men and women are given the run of the island and complete control over their own destinies. Within twenty years—after massive infighting—the three thousand survivors petition to be readmitted into the Fordian world.

Huxley's chief objections, then, to Wells are that he is unrealistic, that his estimate of human nature is completely out of whack, and that his prophecies about the future are therefore dangerously misleading. Not that Wells alone is to be held responsible; he is merely the most visible exponent of a whole complex of attitudes, linking science with socialism and democracy. To some degree at least, Wells belongs to that class of old-style utopians whose conviction it was, as Huxley observed in 1931, that all one had to do was "get rid of priests and kings, make Aeschylus and the differential calculus available to all, and the world will become a paradise." But for Huxley democracy and universal education are not the philosopher's stone, turning lead into gold. Only science can perform this trick, and its price for doing so is prohibitive. Hence, Huxley argues—referring no doubt to himself and to the novel he was just then in the process of writing—"contemporary prophets have visions of future societies founded on the idea of natural inequality, not of natural equality . . . of a ruling aristocracy slowly improved . . . by deliberate eugenic breeding"; and further and even more directly pertinent to the hierarchical society of *Brave New World*, Huxley foresees the next generation's utopia being based on an intellectual caste system "accompanied by a Machiavellian system of education, designed to give the members of the lower castes only such education as it is profitable for society at large and the upper castes in particular that they should have" (*Music at Night*, 150–52).

To be sure, in both *Men Like Gods* and *A Modern Utopia*, there is an active program of eugenics, and in the latter there is even something of a caste separation between the "samurai" and the rest of the population, with further subdivisions within the samurai themselves. However, the samurai are a purely voluntary aristocracy, as are the more loosely organized "intelligences" who direct social and psychological affairs in *Men Like Gods*. A voluntary aristocracy on this scale, however, must have struck Huxley as an absurdity, as at best the equivalent of a voluntary bureaucracy, which is the function of the Alpha individuals in the Fordian world. To ensure stability, the ultimate control of a society must be vested in a very few hands, a condition which is true not merely of the stable Fordian state but also of the stable Pueblo Indian community.

The relation of *Brave New World* to Wells's fantasies is (with the exception of a number of technological details to be dealt with later) of a rather general nature. Though it may have started out as a parody of *Men Like Gods*, Huxley is quite right in insisting that *Brave New World* ended up as something quite different. It is no *Shamela* to Wells's *Pamela*. The only major areas at which the two novels intersect concern the emotions and the Savage. In Wells's utopia, as in Huxley's dystopia, deep feeling is either nonexistent or reprehensible. The explosion that kills three utopians and temporarily opens their world to Wells's mouthpiece, Barnstaple, and a few other less tractable earthlings occasions no grief among their fellows. Pity, in this utopia of pseudo-Nietzschean supermen, is a virtually unknown vice practiced furtively by degenerate throwbacks to primitive modern man. For the rest there is an athletic, no-nonsense attitude about the mental and emotional lives of these demi-gods that must have struck a responsive satirical cord in Huxley. "The daily texture of Utopian life," a revealing passage reads, "was woven of various and interesting foods and drinks, of free and entertaining exercise and work, of sweet sleep and of the interest and happiness of fearless and spiteless love-making."[6] That last item about the love-making, especially, evokes one of the principal features of Fordian civilization.

Barnstaple himself has no importance for *Brave New World*, except insofar as his solitary condition at the end of the novel suggests that of the Savage. Ironically, Barnstaple, bald, pudgy, middle-aged, and married, suffers from neglect where the Savage ails from surfeit. "The loveliness of the Utopian girls and women," Wells rather sympathetically observes, "who glanced at him curiously or passed him with a serene indifference, crushed down his self-respect and made the Utopian world altogether intolerable to him."[7] No fearless and spiteless love-making for him, alas. But one of the other earthlings does seem to have a more vital connection to Huxley's satire, a certain Rupert Catskill who is a thinly veiled caricature of Winston Churchill. Catskill is the most energetic and articulate devil's advocate in the novel. He roundly denounces the serenity of the Utopians to their own faces, calls theirs a life unfit for heroes, lacking in drama and opportunity to experience man's full potential. Eventually he even seizes an outlying castle and proposes to fight to the finish against a degenerate future.

Catskill and his companions, including Freddy Mush (Edward Marsh) and Lord Barralonga (Lord Beaverbrook), are clearly meant to be throwbacks to a feudal past (hence the castle). And of course they are meant to be ridiculous. So they are, but in the event only marginally more so than their opponents. And here appears another parallel to Huxley's world: Catskill's objections to utopia resemble closely those of the Savage, and like Catskill the Savage also makes an attempt to overthrow the established authority, and also prefers the past to the future. Perhaps even the lighthouse to which the Savage retires may be intended as an echo of Catskill's castle. And if so, then we are faced with the somewhat mind-boggling prospect of young Winston as the sire of a New Mexican savage.

However, more even than *Men Like Gods*, *Brave New World* resembles *When the Sleeper Wakes*. Like Huxley's novel, this work is also more an attack on, than an idealization of the future. "Here was no Utopia, no Socialistic state," the Sleeper is made to realize early in this novel. Without entering into the details of its rather absurd, Bellamy-like plot, one can say that the whole quality of the civilization it depicts is quite Fordian. The countryside, for instance, has disappeared from consciousness altogether and daily life has become exclusively urban. The "squat" building of thirty-four stories that sets the scene for the opening of *Brave New World* would fit in nicely here. So would the attitude, at any rate among the managing class, to pleasure and sex. There are, for instance, the so-called Pleasure Cities, "strange places, reminiscent of the legendary Sybaris, cities of art and beauty, sterile wonderful cities of motion and music, whither repaired all who profited by the fierce, inglorious, economic struggle that went on in the glaring labyrinth below." Like the Savage, the Sleeper is repelled (and fascinated) by the sexual license of the new world, refusing offers to inspect a pleasure city more intimately. Like the Savage again, he despises women who make advances. He wants a woman to love rather than merely make love to. And like the Savage he resists all attempts to tamper with the essence of his personality. Invited to submit to the local hypnotic personality controllers, the Sleeper refuses, preferring "very keenly to remain absolutely himself." Similarly, the bosses of the new bureaucracy, the "prominent officers of the Food Trust" and "the controller of the European Piggeries" leave him as unimpressed as the Arch-Songster of Canterbury does the Savage.[8] What they both value is depth of experience, rather than breadth, and for them the two are mutually exclusive. In the jargon of contemporary sociology, they are inner-directed.

*When the Sleeper Wakes* also contains a remarkable series of technological anticipations of the Fordian world, many of which have been catalogued by Mark Hillegas.[9] There is an "International Crèche Syndicate" which falls halfway between a day-care center and a Hatchery and Conditioning Center; there are even infant "incubating cases," a feature that the Sleeper finds particularly disgusting; and there is transatlantic transport vaguely analogous to Huxley's passenger rockets, along with "babble machines" to drum propaganda into the captive minds of the masses. One could go farther, as Hillegas has done, and ransack other Wells novels for more similarities. In *A Modern Utopia*, criminals and deviants are exiled to islands, much as in Huxley's novel; and in *The First Men in the Moon* (1901), there is a termite-like society in which "every citizen knows his place. He is born to that place, and the elaborate discipline of training and education and surgery he undergoes fits him at last so completely to it that he has neither ideas nor organs for any purpose beyond it."[10] Even Huxley's free-martins are matched by the large majority of neuter Selenites.

It is clear that Huxley borrowed a number of the technological aspects of his utopia from Wells, but it would be dangerous to conclude that Wells was Huxley's primary source of scientific information. In the immediate Huxley background, as we have seen, were his brother Julian and various sometime friends such as J. B. S. Haldane and Bertrand Russell. And in any case, the technological details, whether Wellsian or no, are not what matter most. These are only the most superficially memorable aspects of Huxley's novel, and as he himself soon realized he had blundered badly by missing out on one of the most obvious ones, atomic energy. But while this omission is surprising, it certainly does not vitiate the continuing force of his satire. Is Swift's *Gulliver's Travels* no longer of interest because a thorough exploration of the globe has turned up no islands inhabited by Houyhnhnms?

"I would be easy," Huxley wrote in 1931, no doubt a little self-consciously, "but quite uninteresting to catalogue the errors of past prophets. The only significant parts of their prognostications, the only parts of them which we can usefully compare with contemporary prophesyings, are the forecasts of political and social organization. Coaches may give place to airplanes, but man remains very much what he was—a mainly gregarious animal endowed with a certain number of anti-social instincts. Whatever tools he uses, however slowly or quickly he may travel, he must always be governed and regimented" (*Music at Night*, 149–50). Despite all the gadgetry, in other words, the proper study of the novelist remains man. That is why a remark like Gerald Heard's about *Brave New World's* being "obsolete because of the growth and findings of subsequent research" seems quite beside the point.[11]

Huxley, it is true, made no secret of his suspicion of democracy and of the machine, especially when in combination—as, for instance, in Scogan's remarks on this subject in *Crome Yellow* or the essay "Revolutions" in *Do What You Will* (1929). After his first traumatic experience of the U.S.A. in 1926, that suspicion grew even more intense. But surely not, as Mark Hillegas asserts, for selfish reasons.[12] After all, a great deal of Huxley's intellectual and artistic life prior to *Brave New World* (and following it) was taken up with the effort to find an adequate solution to the wearisome condition of this chiefly gregarious but intermittently anti-social creature called man. *Brave New World* is no exception. It is no mere what-would-it-be-like-if-pigs-could-fly fantasy, but a bitter attack on a kind of mentality that was seeking to destroy man and replace him with an anthropoid beast or an anthropoid machine. That after all was the point of the epigraph that Huxley had chosen for his novel from Berdyaev's *The End of Our Time* (1927).

* * *

In one of Huxley's earlier novels, *Point Counter Point*, there is a description of a painting by a character named Mark Rampion (based on D. H. Lawrence) that depicts the evolution of man. It begins with a minuscule monkey and passes, via various stages of primitive man, through Greece, Rome, and the Renaissance, with the figures growing ever larger as they approximate the present. "The crescendo continued uninterrupted through Watt and Stevenson, Faraday and Darwin, Bessemer and Edison, Rockefeller and Wanamaker to come to a contemporary consummation in the figures of Mr. H. G. Wells and Sir Alfred Mond. Nor was the future neglected. Through the radiant mist of prophecy the forms of Wells and Mond, growing larger and larger at every repetition, wound in a triumphant spiral clean off the paper, toward Utopian infinity" (290–91). Needless to say, Lawrence never painted such a picture, though as we shall see there was something in Lawrence that makes it appropriate for Huxley to have attributed it to him. The most obvious allusion here is to Wells's *Outline of History* (1920) which, as A. J. P. Taylor has remarked, tries heroically and fails dismally to trace an evolutionary moral "progress" in the history of mankind. Less obviously, there is another allusion—one that explains the otherwise rather puzzling linkage of Wells to Sir Alfred Mond—to *William Clissold* (1926), the massive novel in which Wells first broached his notion of an "Open Conspiracy." This romantic idea of having the modern movers and makers of business and politics combine to seize power and create the World State represented something of a departure from Wells's usual brand of nonconformist socialism. But then there had always been in Wells a kind of permanently adolescent admiration for the sheer daring and imagination of the capitalist entrepreneur—witness the rather mixed feelings with which the Ponderevo business empire is treated in *Tono-Bungay* (1909). Besides, Wells's disillusion in *William Clissold* is not so much with the ideals of socialism as with the sorry lot of ineffective sentimentalists who are identified with it. "Clissold's direction," John Maynard Keynes noted in his review of the book, "is to the Left—far, far to the Left; but he seeks to summon from the Right the creative force and the constructive will which is to carry him there."[13]

Without mentioning him specifically and by name, it was clear that Wells had a man like Alfred Mond in mind for the job of chief open conspirator. Mond came from a distinguished scientific and financial family; his father had founded the highly successful Mond Nickel Company, partially on the basis of scientific discoveries of his own; his brother, Sir Robert Ludwig Mond, was a distinguished chemist and administrator. Alfred Mond himself expanded his father's company into one of the largest and most powerful industrial enterprises in Britain and eventually fused it and other related concerns in 1926 into Imperial Chemical Industries, which, after Ford Motor Company, was probably the largest privately owned corporation in the world. But Mond was not satisfied to remain a mere businessman. He also pursued a successful political career, serving as an MP from 1906 to 1928, first as a Liberal and later as a Tory. He fitted Clissold's bill precisely, all the more so because, despite his conservatism, he was known to favor such progressive

ideas as profit sharing and because he attributed his success, above all, to his
ability to make his workers believe that his interest was also their own.

That Huxley was not alone in associating Wells's name with Mond's
is evident from Philip Gibbs's *The Day After Tomorrow* (1927). According
to Gibbs, Wells "seems to have lost faith in the advance of democracy to a
flower-strewn Utopia with Men like Gods, and in his recent work [*William
Clissold*] suggests that human progress can only be attained by an intellectual
aristocracy of very rich men, remarkably like Sir Alfred Mond, who will create enormous trusts, discipline the lower classes, and create a new heaven on
earth by scientific organization and divinely inspired committee meetings."[14]

There is no first-hand evidence that Huxley had read *William Clissold*.
The only novel of Wells, aside from the scientific fantasies, that Huxley mentions in his correspondence or in his (prophetic) essay "If My Library Burned
Tonight," is *Tono-Bungay*, and he found that disappointing. That he had some
knowledge of *William Clissold* is, however, strongly suggested by his connection of Wells with Mond. But if he had not read the novel, what was the
source of his knowledge? The answer, I think, is provided by *Point Counter
Point*: from D. H. Lawrence.

Lawrence had not merely read *William Clissold*; he had reviewed it—
though only the first volume—in 1926 for the *Calendar of Modern Letters*. He
condemns the latter half of the book as a duller résumé of the *Outline of History* in words that seem to presage Rampion's drawing: "Cave men, nomads,
patriarchs, tribal Old Men, out they all come again, in the long march of
human progress. Mr. Clissold, who holds forth against 'system,' cannot help
systematising us all into a gradual and systematic uplift from the ape."[15] Lawrence's verdict was that Wells's novel was not a work of art, which in a way is
odd because Lawrence was generally sympathetic to Wells, in part because he
felt that he and Wells had had similar social obstacles to face and overcome.
Perhaps what Lawrence resented here even more than Wells's lack of art was
his glorification of the modern businessman.

It is tempting to think of Lawrence and Huxley discussing and condemning Wells together, especially the Wells of *William Clissold*; but again there is
no real evidence that they did. There is only the hint of *Point Counter Point* and,
even more tantalizing, the poem "Wellsian Futures" in *Pansies* (1929):

> When men are made in bottles
> and emerge as squeaky globules with no bodies to speak of,
> and therefore nothing to have feelings with,
>
> they will still squeak intensely about their feelings
> and be prepared to kill you if you say you've got none.[16]

What makes this poem especially interesting with regard to Huxley (aside from the fact that *Brave New World* contradicts it outright) is that there is nothing about babies made in bottles anywhere in Wells. Huxley, on the other hand, had already raised the possibility twice, once in *Crome Yellow* and again in *Proper Studies* (1927), and Lawrence had certainly read the latter book. There is more than a slight possibility, therefore, that Lawrence got the scientific information for his poem from Huxley. As it happens, there is circumstantial evidence to support this hypothesis in Julian Huxley's *Memories* (1970), where Huxley's brother mentions lively discussions of "evolutionary and physiological ideas, including the idea of mankind's genetic improvement."[17] These discussions took place at Diablerets in the winter of 1927–28, when Lawrence was also present. In fact it was almost certainly at one of these sessions that Lawrence delivered his famous outburst against evolution.

If what I have argued here is true, then Lawrence bears a considerable, if indirect responsibility for the figure of Mond/Wells in *Brave New World*. Nor is that his only responsibility. In an essay, rather oddly entitled "Man Must Work and Woman as Well" (November 1929), Lawrence examines what he sees as the modern anti-work ethic. Progress, for modern men and women, has come to mean less work and more pay. No longer is there pride or joy in creation through work. The new ethic is the ethic of enjoyment, with more films, dances, golf, tennis and "more getting completely away from yourself." This, according to Lawrence, is the "plan of the universe laid down by the great magnates of industry like Mr. Ford."

Science and technology, however, have not been able to keep pace with the new ethic. The abstract desire for increased enjoyment is frustrated by the practical reality of inadequate labor-saving machinery. There is not even a satisfactory mechanical dishwasher, much less "babies bred in bottles and food in tabloid form." As a consequence, there is an enormous resentment at having to remain physical and laborious when one so ardently wishes to be mechanical and "joyous."

The new ethic also has an inevitable impact on the old moral and social order. Traditional institutions like marriage and the family are withering away along with the old work ethic. There is a fundamental change in instinct. Sexuality turns into promiscuity. People turn away from actual reality in favor of a pseudo-reality mediated by machines: "We don't *want* to look at flesh and blood people—we want to watch their shadows on a screen. We don't *want* to hear their actual voices: only transmitted through a machine. We must get away from the physical."[18]

The connection of these ideas with *Brave New World* is obvious. They are not, of course, ideas that are original with Lawrence. With a few changes of emphasis and chronological context, they could easily have been stated by Carlyle or Ruskin. But originality is not the point here. The point is that Lawrence was intensely preoccupied with the deterioration of the social and moral nature of modern man in ways that closely resemble Huxley's own preoccupations. This similarity of viewpoint—with an identical focus in several striking instances: ectogenesis, the compulsion for enjoyment, the mechanization of man, the substitution of sensation for feeling—suggests a close interchange on these subjects between Lawrence and Huxley, an interchange that surely did not move only in one direction.

Lawrence also exercised another and quite different influence on *Brave New World*. For just as behind Mond and behind the whole technological world that he controls stands H. G. Wells, so behind the Savage and the New Mexican Pueblo stands D. H. Lawrence.

When Huxley began work on *Brave New World*, he had never been to New Mexico. That he had not seems in fact to have troubled him, since nearly thirty years later he recalled having "had to do an enormous amount of reading up on New Mexico, because I'd never been there. I read all sorts of Smithsonian reports on the place and then did the best I could to imagine it."[19] His path passed near New Mexico a couple of years later during the travels described in *Beyond the Mexique Bay* (1934), but he did not actually set foot there until 1937.

If, however, Huxley had not been to New Mexico and if, for that reason, he had to do a good deal of boning up on it, one wonders why he bothered. If it was underdeveloped or non-Western societies he was after, he had already seen several such during his travels in the Far East in 1926. Why then? Perhaps in order to have a peculiarly American locale to match the American flavor of the Fordian world? Yes, possibly, though this suggestion still does not account specifically for New Mexico. Why not Arizona instead, or even Texas or Florida, or any other American state with a sizable Indian population?

The real answer is Lawrence. By the time Huxley came to know him intimately, Lawrence had already, to be sure, closed the New Mexican chapter of his life, but he had by no means forgotten it. "In later years," Huxley wrote in his preface to Knud Merrild's *A Poet and Two Painters* (1938), a memoir about Lawrence in New Mexico by a Dane who had lived there with him, "he [Lawrence] often talked of the place—talked with a mixture of love and dislike; nostalgically longing to be back in that ferociously virgin world of drought and storm, and at the same time resenting its alienness and lunar vacancy."[20] New Mexico, it seems safe to assume, existed for Huxley (that is, before he delved into the Smithsonian reports) only insofar as he had heard of it from Lawrence.

Lawrence, however, did not merely talk about New Mexico; he had also written of it. Though he saved his best energies for the old Mexico—much to the dismay of Mabel Dodge-Luhan who had lured him to Taos to be a sort of combined poet-in-residence and genius loci—he did compose several impressionistic sketches about the Indians and landscape of New Mexico.

The sketch that seems most immediately relevant to the Pueblo section of *Brave New World* is entitled "The Hopi Snake Dance," and it gives Lawrence's reaction to the most dramatic of all the Pueblo Indian dances. The outward trappings of the dance seemed to Lawrence merely spectacular circus tricks with snakes dangling from the performers' mouths but he was profoundly impressed by the gripping rhythmic nature of the ritual, symbolized by the continuous beating of the drum and the pad of human feet. Here was the real heart of the Indian, Lawrence thought; here was his eternal assertion that god and life are one.

The other sketches play variations on much the same theme, usually with a heavy accompaniment of the percussion instruments. Not that Lawrence naively idealizes the life of the Indian. He aggressively demands the "debunking" of the Indian and maintains that "it is almost impossible for the white people to approach the Indian without either sentimentality or dislike."[21] Even so, one suspects that Lawrence felt that he himself had managed to achieve the nearly impossible. Certainly he felt that he had made contact with something that was older and stranger and more godlike than anything he had known before. "I had no permanent feeling of religion," he writes in "New Mexico," "till I came to New Mexico and penetrated into the old human race-experience there." And elsewhere in the same essay he even goes as far as to say that "New Mexico was the greatest experience from the outside world that I ever had. It certainly changed me forever. Curious as it may sound, it was New Mexico that liberated me from the present era of civilization, the great era of material and mechanical development."[22]

Understatement was, of course, not Lawrence's strong point, but undoubtedly New Mexico left its mark on him. For a brief period Lawrence even convinced himself that he was an integral part of New Mexico, living high up on his ranch, surrounded by his women and his cow, with the Indians just a few steps away. This is probably the New Mexico about which Lawrence "often" spoke to Huxley, for no matter how strenuously Lawrence might have wished to debunk the Indian, he was an iconophile, not an iconoclast. It was Huxley who was the debunker.

There are signs that Huxley was debunking Lawrence even when their friendship was at its height. Lawrence must have been at least partly on his mind when Huxley wrote in "The Cold-Blooded Romantics" (1928) that "the modern artist seems to have grown down; he has reverted to the preoccupation of his childhood. He is trying to be a primitive. So, it may be remembered, was the romantic Rousseau. But whereas Rousseau's savage was noble, refined, and intelligent, the primitive our modern artists would like to resemble is a mixture between the apache and the fifteen-year old schoolboy."[23] Reading this, one is reminded of the scene in "Indians and the Englishman" where Lawrence is confronted in the dusk by an Apache who, he is convinced, wishes to murder him. Here they are, the twin spirits of Lawrence: Natty Bumppo and the primitive blood-consciousness.

Certainly by the time Huxley was writing *Brave New World*, he was sure that Lawrence's primitive utopia no longer cut any ice, or at any rate no more than Wells's technological one. "In beating the West with an extreme-oriental stick, contemporary writers like Lowes Dickinson and Bertrand Russell have only revived a most respectable literary tradition," Huxley observed in 1931. "The primitive and prehistoric Utopias of D. H. Lawrence and [Grafton] Elliot Smith have as good a pedigree. Our ancestors knew all about the State of Nature and the Noble Savage." It had all been tried before and had failed, so runs the implication, so why try and fail again? Here Lawrence's utopian vision is degraded (or should one say debunked?) to the point of being just another literary stone piled on an already ruinous edifice. Later on in the essay, Lawrence is degraded even further, to the level of a fad (as he is in *Eyeless in Gaza*). "With every advance of industrial civilization," Huxley predicts, "the savage past will be more and more appreciated, and the cult of D. H. Lawrence's *Dark God* may be expected to spread through an ever-widening circle of worshippers" (*Music at Night*, 141–42, 147). Now Lawrence is the fashionable cultist, no longer the prophet of a new religion. And now the connection is made explicit: Lawrence is the savage past.

\*    \*    \*

The savage past or the Fordian future? That is the question which *Brave New World* poses. The Malpais (literally "bad country" in Spanish) of prehistory or the ironically "Buenpais" of post-history? The choice is between two evils. Not that Lawrence is to be exclusively identified with the one or Wells with the other; that would be to simplify excessively the complexity of Huxley's vision, and to err by trying to make a partial truth do the work of a whole one. Huxley's Pueblo Indians, closely related as they are to Lawrence's, also have other ancestors. The fragmentary tales they tell derive, for instance, not from Lawrence but from Frank Cushing's *Zuñi Folk Tales* (1901), which seems also to be the source of many of Huxley's Indian names, including Mitsima and Waihusiva, not to mention the Smithsonian reports.[24]

No, though Lawrence's experience of New Mexico and Lawrence's antipathy to science, to social regimentation, and to promiscuous sexuality surely helped shape the spirit of the Savage, it would be wrong to identify him with Lawrence too completely. For one thing, it is important to note that Huxley transformed the Pueblo Indians, in one respect at least, almost as much as he did our own world. The Pueblo Indians—as the Smithsonian reports, among others, make clear—are anthropologically a separate entity from the Penitentes. According to Elsie Clewes Parsons's massive study of Pueblo Indian religion—not published in book form until 1939 but a considerable proportion of which had already appeared as articles by the end of the twenties—the Penitentes are "an organization [that] the Indians observe with interest as comparable to their own esoteric groups."[25] But there is no mingling of the two, certainly nothing like the fusion that exists in *Brave New World*. Huxley was, of course, aware of this fact and in his foreword described the religion of his Indians as "half fertility cult and half *Penitente* ferocity" (p. viii).

The fertility cult is Indian and, as one might expect, the snake dance is part of that cult. How closely this feature of Pueblo Indian life was linked with Lawrence in Huxley's mind may be appreciated from H. K. Haeberlin's observation that "the Great Serpent of the Pueblo is commonly known as the 'plumed serpent.'" So too with the *sipapus*, the openings in the floor of the *kiva*, which play an important part in Huxley's description of the snake dance. It is there that the deities of germination and fertility reside. And associated with these deities are also the war gods, "Püükon and his less important [twin] brother."[26]

"Püükon" is obviously Huxley's Pookong, but in *Brave New World* his twin brother has been replaced by Christ, and along with Christ have also come the Penitentes. To be sure, there are certain points of historical contact between the native Indian rites and those of the Penitentes, some of which may possibly derive from Spanish influence at the time of the Conquest. Both groups practice fasting, continence, and flagellation. The use of emetics is, however, a peculiarly Indian custom, and, though the Indians do practice whipping, it is very mild indeed compared to the Penitentes. The Pueblo Indians would certainly never tolerate sadism of the kind that climaxes the snake dance in *Brave New World*. Their whippings take place at initiation ceremonies only and then always in groups, with each youth accompanied by an adult sponsor who is sometimes also whipped. The maximum number of strokes is usually four and there is no attempt on the part of the person being struck to conceal pain. Furthermore, no Pueblo Indian would go out alone into the desert and commit an act such as the Savage describes. "Once," he tells Bernard Marx, "I did something that none of the others did: I stood against a rock in the middle of the day, in summer, with my arms out, like Jesus on the Cross" (93).

What is Huxley's point here? Why does he insist on combining an Indian fertility cult with a Christian penitential ritual? If it is merely to suggest that the forces of life are balanced by those of death—Huxley, one remembers, is often accused of Manichaeanism—then he could have portrayed that balance with much less effort by means of the Aztecs of the Old Mexico. Sir James Frazer's *Sacrificial God* is full of horrific examples.

Then why? Because, I suspect, he wishes to make a point about the relation of life to death that he could not have done using the Aztecs. The Aztecs practiced human sacrifice in order to preserve the life of their gods; for them death was merely another aspect of fertility. This is one of the chief reasons why Lawrence rooted his dark god in the *old* Mexican soil. But here again Huxley is debunking Lawrence. Life, Huxley implies, is life, never to be confused with death—unless it is the everlasting life, the life beyond death. Lawrence, as Huxley knew, disliked Christianity and may have feared it. Characteristically, he tried to shut himself off from all contact with the Penitentes during his stay in Taos. As Eliot Fay, who was in Taos at the same time as Lawrence, recalled years later, he would close the windows of his room whenever the Penitentes began their evening chants and cries.[27]

There is another and perhaps more important reason why Huxley may have chosen to put the Penitentes into his novel. *Brave New World* portrays a future and a past that differ from the present in that they have no history. Our Ford's remark that "History is bunk" applies with equal force to the Pueblo and to the London of A.F. 632. Both are stable societies that can tolerate no change and therefore possess no history. Now, the one relatively stable institution known to the West in modern historical times is the Church. Significantly, Christianity is the most important shared element of both the Fordian and the Pueblo societies.

This may be less apparent in the new world, but it is no less true. The Solidarity Service that forms a counterpart of the Pueblo Snake Dance is an obvious parody of the mass. The loving-cup of strawberry ice-cream soma is based on the bread and wine of the holy communion. ("All the advantages of Christianity and alcohol; none of their defects" (36), is how Mustapha Mond defines soma). The Solidarity hymns appear to echo Wesley's, and there is even an oblique reference to the Holy Spirit in the "enormous negro dove" at the close of the service. Like the Snake Dance, the Solidarity Service also has an underlying sexual meaning, though here it would be more appropriate to call it a sterility rite. When the drums begin to beat at the Reservation, Lenina's first thought is of the Solidarity Services. "'Orgy-porgy,' she whispered to herself. These drums beat out just the same rhythm" (75).

Christianity is an essential element in both of the worlds Huxley depicts. But—and this is a crucial distinction—it is not the same Christianity. In the one instance, it is the Christianity that maintains that we inhabit a vale of tears and that we should mortify the flesh in this life in order to store up credit in the next; on the other, it is the Christianity that promises a paradise on earth. The one is Christianity in rags, with flagellation and retreats into the desert; the other Christianity in riches, with everybody "happy" and the peace of the world insured by ten semi-apostolic World Controllers. "Suffer little children" (38), Mustapha Mond admonishes the DHC who has disturbed the little girls and boys at their erotic play.[28]

At the end of *Brave New World*, secular and fanatic Christianity meet and join. The Savage's flagellation of himself and Lenina, echoing the dance at the Pueblo, merges with the orgy-porgy dance of the visiting Fordians and culminates in a fertility-sterility rite in which the Savage finally yields his principles and himself. The only purification for that sin, he realizes on the following day, is death. Such is the result of the Controller's "experiment." Pueblo is Pueblo, and Ford is Ford, and ne'er the twain shall meet, for if they do disaster ensues. Stability lies at the extremes, not at the middle; in machine and in monster, not in man. The choice is between the chiliastic horrors of the Wellsian future or those of the Lawrentian past, both of which exclude the (by comparison lesser) day-to-day trauma of Huxleyan—or human—present.

And what does Huxley mean to suggest by all this? Perhaps, as he once wrote to his brother Julian, "all's well that ends Wells" (L. 103). To which he might later have added that finishing off Lawrence, as a social philosopher at least, was not a bad idea either.

## NOTES

1. George Wickes and Ray Frazer, "Aldous Huxley," *Writers at Work, The "Paris Review" Interviews*, 2d ser. (London: Secker & Warburg, 1963), p. 165. That Huxley knew and in some sense admired Wells's scientific fantasies is confirmed by his essay, "If My Library Burned Tonight," *Home and Garden* 92 (November 1947): 243. It is perhaps also worth noting that *Men Like Gods* was reviewed in *Nature* by Julian Huxley, who was later to collaborate with Wells on *The Science of Life* (1931).

2. Derek Patmore, *Private History* (London: Jonathan Cape, 1960), p. 154. Patmore goes on to describe how Wells, "ever an ardent socialist . . . was certain that social progress would cure the evils that men were so easily prone to, and when we discussed the works of such writers as Aldous Huxley he said to me savagely: '*Brave New World* was a great disappointment to me. A writer of the standing of Aldous Huxley has no right to betray the future as he did in that book. When thinking about the future, people seem to overlook the logical progress in education, in architecture, in science.'" H. G. Wells, *The New World Order* (New York: Knopf, 1940), p. 126; and Klaus Mann, *Der Wendepunkt, Ein Lebensbericht* (Frankfurt am Main: Fischer, 1952), p. 439. Huxley and Wells did, however, continue to correspond occasionally, and in late 1933 Huxley even joined Wells as one of the vice-presidents of the Federation of Progressive Societies and Individuals.

3. H. G. Wells, *Seven Famous Novels* (Garden City, N.Y.: Garden City Publishing Company, 1934), p. ix.

4. Quoted in W. Warren Wagar, *H. G. Wells and the World State* (New Haven, Conn.: Yale University Press, 1961), p. 48.

5. H. G. Wells, *Tales of Space and Time* (Leipzig: Tauchnitz, 1900), pp. 240–41.

6. H. G. Wells, *Men Like Gods* (New York: Macmillan, 1923), p. 266.

7. Ibid., p. 291.

8. H. G. Wells, *When the Sleeper Wakes* (New York: Harper's, 1899), pp. 69, 167, 216.

9. Mark Hillegas, *The Future as Nightmare, H. G. Wells and the Anti-Utopians* (New York: Oxford, 1967), pp. 111ff. Huxley's fictional history of the new world state may derive from—and parody—Wells's brutal utopia, *The World Set Free* (1914), in which, just as in Huxley's novel, liberation only takes place after the world is utterly devastated. In Wells's case this occurs by means of atomic bombs, which keep on exploding and releasing radioactive vapor for decades, and so render the sometime principal cities of the world uninhabitable.

10. H. G. Wells, *The First Men in the Moon* (London: George Newnes, 1901), p. 304.

11. Gerald Heard, "The Poignant Prophet," *The Kenyon Review* 27 (Winter 1965): 57.

12. Hillegas, *Future*, p. 120.

13. Reprinted in *H. G. Wells, The Critical Heritage*, ed. Patrick Parrinder (London: Routledge & Kegan Paul, 1972), p. 288.

14. Philip Gibbs, *The Day After Tomorrow* (London: Hutchinson, [1927]), p. 235.

15. D. H. Lawrence, *Selected Literary Criticism*, ed. Anthony Beal (London: Heinemann, 1955), p. 136.

16. D. H. Lawrence, *Poems* (Geneva: Heron, 1964), 1:501.

17. Julian Huxley, *Memories* (New York: Harper & Row, 1970), p. 160.

18. This essay has been reprinted in D. H. Lawrence, *Phoenix II*, ed. Warren Roberts and H. T. Moore (New York: Penguin, 1978), pp. 583–90.

19. Wickes, "Huxley," p. 165.

20. Aldous Huxley, preface to Knud Merrild, *A Poet and Two Painters* (London: George Routledge, 1938), p. xvi.

21. D. H. Lawrence, *Mornings in Mexico* (London: Martin Seeker, 1927), p. 101. Huxley read this work in October 1927 and liked it.

22. D. H. Lawrence, *Phoenix*, ed. E. D. McDonald (London: Heinemann, 1936), pp. 144 and 142.

23. Aldous Huxley, "The Cold-Blooded Romantics," *Vanity Fair* 30 (March 1928): 104.

24. The name "Popé," however, alludes to Popé of San Juan, a leader in the great 1680 Pueblo Indian rebellion against the Spaniards. By "Smithsonian Reports" Huxley means the *Annual Report of the Bureau of Ethnology*, which since 1880 has frequently published detailed studies of Pueblo Indian culture, notably by Tilly E. Stevenson, J. P. Harrington, and Leslie A. White. For general information Huxley may also have relied on Pliny Earle Goddard's *Indians of the Southwest* (New York: American Museum of Natural History, 1913), which along which geographical and historical information contains a good description of the Snake Dance. The

nonexistent pueblo of "Malpais" in *Brave New World* does not resemble physically the Zuñi pueblo at Thunder Mountain, but rather the linguistically unrelated pueblo of Acoma, over which Bernard and Lenina fly on their way to Malpais. I have been unable to determine if all the Zuñi words that the Savage occasionally bursts out with are actually Zuñi. There are, however, some resemblances between the Savage's language and the samples of Zuñi given in Ruth L. Bunzel's *Zuñi Texts*, Publications of the American Ethnological Society, vol. 15 (New York: Stechert, 1933).

At least one of the words used by the Savage—*hani*—occurs in Frank Hamilton Cushing's *My Adventures in Zuñi* (Santa Fé, N.M.: The Peripatetic Press, 1941), p. 134, originally published in 1922–23. The word is there glossed as a sister's younger brother. According to Stanley Newman's *Zuñi Dictionary* (Bloomington: Indiana Research Center in Anthropology, Folklore and Linguistics, 1958), *hanni* means a sister's younger sibling. The Savage appears to use the word as an insult, a usage not confirmed by either Cushing or Newman.

Huxley may also have consulted Cushing's "Outlines of Zuñi Creation Myths," *Annual Report of the Bureau of Ethnology* 18 (1891–92): 325–447, for some of the Pueblo names and legends.

25. Elsie Clewes Parsons, *Pueblo Indian Religion* (Chicago: University of Chicago Press, 1939), 1:159.

26. H. K. Haeberlin, "The Idea of Fertilization in the Culture of the Pueblo Indians," *Memoirs of the American Anthropological Association* 3 (1916): 24 and 234. Goddard, *Indians*, p. 118, uses the spelling "Pookong," as Huxley does.

27. Elliot Fay, *Lorenzo in Search of the Sun* (London: Vision Press, 1955), p. 71.

28. There are other echoes of the Christ story as well. Helmholtz Watson's joining the Savage to fight the Deltas recalls Peter's defense of Christ, just as Bernard Marx's later attempt at disassociation recalls his betrayal. The identification with Christ among the Penitentes is immediate and explicit. One of the members is chosen to bear the cross, upon which he is later bound and raised. See Ruth Benedict, *Patterns of Culture* (London: Routledge & Sons, 1935), pp. 90–91.

HANS J. RINDISBACHER

# Sweet Scents and Stench: Traces of Post/Modernism in Aldous Huxley's Brave New World

"There isn't any need for a civilized man to bear anything that's seriously unpleasant."

Mustapha Mond

It is without a doubt Patrick Süskind's 1985 best-selling novel *Das Parfum* that put olfactory perception, both of stenches and perfumes, on the popular cultural map of our time.[1] This book touched a sensitive nerve, so to speak, eager to respond. All that seems required at this time for the sense of smell to come fully into its own is some technical invention of a cultural magnitude similar to the movie camera or sound recording and replay systems. Imagine the possibilities this could open up—possibilities which Aldous Huxley, among very few others, already toyed with in his technofantasy *Brave New World* more than sixty years ago.[2]

Three times in his life Huxley created a scenario for a possible future state of humankind. *Brave New World*, 1932, the earliest such proposition, is the most science-fictional and futuristic; *Ape and Essence* from 1948 the most 'realistic,' bleak, and pessimistic about humankind; and *Island* from 1962 the most practically, almost feasibly utopian in its realization of true humanity. In each case Huxley, like every writer, had to choose the means of literary representation best suited to his purposes; he had to create in language a universe graspable by the human imagination through the medium of the senses, for

From *Now More Than Ever: Proceedings of the Aldous Huxley Centenary Symposium, Münster 1994*, edited by Bernfried Nugel, pp. 209–23. Copyright © 1995 by Peter Lang.

all imagination, however utopian or scientific-fictional, remains inextricably bound to the capacities of human sensory perception. Even the most fantastic universe is but an extension or a distortion of human sensory capacities.

Centering on *Brave New World* and the nature of its modernity and the modernist and postmodernist aspects in its strategies of representation, the present inquiry will draw on *Ape and Essence* and *Island* for comparison and contrast. The entry point into the text of *Brave New World* en route to answering the issue of its modernity or postmodernity is through Huxley's handling of olfactory perception. Among the many possible facets of the sense of smell in biology, neurology, physiology, as well as cultural history, linguistics, and the general progress of civilization, the focus here will be on cultural, historical, and literary aspects.

Before turning to Huxley, it may be in order to sketch a brief history of the sense of smell over the past two centuries in Western literature and emphasize the two most relevant aspects of that mode of perception for a literary context. Both concern its verbal codification. First, there is the almost complete lack of an abstract vocabulary for smells as it exists for vision, in particular for colors and shapes. We therefore commonly refer to smells in terms of their origins ('it smells like . . . ;' 'the smell of . . .'). Second, although we lack a particular vocabulary, we seem to have little difficulty in or doubt about referring to smells in the basic binary categories of *good* and *bad*, which are anthropologically determined, but socio-historically modified.[3]

Regarding the first contention, the rather precarious grounding of olfactory perception in language, Dan Sperber once made the following astute observation:

> Even though the human sense of smell can distinguish hundreds of thousands of smells and in this regard is comparable to sight or hearing, in none of the world's languages does there seem to be a classification of smells comparable, for example, to colour classification. Ethno-linguists systematically describe colour classifications, often containing several hundred terms ordered under a small number of basic categories [ . . . ]. We would search in vain for a similar work on smells; perhaps this is a sign of lack of imagination on the part of scholars, but more likely it is because there is nothing for such a work to be about [ . . . ]. There is no semantic field of smells. The notion of smells only has as lexical sub-categories general terms such as "stench" and "perfume." Our knowledge about different smells figures in the encyclopaedia not in an autonomous domain, but scattered among all the categories whose referents have olfactive qualities.[4]

Sperber, therefore, prefers to talk about smells as a symbolic rather than a semiotic system. The latter for him aims at simplicity, unambiguity, i.e. freedom from contradiction, and ideally a one-on-one relation of signifier and signified. The symbolic system, in contrast, is associative, evocative, multi-referential, and far from unambiguous. It is only in a limited sense a system of communication; it connotes more than it denotes its objects.

The second point, above, the binary division of the olfactory spectrum into a good and bad part, we best address with a hypothesis about the origin of these two categories. It is Sigmund Freud who provides the starting point. His theorizing about the sense of smell places olfaction in a teleological process that leads, in fact has already led, to its virtual demise as a culturally relevant mode of perception. The decisive step in this course of developments, according to Freud's admittedly speculative remarks, occurs some time in prehistory when humans begin to walk upright.[5] The olfactory, before this event the guiding sense in man's sexual behavior (as can be observed to this day in animal behavior as exhibited, for instance, by dogs), loses its function of regulating male–female attraction, which is taken over more and more by vision. Indeed, we fall in love at first sight, not at a first whiff—or if we do so we prefer not to talk about this.

To elucidate this point further, we may also draw on Freud's concept of *Eros* and *Thanatos* that can be fruitfully linked with his remarks on the sense of smell. Bad smells signify repulsion, corruption, decay, and ultimately death. The final reference point is the decomposing human body, a universal source of alarm and revulsion. For this our cultural history provides numerous examples, for instance in the accounts of Nazi death camp survivors.[6] The underlying forces and the fear associated with them are of disintegration, of the dissolution of bonds (both concrete, biochemical as well as figurative), which set free odors. Our modern obsession with body odor and its commercial presentation as destructive of an individual's social life if not counteracted, is only one manifestation of this primordial nexus. Good smells, on the other hand, mean attraction, eroticism, sexuality, birth, life; they mean the creation of bonds. The modern perfume industry is explicitly marketing this (erotic) attraction, irresistibility, and charisma. The mythical figure symbolizing attraction is *Eros*.[7] Freud's model also accounts for the gender coding of smell. The eternal feminine—as well as female—that attracts 'us,' the male, may well be its aroma. Indeed our cultural semiotics tends to cast the male as the smeller, the female as the olfactorily perceived object.

Freud's, however, is not the whole story. The sense of smell does not simply atrophy once its central function of regulating sexuality is allegedly diminished. The loss of importance that Freud diagnoses is certainly not one of actual physiological capacities but rather one of social functionality.

Theodor W. Adorno and Max Horkheimer in *Dialectic of Enlightenment*[8] propose a view different from, yet complementary to Freud's, of the essential functioning of smell and the combination of fear, shame, and desire that modern civilization associates with this sense:

> Of all the senses smelling, which is stimulated without objectifying, testifies most clearly to the urge to abandon and assimilate oneself to the Other [ ... ]. In the act of seeing one remains oneself, in smelling one dissolves [ ... ]. Civilized man is permitted such pleasure only when it can be justified in the name of real or seemingly practical purposes. The tabooed drive can only be indulged when it is unmistakably clear that such indulgence aims at its eradication.[9]

This is a good summary of the general cultural attitude toward olfactory perception since the Enlightenment and in particular of the views of Immanuel Kant. For him the sense of smell leads humankind to clean up its environment and eliminate sources of stench; it undermines its own *raison d'être* in the process. Both Kant's and Hegel's aesthetics exclude olfaction, and both thinkers build their paradigms on vision instead.[10]

It is a combination of anthropological and psychoanalytical thought patterns on the one hand, and cultural-historical developments understood as a process of enlightenment on the other (with all its deviations and detours) that provides the most complete explanatory model for the cultural role of olfaction. This 'process of civilization' can in fact be understood as a 'project of deodorization' of both the public and the private spheres, of cleaning up the olfactory environment in order to reinfuse it with new, standardized, accepted good smells. Alain Corbin has done pioneering work in this regard in his book *The Foul and the Fragrant*.[11]

In addition to this elementary anthropological, psychoanalytical, and philosophical grounding of olfaction, we also need to equip ourselves with a thumbnail sketch of olfactory literary history before addressing *Brave New World*. In the framework of modern European literature of the past one hundred and fifty years or so, the sense of smell bursts onto the scene first in French literature with Baudelaire.[12] It becomes an accepted medium of representation in the course of the nineteenth century, with Zola's realism/naturalism forming a climax in the 'realistic' use of olfactory perception—in contrast to the subsequently emerging 'aestheticist' or 'decadent' uses of olfaction in authors such as Huysmans and Wilde.[13] In German bourgeois realism, on the other hand, and in more 'Victorian' modes of writing in general, there are strong forces of resistance at work, specifically regarding the representation of the two most critical areas of olfaction, sexuality and death, *Eros* and *Thanatos*.

As the sense of smell is highly subjective, evocative, and apt to trigger memory, its effects—even literary ones—cannot be as easily anticipated and calculated by the author as the effect of descriptions and characterizations based on vision. The linguistic reference structure of olfaction ('the smell of . . . ;' 'it smells like . . .') inevitably breaks the smooth, authorially controlled surface of realistic texts and refers the reader to the chaos of the very object world that the text is designed to keep in check. To writers of bourgeois and Victorian inclinations who try to come to terms with the rapidly changing and modernizing world of the second half of the nineteenth century olfactory perception appears unsuitable for the overall project of mapping social and literary-aesthetic norms onto the individual reader. There is always something liminal, scandalous, provocative about this sensory mode which, through both its ultimate reference points for good and bad smells, sexuality and death, remains insolubly connected with the human body. Olfactory references, therefore, are sparse. But the olfactory medium and the cultural unfolding of olfactory perception do provide an excellent entry point into the politics of the body, an issue that has triggered much academic interest in recent years. It is at the good end of the olfactory spectrum that the cultural historical battles over the human body have been raging most fiercely. Tendentially, natural smells (squeamishly reduced to just two letters, 'b.o.') have come to be understood as bad, whereas artificial smells have turned into our standards for good. The vast perfume and deodorant industry testifies to this development.

Sexuality and its aromas, anthropologically speaking, must belong to the realm of attraction. It is precisely sexuality, however, that has experienced the most drastic socio-cultural pressures over time in many respects, not just olfactory, and the associated natural smells have been pushed into the negative half of the olfactory spectrum. They are repulsive. The gap between their low public standing and their secret personal appreciation as erotically attractive, however, is significant. Publicly, odors can cross this gap only in disguise, in the form of perfume, the *ersatz* body odor. Natural smells, the archaic odors once regulating sexual behavior, are of course still with us. The only effect the civilizing process has had on them is a 'revaluation of all values,' in calling good the artificial and bad the natural—although deep down we may still know better. The ancient link of certain body odors to erotics has never really been broken. For centuries perfumery has claimed to conceal what it was in fact revealing; it has highlighted what it was pretending to cover over. Perfume is the last piece of clothing to come off (in fact, in its most natural form of body odors it does never come off completely) in the historical process of undressing the human (female) body in Western culture. Perfume is the smell of pudenda by a different, respectable name. Perfumery, therefore, is the transferred discourse on the tabooed odors of sexual attraction.

In terms of cultural history, it is of course only in the latter part of the nineteenth century and around the turn of the twentieth century that the actual physical environment has been sufficiently cleaned up for the good spectrum of olfaction to unfold its full potential. Only the stage of cleanliness reached around that time has allowed the deliberate application of perfumes to create its own, heady, heavy, erotic and seductive atmosphere. The concrete physical world—workplaces, city streets, homes, as well as clothing and human bodies—are now sufficiently free from those stenches and bad odors that naturally emanated from objects or processes as their unintentional by-products—to the growing disgust of people. Perfumes and good scents now begin to play their quintessentially modern role, not of masking bad odors and of covering up stenches and miasma, but of self-indulgently and playfully filling public, personal, and intimate spaces. Thus a new and liberated literary mode of olfactory representation emerges with decadence and aestheticism. With its modernist roots in Baudelaire, this new mode of olfactory representation is continued by authors such as the French Symbolists, Huysmans and Oscar Wilde, but even Rilke and Thomas Mann are influenced by it. What we find in their writings is the deliberate use of olfactory instances and explicit allusions to eroticism and sexuality for aesthetic effect.

In the 1920s and 1930s a new 'tone' is entering the literary use of olfactory perception, with *Brave New World* marking the crossroads of modernism and postmodernism—as we are now able to see in retrospect.[14] This novel as a whole rests essentially on modernist parameters, on technology, centralization, rationalization, social engineering, etc. But Huxley is among the very first authors to integrate even olfactory perception into this modernist-utopian framework. In doing so, he goes far beyond the literary and historical parameters common for this sensory mode up to his time. He employs the hedonistic-sensual and deliberately playful aspects of olfactory perception in his utopian world as a technocratic means of social control. He thereby anticipates a development in the olfactory realm that has only recently been discussed with any degree of seriousness, the so-called "environmental fragrancing systems," whose "dark side is mind control."[15]

There are passages in *Brave New World*, however, where olfactory perception refuses to go along with the technocratic function that Huxley assigns to it and instead shows its atavistic and anarchic potential both in individuals and in state institutions. It is precisely in these instances that the forced utopian integration, along modernist lines, of olfaction into thoroughly rationalist parameters breaks down. Olfactory perception, by touching on its most archaic reference points, reveals itself as a thoroughly postmodern mode of textual representation, emphasizing metonymy, syntagm, combination and contextualization.[16] In its archaic anthropological connections olfaction involves chance, individuality, desire, even anarchy; in its historically more recent pleasant forms it means play, allusion, dispersal, rhetoric, surface, and irony.[17] Thus in all three categories—textual representation, anthropological roots, and historical process—olfactory perception comes down squarely on the postmodern side of any comparison between modernist and postmodernist paradigms. The crucial aspect of olfactory representation in *Brave New World* is the assignment to it of a socially stabilizing function within a modernist-technological universe. This creates a unique and revealing intersection of modernism and postmodernism. No longer are olfactory phenomena something to be *eliminated* by the system as potentially disruptive, but rather something to be *employed*, if not exploited, by it.[18] They become a tool for the manipulation of the masses, agents in the struggle for political control. In this role, however, the whole history of the sense of smell is brushed against the grain and olfaction charged with a function that it simply cannot fulfill. Significantly, it is John, the half-savage who, in his interaction with Lenina, exhibits all the archaic, individual, sexual aspects of olfaction that its official application in the universe of *Brave New World* seems to have overcome.

Into Huxley's dualistic concept, within which the technofantasy land forms the futuristic fictional standard and the Indian reservation in Arizona represents a backward stage of civilization, the existing world of the 1930s (and still, to a large extent, that of the 1990s) inserts itself as an intermediate standard by which to gauge both. Here is not the place to discuss Huxley's vision in its historical and political context or to debate the extent to which *Brave New World* has or has not become reality, but rather to take notice of how the two contrasting realms are evoked narratively and descriptively, focusing on olfaction. To put it simply: the old world stinks, the new is full of pleasant scents. Although the key element of social stability and intellectual inertia in the new world is the drug *soma*, olfaction has developed its own technological apparatus and is implemented effectively as a political instrument for social and psychological purposes. It plays a considerable part in the enterprise of creating stability, thanks to its various advanced application technologies. For instance, in order to quell the near-riot that breaks out among the Delta menial staff at the Park Lane Hospital after John throws out their *soma* rations, the police "pumped thick clouds of soma vapour into the air" (*BNW*, 256). The general use of the pills and the distribution of the active ingredient in breathable (though not olfactorily marked) form are shown to complement each other. The state of sanitation and medical and hygienic standardization in the Brave New World thus extends from the institutionalized drug consumption to pregnancy substitutes, the talcum powder hoses with the eight different scents, and the eau de cologne taps (*BNW*, 42) in the women's lounge at the Central London

Hatchery, where Lenina Crowne and the other major characters work; and it extends to the moment of death which, as we learn from the events surrounding Linda's dying, takes place in an atmosphere of regularly changed artificial scents (*BNW*, 238, 239, 244). To this ever-pleasant and sensorially stable atmosphere the scent organ, for instance at the "Westminster Abbey Cabaret"—"London's Finest Scent and Colour Organ"—contributes its own not inconsiderable share (*BNW*, 90). The scent organ, or rather the lack thereof at the North Pole vacation facility, helps swing Lenina's opinion in favor of Bernard Marx and the trip he suggested to take with her to North America rather than to Arctica, thus making possible a visit to the Arizona Savage Reservation (*BNW*, 103). The trip turns out to be a disaster, not lastly in respect to the olfactory. Their Indian guide smells (*BNW*, 121). In fact everything "primitive" smells, and as they are climbing up the rocky slope to the Indian village perched on top of a mesa, all is "oppressively queer, and the Indian smelt stronger and stronger" (*BNW*, 127). Twice Lenina is forced to hold "her handkerchief to her nose" (*BNW*, 128, 131). Other scenes are so unbearable or embarrassing for her that she has to turn and look away or cover her face with her hands (*BNW*, 130, 135). The unbeautified and non-standardized world has become unacceptable in its physical reality to the new-world inhabitants, the more so, as Lenina has left her *soma* pills at the hotel and has to face reality without the protection of the customary drug haze. Linda, the new-world woman, whom Bernard and Lenina find living among the Indians and whom they end up taking back to their civilization, together with her son John, positively reeks of mescal (*BNW*, 148, 155). Back in the Brave New World Linda will spend the rest of her days in a *soma* haze, with "the patchouli tap just dripping" (*BNW*, 184). Patchouli to her is "more than scent;" it "was the sun, was a million sexophones, was Popé making love, only much more so, incomparably more, and without end" (*BNW*, 185). At the reservation the twilight of her hut "stank" (*BNW*, 139), and when she approached Lenina, she "smelt too horrible, obviously never had a bath, and simply reeked of that beastly stuff that was put into Delta and Epsilon bottles" (*BNW*, 139–140). John, who was born and grew up on the Savage Reservation, loves the stories his mother has been telling him all these years of the unattainable new world, of the "pictures that you could hear and feel and smell, as well as see, and another box for making nice smells" and of everybody always being happy "and no one ever sad or angry [ . . . ] and everything so clean, and no nasty smells, no dirt at all" (*BNW*, 151). It is no wonder that he is attracted to Lenina, the dream-come-true girl, and gets into a veritable frenzy over her scents when he breaks into her hotel room to check whether she and Bernard are still there to take him and his mother away to the new world as they had promised:

A moment later he was inside the room. He opened the green suit-
case; and all at once he was breathing Lenina's perfume, filling his
lungs with her essential being [ . . . ] [he] kissed a perfumed acetate
handkerchief [ . . . ]. Opening a box, he spilt a cloud of scented
powder. His hands were floury with the stuff. He wiped them on
his chest, on his shoulders, on his bare arms. Delicious perfume!
He shut his eyes; he rubbed his cheek against his own powdered
arm. Touch of smooth skin against his face, scent in his nostrils of
musky dust—her real presence. "Lenina," he whispered. "Lenina!"
(*BNW*, 170)

This orgiastic scene is a clever double take. It allows us to see the new world
as the scented paradise from the perspective of the (half) savage; and it glar-
ingly highlights the erotic misunderstanding unfolding here. John goes wild
over Lenina's scents because, for him, they are unique.[19] They mark "her
essential being." The reader knows, however, that in the new world the very
opposite is true: the standardized scents of the powder hose and scent tap
are ubiquitous and designed precisely to eradicate differences, to deconstruct
eroticism as the individual and personal. They help preserve the state of
institutionalized absence of jealousy, an emotion that has become obsolete
in an environment in which erotic attraction has been replaced by the much
more convenient psychosexual hygiene.

Huxley's new world is one of sexual promiscuity that is not only desired
but virtually required. The artificial scents wafting through this universe function like perfumes in that they refer to nothing but themselves, but ultimately,
or rather, originally, refer to sexuality as such. The difference with perfumes
as we still use them in the late twentieth century lies in their public application as *dampers* rather than their personal use as *highlights* of individuality. Only John, the savage, still operates on this older pattern, whereas the
citizens of the Brave New World have lost that original sense of smell. Their
excitement at the feelies (while "the scent organ was playing a delightfully
refreshing Herbal Capriccio" as an opener [*BNW*, 198]) is a communal turn-
on, directed at nobody in particular. John, however, thinks of Lenina still as
a unique person, not lastly characterized by her smell, "her essential being,"
while he, for her, at first seems just another object of desire. It is to her great
frustration that she finds herself actually liking him, while he rejects the new-
world standard of sexual interaction (there is no emphasis on smell in this
case). In the disastrous, unconsummated love scene between the two smell is
present in the Shakespeare quotes that John mumbles to himself (about that
"sulphurous pit" and the "burning, scalding" and the "stench" encountered
below women's girdles) after Lenina has escaped into the bathroom; but "her

perfume still hung about him," too, in actual reality, and "his jacket was white with the powder that had scented her velvety body" (*BNW*, 233). "Impudent strumpet" is all he can think of in reaction.

If *Eros* is indeed the constructive and binding force of civilization as Freud claims, it is in the scene at Lenina's hotel on the Reservation, where we still encounter it as this force of individual attraction between the sexes— and indeed in its oldest, unsublimated medium, the olfactory. This, however, is only true in John's world. Lenina's, and the whole Brave New World, has succeeded in the very annihilation of this force through the mass application of de-individualized olfactory standards in the name of maintaining social stability. The olfactory is back in the public sphere, as it was in the eighteenth and nineteenth centuries, but this time not as a public-health concern as in those earlier scientific discourses, nor as an expression of a sensory and perceptual revolution (in which form it found its way into literature), but rather, within literature, as an as yet utopian political instrument.

Later on in Huxley's book, the Controller agrees with John that *Othello* is "better than those feelies." But he maintains that they are "the price we have to pay for stability." Instead of *Othello* "we have the feelies and the scent organ" (*BNW*, 264). What is considered art in the new world points only to itself; the feelies and the scent organ lack the referential capabilities of the work of art as we know it. The feelies (and their olfactory component with them) are not products of sublimation, they do not even induce sublimation: they function as the permanently open safety valve of the sensual and erotic plumbing system. This is Freud taken to the extreme, to the point of revaluating all values where, among other things, smell shifts its impact from its passive reception in the individual and erotic sphere to aggressive dispersion with an anaesthetic purpose in the public realm. That is how 'emotionally engineered' smells find their political application.[20]

In olfactory terms the civilization of *Brave New World* has reached a final stage. Its environment is clean and artificial; the sensory spectrum of the atmosphere has shifted to the exclusively pleasant; and what could be offensive exists only in the Savage Reservations. The family home, negatively characterized as a locus of smell, has been overcome; sexuality and placebo-procreation have been made part of the public domain.[21] There is nothing personal, intimate, erotic about them any more, and odor thus has lost its original sexual connotation. There are, however, characteristic instances where the old sensitivity for smells resurfaces. The political system of *Brave New World* has not quite succeeded in wiping out all the archaic olfactory patterns. It has indeed managed to manipulate technologically and by means of political indoctrination the spectrum generally available to its citizens and their evaluating mechanisms, but as a consequence everything penetrating from outside (in whatever limited form an outside still exists) is cause for both disgust and alarm. It is revealing that the very act that guarantees the stability of the system, the molding of the bottled embryos into their various castes, is associated with a stink, "a whiff of asafoetida" (*BNW*, 31), which is used in the conditioning of the lower castes, along with hypnopaedia, to which all castes are exposed. Characteristically, too, when Lenina meets Linda for the first time on the occasion of her visit to the reservation, she "stiffened and shrank" from Linda's "reek of embryo-poison" (*BNW*, 142). The political manipulators of *Brave New World* control and manufacture the good part of the olfactory spectrum; the bad part, however, still emerges against their will, escapes from acts and processes of an ethically questionable nature—as has always been the case.[22] It is interesting to notice in this context that the disposal of the dead in this new world is specifically mentioned as a process of recycling, as it were, and characterized, by implication, as odor-free (*BNW*, 86–87).

In conclusion, let us turn to *Ape and Essence* and *Island* to complement our understanding of Huxley's uses of olfactory perception in his utopian writing.[23] In both novels, Huxley's use of smells is much less spectacular and futuristic than in *Brave New World*. In *Ape and Essence* the binary set-up of a civilized and a savage part of the world is drastically reversed in its proportions: the whole world, except for New Zealand, has reverted to a state of neo-primitivism after "the Thing," the nuclear holocaust. The focus of Huxley's interest is, as in so much of his writing, on social organization, with its primary aspects of religious (ideological) and sexual control. Smells play a minor role, and those instances we do find fit into the archaic binary reference structure of sexuality and death, with the former appearing in its uncivilized natural state, unbeautified by perfumes—yet all the more attractive to Alfred Poole, the visitor from New Zealand to the primitive culture that survives and is re-emerging in the ruins of Los Angeles. "Loola *au naturel* with a musky redolence which, on second thoughts, has something really rather fascinating about it"[24] will in fact help Poole liberate himself from the somewhat Victorian erotic standards that his mother had inculcated into him. A little later "the wine within and, without, the musky reminder" do it for him: "Dr. Poole takes her face between his hands and kisses her on her mouth" (*AE*, 88). The stench of death on the other hand is present in the "malodorous twilight" (*AE*, 92) of the former Biltmore Coffee Shop, where the young women with their deformed babies are kept that are going to be slaughtered during the subsequent religious ceremony. "Here the stink was overpowering, the filth beyond description" (*AE*, 100). In this most dystopic of Huxley's three accounts of future society even the erotic is of an ambivalent nature—at least for the late twentieth-century lovers of bodily cleanliness: it is musky.

In *Island*, the binary set-up of Huxley's universe is different again—and so is its mood. Pala is a truly positive, hopeful utopia, a society that in fact might almost exist even at present—if it were not relentlessly set upon and, at the end of the novel, taken over and destroyed by the world that surrounds it—a world very much like our own. Pala is a gentle, human, and humane society that, among other things, emphasizes a Buddhist-inspired mind–body totality that makes it much more openly sensual and aware of sensory perception than our own culture. Olfaction, however, although firmly planted in the general sensory spectrum, is used conventionally, with Eros and *Thanatos* as its open reference points. Thus Will Farnaby, at the very outset of the novel—and at that point thinking back to England—realizes clearly why he abandoned Molly, his wife, and went for Babs instead, for "what he wanted was a different perfume, was the warmth and resilience of a younger body."[25] The pink alcove, where Babs and he used to make love, haunts him throughout the story and is conjured up in its ambivalence of attraction and horror, together with "that delicious smell in the darkness [ ... ] the skills, the reflexes, and, within its aura of musk" Babs's body, "agonizing in the extremity of pleasure" (*Isl*, 271). Professionally, however, Will, the journalist, has followed another smell, "the smell of death from one end of the earth to the other." And in his memory the two have mixed when suddenly, "through the stench of death, mingled and impregnated with the stench of death, he was breathing the musky essence of Babs" (*Isl*, 272). He even remembers a little joke he used to make "about the chemistry of purgatory and paradise" (*Isl*, 272) and goes on to name three chemical compounds that olfactorily represent these two realms for him.[26] Death is present as smell also when his beloved dog Tiger dies (*Isl*, 273); old people smell bad in general (*Isl*, 274), and his favorite aunt Mary is also dying in a "strange, aromatic smell of contaminated blood" hanging about her (*Isl*, 276). Thus we find again love and death, the reference points of olfactory perception in Western culture. In between, however, there is another realm of olfaction, not uncommon in the history of culture, but not encountered in the works discussed so far: the spiritual. As a liminal sense par excellence, the olfactory mediates between this world and another, as it were; and not only in Christian religion is the divine veiled in scents. It is incense, on several occasions, that appears as the aroma of the spiritual, the merest trace of matter that connects this world with the next.

Most unusual perhaps—yet in itself not without a precursor—is "the heavenly smell of enlightenment" (*Isl*, 243) that is released when children of Pala get rid of their anger and frustration through certain breathing techniques and thereby convert their negative feelings into positive ones. This smell of enlightenment is like "champak, like ylang-ylang, like gardenias—only infinitely more wonderful" (*Isl*, 243). The precursor to Huxley who linked the enlightenment spirit with olfaction was Hegel; he once said: "The communication of pure knowledge is comparable to the dispersion of a scent in a nonresisting atmosphere. It is an all-out contagion that initially goes unnoticed by the uncaring element into which it spreads. Therefore, there is no defense against it."[27]

If only, one might wish, the process of enlightenment had relied more on this method of *insinuation* ...

## Notes

1. Patrick Süskind, *Das Parfum* (Zurich, 1985). Engl. *Perfume*, transl. John E. Woods (New York, 1986).

2. *BNW* (New York, 1946). Here the public and private spheres have been cleansed of unpleasant odors and are periodically infused with good smells from specialized equipment.

3. As with the sense of taste, whose categories of 'bitter' and 'sour' may have served early humans as warning criteria in food selection, certain smells may have functioned in similar ways and led to near-insoluble indexical pairings, such as of smoke and fire. In contrast, the preference for certain types of perfumes at certain times in history—the craze for musk in the eighteenth, the predilection for floral notes in the nineteenth century, for example—testifies to a degree of freedom in olfactory semiotics.

4. Dan Sperber, *Rethinking Symbolism* (Cambridge, 1975), 115–116.

5. See Sigmund Freud, *Civilization and Its Discontents*, ed. and transl. James Strachey (New York, 1961), section 4.

6. Limited space does not allow a full discussion of this issue here, but it is noteworthy how in many survivors' accounts the stench that reigned in the camps, and specifically the smoke from the crematoria, serve as an indelible symbol of the complete breakdown of civilization, a return to utter primitivism. For a fuller discussion of this issue and the development of the literary uses of olfactory perception in general see my monograph: *The Smell of Books: A Cultural-Historical Study of Olfactory Perception in Literature* (Ann Arbor, 1992). Hereafter, *The Smell of Books.*

7. *Thanatos* and *Eros* are used here in analogy to, if not identical with, Freud's usage of these two figures of thought in *Civilization and Its Discontents.*

8. Max Horkheimer/Theodor W. Adorno, *Dialektik der Aufklärung* (Frankfurt a.M., 1971; 1947). Hereafter, *Dialektik.*

9. *Dialektik*, 165; my translation.

10. It is revealing in this context that the 'higher senses' as they are often called, vision and hearing, have developed their own social infrastructure (so that one can learn about them) and their realms of art and aesthetics. Of the 'lower senses,' taste and smell, only the former, in the culinary, approaches the artistic, whereas perfumery, the 'art' associated with the latter, is often seen as bordering on artifice.

11. Alain Corbin, *The Foul and the Fragrant: Odor and the French Social Imagination* (Cambridge, MA, 1986), originally published as *Le miasme et la jonquille*, 1982. For another very readable cultural-historical account of olfactory perception, setting out from biology, see D. Michael Stoddart, *The Scented Ape: The Biology and Culture of Human Odour* (Cambridge, 1990).

12. This cut-off is, of course, arbitrary. Olfactory perception has been noted, commented on, and, in fact, theorized since classical antiquity. It also plays a persistent role in religious contexts, Christian as well as others. Thus having had to limit the scope of my inquiry, I focused on modernity. This is also the time when good smells are beginning to gain the upper hand in both personal and private realms and thus allow for growing aesthetic free play.

13. See J. K. Huysmans, *Against the Grain* (*À Rebours*), and Oscar Wilde, *The Picture of Dorian Gray*. For both authors odors are no longer the 'natural' emanations of objects, but become themselves artificial and artistic objects of aesthetic creation and literary discourse.

14. As early as 1911, for instance, the German writer and philosopher Salomon Friedländer undertakes olfactory explorations that turn the representational history of that sensory mode upside down. The most uncanny among them is a science-fictional piece about purifying the air of the whole world. In this totalitarian project large parts of the world population would be exterminated. Mynona (pseud. for Salomon Friedländer), "Von der Wollust über Brücken zu gehen," *Die Aktion* (11 September 1911), collected in: *Rosa, die schöne Schutzmannsfrau und andere Geschichten*, ed. Ellen Otten (Zurich, 1965).

15. *Wall Street Journal* (13 October 1988), section B.

16. On the aspect of contextualization see, for instance, Trygg Engen, "La mémoire des odeurs," *La Recherche* (February 1989), 176. Engen, a specialist in sensorial psychology, has been one of the more persistent researchers in matters of olfaction in recent years. His *Odor Sensation and Memory* (New York, 1991) provides a recent very readable overview of the field.

17. For a set of contrastive terms see, for instance, Ihab Hassan, "The Culture of Postmodernism," in: *Modernism: Challenges and Perspectives*, eds. Monique Chefdor/Ricardo Quinones/Albert Wachtel (Urbana/Chicago, 1986). Hassan provides a comparative chart of those key aspects of modernism and postmodernism that are widely accepted for a categorical distinction of these two styles and modes of thinking.

18. This shift is predicated on the binary structure of the realm of olfaction itself: what was to be eliminated has always been the bad part of the olfactory spectrum which, as a rule, emerges as an unintended by-product of human activities. The Huxleyan universe deliberately produces only the good part of the spectrum. Notice also the duality in the verb "to smell" itself, denoting both the (passive) emanation of odors from an object and the active sampling of odors by a subject. There is—at least in literature—no space for neutral odors; they are 'silent.' Between good and bad, *tertium non datur*.

19. These and subsequent remarks on John are not meant to provide a full socio-psychological interpretation of his character. In general he is much more in between worlds, times, and symbolic systems than his olfactory behavior would make him appear.

20. Capping the alteration of values depicted in the Huxleyan universe is the fact that the concept of what was formerly known as the *home*, the family, the male and female couple caring personally for a number of children, has become anathema and is transferred onto the savage side and depicted as—among other disgusting things—a place of bad odors. "Home, home—a few small rooms, stiflingly overinhabited by a man, by a periodically teeming woman, by a rabble of boys and girls of all ages. No air, no space; an understerilized prison; darkness, disease, and smells"

(*BNW* 41–42). This is the final blow to the (romantic) home as a place of origin and belonging, and the rejection is emotionally couched in a gesture of physical and sensual disgust. Its practical social consequence is hatchery rearing. The home is replaced in Huxley's work by the anonymous industrial process of artificial gestation.

21. While Huxley continues his critique of the traditional Western nuclear family in *Island*, this criticism seems much more 'constructive,' seeking a solution no longer in technology, but in the system of the Mutual Adoption Clubs.

22. We encounter the same olfactory constellation in the Nazi death camps, with the difference that the powers in control there are not manufacturing pleasant smells to *control* a population, but are clearly aware of the stench generated by *eradicating* a population. Important material on this issue can be found in Robert Jay Lifton, *The Nazi Doctors: Medical Killing and the Psychology of Genocide* (New York, 1986). See also Jadwiga Bezwinska (ed.), *KL Auschwitz Seen by the SS: Höss, Broad, Kremer* (New York, 1984); and my own *The Smell of Books*, especially ch. 4.

23. An even more general frame of reference for my arguments is provided, of course, by Huxley's life-long interest in the working of the human brain, matters of neurology, perception, and mind–body interaction.

24. *AE* (New York, 1948), 82.

25. *Isl* (New York, 1962), 3.

26. To characterize purgatory in olfactory terms he would use tetraethylene diamine and sulfureted hydrogen; for paradise, symtrinitropsibutyl toluene, "with an assortment of organic impurities" (*Isl*, 272). Tetraethylene diamine smells like a cross between rotting fish and ammonia; but symtrinitropsibutyl is not a 'real' name (i.e., it does not follow the nomenclatural rules). 'Trinitro-' and 'butyl-' are meaningful prefixes, but 'sym-' and 'psi-' are not. Toluene itself smells like airplane glue or turpentine, but any substituents on it would undoubtedly alter its aroma.

27. G.W.F. Hegel, *Gesammelte Werke*, ed. Westfälische Akademie der Wissenschaften (Hamburg, 1968–), IX, 295 (my translation).

MARIO VARRICCHIO

# *Power of Images/Images of Power in* Brave New World *and* Nineteen Eighty-Four

Two of the most important dystopic novels of our century, *Brave New World* and *Nineteen Eighty-Four*, make use of cinema and television to draw an extremely pessimistic picture of humanity's future, emphasizing their role as essential means for distorting reality and, in the case of the Fordian society,[1] also for providing artificial pleasures which dim the mind. The big and the small screen—Huxley dedicates more space to the former while Orwell to the latter—perform a crucial political function by preventing and repressing protest and, more generally, by conditioning and inhibiting oppositional forces in a fashion that ominously foreshadows the present. This is particularly striking in Huxley's work, published as early as 1932. While for Orwell it was comparatively easy, after World War Two, to predict the potential twisting power of television, Huxley was able to see beyond cinema, the most popular visual medium of his age, envisaging the consequences of the invention of the small screen.

In the standardized societies depicted in both novels the media uphold conformity, denying individuals their own privacy and personal feelings. Simultaneously, they strengthen powers capable of controlling every single facet of their subjects' lives by depriving them of all critical attitude. Both societies have been emptied of a sense of history and of memory of the past. In Airstrip One, the emptiness is filled by a host of images of propaganda

From *Utopian Studies* 10, no. 1 (1999): 98–114. Copyright © 1999 by the Society for Utopian Studies.

whereas in the Fordian world it is shallowness and sensationalism which nullify any possible counteraction, acting as disabling drugs.

Peter E. Firchow points out that Huxley's antiutopia possesses many of the typical aspects of the American society contemporary with him: "that the United States is the present model for Huxley's vision of the future emerges [ ... ] clearly from an essay entitled, 'The Outlook for American Culture, Some Reflections in a Machine Age', published in 1927 [ ... ] one of the most ominous portents of the American Way of Life is that it embraces a large class of the people who 'do not want to be cultured, are not interested in the higher life. For these people existence on the lower, animal levels is perfectly satisfactory. Given food, drink, the company of their fellows, sexual enjoyment, and plenty of noisy distractions from without, they are happy'" (455). Bernard Crick remarks that Orwell drew on the features of the totalitarian regimes which developed in the Soviet Union and Germany in the 1920s and 1930s and on his personal experience of life in Britain in the aftermath of World War Two. He was also affected by the thesis expressed by James Burnham's *The Managerial Revolution* (1941) according to which, in industrially developed countries, there is a trend towards the establishment of hierarchical and technocratic forms of society (7–10; 20–23; 46–47 and *passim*). In particular, the resumption of BBC television broadcasting played a role in Orwell's prominent use of the telescreen: apart from alluding to the USSR, "the general reeling off of triumphant and possibly imaginary production statistics was familiar to wartime listeners to the BBC itself" (21). In Orwell's work the theme of images is reinforced by the use of visual metaphors and of metaphors of the screen as a "frame," which projects and delimits pictures at the same time.

## New Media for New Worlds

In *Brave New World* the first allusion to the cinema is made right after the initial sequence of the visit to the Conditioning Centre, when the Assistant Predestinator asks Henry Foster if he will go see the new, sensational *feely*: "'Going to the Feelies this evening, Henry?' enquired the Assistant Predestinator. 'I hear the new one at the Alhambra is first-rate. There's a love scene on a bearskin rug; they say it's marvellous. Every hair of the bear reproduced. The most amazing tactual effects'" (30). The new "films," which also stimulate the senses of touch and smell, are perfectly in tune with the hedonistic social picture that takes shape before the reader's eyes: together with the children's erotic play (26–27) and the conversations between Lenina and Fanny and between Henry and the Assistant Predestinator, they characterize a world which reifies individuals and predetermines the satisfaction of sexual desires. Intercourse, frequently practised with changing (and interchangeable) partners, is seen in terms of possession, or rather of "use" (39; 51). As a matter of fact, the adjective which defines female beauty—*pneumatic*—reveals much about the values of the Fordian world. Desire is dead in the Brave New World: to admit the existence of it would mean to recognize the failure of the ideal State. That is why all fundamental needs, above all those related with the sexual instinct, are immediately satisfied except for the desire for freedom, which has inevitably been suppressed (Meloni 118).

The cinema plays an important role throughout the story, but especially in the second half of it. In addition to the long narrative stretch devoted to the "cinematographic" experience of the Savage, references to motion pictures are numerous. The first contact John has with them occurs in the Geography Room of the Alpha Plus school, where he attends the screening of a "documentary" on the life in the Reserve. The light from the projection recalls the cold sinister illumination of the laboratories and provides Bernard Marx with the opportunity to make advances to the Head Mistress, while the images of the rites performed by the natives set off the students' hilarity. Much to its discredit, the cinema here prompts derision and favours promiscuity:

> A click; the room was darkened; and suddenly, on the screen above the master's head, there were the *Penitentes* of Acoma prostrating themselves before Our lady, and wailing as John had heard them wail, confessing their sins before Jesus on the cross, before the eagle image of Pookong. The young Etonians fairly shouted with laughter. Still wailing, the *Penitentes* rose to their feet, stripped off their upper garments and, with knotted whips, began to beat themselves, blow after blow. [ . . . ] In the cinematographic twilight, Bernard risked a gesture which, in the past, even total darkness would hardly have emboldened him to make. Strong in his new importance, he put his arm round the Head Mistress's waist. It yielded, willowily. He was just about to snatch a kiss or two and perhaps a gentle pinch, when the shutters clicked open again. (146–147)

Cinema is also associated with superficiality. Among the things Fanny Crowne envies of Lenina is the fact that she has been on the *Feelytone News* because of her special relationship with the Savage, "visibly, audibly and tactually appeared to countless millions all over the planet" (149). Prophetically, Huxley foreshadows in this sort of newsreel the predominantly lurid character of contemporary television.

The vulgar nature of the cinema is then shown in full. John's experience at the *feelies* begins with scented songs played by *synthetic music machines*: "The scent organ was playing a delightfully refreshing Herbal Capriccio—rippling arpeggios of thyme and lavender, of rosemary, basil, myrtle, tarragon [ . . . ] In the synthetic music machine the soundtrack roll began to unwind. It was a trio for hyper-violin, super-'cello and oboe-surrogate that now filled the air with its agreeable languor" (150–151). Then, as the lights of the Feely House go down:

> [ . . . ] fiery letters stood out solid and as though self-supported in the darkness. THREE WEEKS IN A HELICOPTER. AN ALL-SUPER-SINGING, SYNTHETIC-TALKING, COLOURED, STEREOSCOPIC FEELY. WITH SYN-CHRONIZED SCENT-ORGAN ACCOMPANIMENT.
>
> "Take hold of those metal knobs on the arms of your chair,' whispered Lenina. 'Otherwise you won't get any of the feely effects."
>
> The Savage did as he was told.
>
> Those fiery letters, meanwhile, had disappeared; there were ten seconds of complete darkness; then suddenly, dazzling and incomparably more solid-looking than they would have seemed in actual flesh and blood, far more real than reality, there stood the stereoscopic images, locked in one another's arms, of a gigantic Negro and a golden-haired young brachycephalic Beta-Plus female.
>
> The Savage started. That sensation on his lips! He lifted a hand to his mouth; the titillation ceased; let his hand fall back on the metal knob; it began again. The scent organ, meanwhile, breathed pure musk. Expiringly, a soundtrack superdove cooed "Oo-ooh"; and vibrating only thirty-two times a second, a deeper than African bass made an answer: "Aa-aah." "Ooh-ah! Ooh-ah!" the stereoscopic lips came together again, and once more the facial erogenous zones of the six thousand spectators in the Alhambra tingled with almost intolerable galvanic pleasure. (151–152)

The *feelies* episode establishes a synthesis between technology and social life. It is one of the three stages, undoubtedly the climactic one, that best embody the spirit of the Fordian age along with the Conditioning Centre tour—where emphasis is laid on technology and biogenetics—and the Solidarity Service—an example of "communal" life which also provides Huxley with the opportunity to mock the new religion.

The passage narrating Lenina's advances to the Savage makes it clear how artificial and deindividualized life is in the Fordian era and how relevant is the role played by the cinema in determining its nature. John's sensations in coming into contact with the young woman's body remind him of the *feelies* thus making this experience, mediated by them, become unnatural to him. The reader witnesses here an all-out attack of organized society on what is most private and personal. The cinema, indeed, proves to be an internalized component of the political apparatus: "And suddenly her arms were round his neck; he felt her lips soft against his own. So delicious soft, so warm and electric that inevitably he found himself thinking of the embraces in *Three Weeks in a Helicopter*. Ooh! ooh! the stereoscopic blonde and ahh! the more than real blackamoor. Horror, horror, horror . . ." (174).

John and Mustapha Mond, the *World Controller*, discuss the social role of cinema in the didactical chapter preceding the conclusion of the novel. When the Savage numbers the *feelies*, vulgar and banal as compared to the profundities of tragedy, among the horrors of the New World the Controller points out that they do not have, nor are they supposed to have, other meaning than themselves (200–201). In his desperate battle against vacuity John quotes *King Lear*, resorting to what constitutes for him (but Huxley's voice is also to be heard here) the quintessence of Culture. The Savage has a transcendental idea of culture, which he sees as a natural heritage, an old wisdom transmitted throughout the centuries. This heritage is contrasted to cold dialectic, whose purpose is to restrain thought, setting limits and establishing boundaries. John portrays the world in absolute terms: on one side programmed integration, with all its negative consequences, on the other naturalness which, even though repressed, can be summoned up by reason. He does not understand the complexity of the structures which regulate the Fordian society and denies the reification of spirit, hoping to be able to modify the web of power thanks to personal will and perseverance (Bertinetti, Deidda and Domenichelli, 49–50). The deceptiveness of such a hope is shown by Mond's discouraging reply, which reveals that the new society does not confine itself to self-representation and not only rejects the past but filters and reinterprets it according to its own laws, transforming it completely: "But where would Edmund be nowadays? Sitting in a pneumatic chair, with his arm round a girl's waist, sucking away at his sex-hormone chewing-gum and looking at the feelies" (215). One more enlightening episode is worth considering: hidden in the woods, an expert operator shoots the Savage's self-flagellation and makes a "film" out of it. The rich sample of technical terms and the detailed description of the process of shooting emphasizes the metamorphosis of personal tragedy into a spectacle for the masses. In this example of journalistic malpractice Huxley demonstrates, once again, his ability to predict today's cynical exploitation of suffering as a means to increase ratings:

> Patience and skill had been rewarded. He had spent three days sitting inside the bole of an artificial oak tree, three nights crawling on his belly through the heather, hiding microphones in gorse bushes, burying wires in the soft grey sand. Seventy-two hours of profound discomfort. But now the great moment had come [ . . . ] "Splendid," he said to himself, as the Savage started his astonishing performance. "Splendid!" he kept his telescopic cameras carefully aimed—glued to their moving objective; clapped on a higher power to get a close-up of the frantic and distorted face (admirable!); switched over, for half a minute, to slow motion (an exquisitely comical effect, he promised himself); listened in, meanwhile, to the blows, the groans, the wild and raving words that were being recorded on the sound-track at the edge of his film, tried the effect of a little amplification (yes, that was decidedly better) [ . . . ] (what astonishing luck!) the accommodating fellow did turn round, and he was able to take a perfect close-up.
>
> "Well, that was grand!" he said to himself when it was all over. "Really grand!" He mopped his face. When they had put in the feely effects at the studio, it would be a wonderful film. Almost as good, thought Darwin Bonaparte, as the *Sperm Whale's Love-Life*—and that, by Ford, was saying a good deal!
>
> Twelve days later *The Savage of Surrey* had been released and could be seen, heard and felt in every first-class feely-palace in Western Europe. (230–231)

Unlike Huxley, Orwell does not place films in the foreground, preferring to reserve much more space to the *telescreen*. The main function of cinema in *Nineteen Eighty-Four* is one of political propaganda. Witness to this is the alteration of films, as well as newspapers and pictures, effected both routinely (e.g. 190) and under special circumstances: during the Hate Week, for instance, the sudden change of alliances compels the members of the Party to perform a *tour de force* in order to change all the documents testifying to the previous association with Eastasia (314).

Not only is the cinematographic medium controlled by the members of the Party, and employed to influence their own thinking, but it is also meant to provide the proles with the kind of obscene entertainment suitable to maintain a peaceful social order. The Records Department of the Ministry of Truth, in fact, includes a section specifically devoted to the production of pornographic films (193). William Plank draws an interesting parallel between the proles and the citizens of the Fordian society. In Oceania the "problem" of sexual drive is solved by repressing the instincts of the clerical workers while granting free vent to, and indeed encouraging the satisfaction of, the desires of the lower classes: "Orwell's proles, erotically nourished with state-produced pornography, are the equivalent of the citizens of *Brave New World* who are encouraged to be openly erotic [ . . . ] The erotic feelies in *Brave New World* are likewise a control device, a massified orgasm" (33). Gruesome "entertainment," on the other hand, is directed to everybody. When asked if he has attended the hangings, Winston replies he will see them "on the flicks" (198): more than real films, the "flicks" are propaganda newsreels (most, if all of them, commissioned by the Party), a typical product of totalitarian regimes and military conflicts. A good description of this strange kind of amusement is provided in a page of Winston's diary. The gory shots of the "war films," as he defines them, stimulate the elated response of an audience conditioned to the point of enjoying the sight of a child's arm severed by a bomb (except for the indignation of a prole woman, a feeling allowed to the members of her social group). On this occasion, the cinema is shown in all its socio-technical facets. The explicit mention of video cameras, the precise description of the shots and of the process of filming and, finally, of the audience's reaction, illustrate the production of the images (the technical aspect of the cinema), the images themselves (the spectacular aspect) and the effect of their reception (the sociopolitical aspect):

> *April 4th, 1984. Last night to the flicks. All war films. One very good one of a ship full of refugees being bombed somewhere in the Mediterranean. Audience much amused by shots of great huge fat man trying to swim away with a helicopter after him. first you saw him wallowing along in the water like a porpoise, then you saw him through the helicopters gunsights, then he was full of holes and the sea round him turned pink and he sank as suddenly as though the holes had let in the water, audience shouting with laughter when he sank. then you saw a lifeboat full of children with a helicopter hovering over it. there was a middle-aged woman might have been a jewess sitting up in the bow with a little boy about three years old in her arms. little boy screaming with fright and hiding his head between her breast as if he was trying to burrow right into her and the woman putting her arms round him and comforting him although she was blue with fright herself, all the time covering him up as much as possible as if she thought her arms could keep the bullets off him. then the helicopter planted a 20 kilo bomb in among them terrific flash and the boat went all to matchwood, then there was*

*a wonderful shot of a child's arm going up up right up into the air a*
*helicopter with a camera in its nose must have followed it up and there*
*was a lot of applause from the party seats but a woman down in the*
*prole part of the house suddenly started kicking up a fuss and shouting*
*they didnt oughter of showed it not in front of kids they didnt it aint*
*right not in front of kids it aint until the police turned her turned her*
*out i dont suppose anything happened to her nobody cares what the proles*
*say typical prole reaction they never*—(163. Emphasis in the original)

In the first chapter of Goldstein's book, "Ignorance is Strength", a work actually written by the members of the Inner Party, there is a clear allusion to the role of mass media in manipulating public opinion. The cinema is among them, though it is acknowledged that political control has been ensured, above all, by the evolution of television: the invention of the telescreen, a device which can transmit and receive at the same time, is rightly considered of the utmost importance for the maintenance of a police State (335).

The obsessive presence of the telescreen in the Orwellian world makes it the core of any analysis of the role of media in the novel. The screen, immediately introduced into the narration, is described as an oblong metal plate resembling an opaque mirror from which a fruity voice continuously emanates (157). Piercing sounds and military music are also what it often transmits (see, for example, 162, 178).

As he had previously done with cinema, Orwell dwells upon the images of the telescreen showing in a precise and unequivocable manner its function and purpose. Once the Two Minutes Hate are over, Oceania no longer hides secrets for the reader. The distorted use of the medium and the ideological artificiality of the message determine an aural and visual Pavlovian reaction on the part of the audience. The Two Minutes start with a screeching sound and finish with the appearance of Big Brother restoring calm and serenity. The spectators' emotional involvement is complete, while all critical attitude is absent: "The next moment a hideous, grinding screech, as of some monstrous machine running without oil, burst from the big telescreen at the end of the room. It was a noise that set one's teeth on edge and bristled the hair at the back of one's neck. The Hate had started.

As usual, the face of Emmanuel Goldstein, the Enemy of the People, had flashed onto the screen. There were hisses here and there among the audience" (165–166).

The narration is interrupted by digressions on the figure of Goldstein, only to resume and reach its climax. Frenzy and hate are replaced by ecstasy when Big Brother's face and the Party's slogans fades in:

In its second minute the Hate rose to a frenzy. People were leaping up and down in their places and shouting at the tops of their voices in an effort to drown the maddening bleating voice that came from the screen. The little sandy-haired woman had turned bright pink, and her mouth was opening and shutting like that of a landed fish. Even O'Brien's heavy face was flushed. He was sitting very straight in his chair, his powerful chest swelling and quivering as though he were standing up to the assault of a wave. The dark-haired girl behind Winston had begun crying out "Swine! Swine! Swine!", and suddenly she picked up a heavy Newspeak dictionary and flung it at the screen. [ . . . ]

The Hate rose to its climax. The voice of Goldstein had become an actual sheep's bleat, and for an instant the face changed into that of a sheep. Then the sheep-face melted into the figure of a Eurasian soldier who seemed to be advancing, huge and terrible, his sub-machine-gun roaring, and seeming to spring out of the surface of the screen, so that some of the people in the front row actually flinched backwards in their seats. But in the same moment, drawing a deep sigh of relief from everybody, the hostile figure melted into the face of Big Brother [ . . . ] Then the face of Big Brother faded away again and instead the three slogans of the Party stood out in bold capitals:
WAR IS PEACE
FREEDOM IS SLAVERY
IGNORANCE IS STRENGTH
But the face of Big Brother seemed to persist for several seconds on the screen, as though the impact that it had made on everyone's eyeballs was too vivid to wear off immediately. (168–170)

In *Part I* of the novel everything happens in front of a screen. The very term "telescreen" recurs dozens of times, often repeated on the same page, thus driving its pervasive presence home to the reader. Rather than something to be watched—the "recreational" aspect of the cinema, ironical as it may be, is totally missing—the screen is an instrument to spy on people, the extension of the Police eye, an essential element of the heavy-handed, brutal nature of the totalitarianism shown in *Nineteen Eighty-Four*.[2] It is worth noting that, in Oceania, the Party's methods of maintaining order are very different from those employed in the fordian world. While the Orwellian society resorts to repression and comparatively rudimentary techniques, the Fordian world relies on a much more sophisticated technology. In many respects, Oceania resembles the crude contemporary authoritarian States mentioned by Huxley in his "Foreword" to the 1958 edition of *Brave New World* whereas the Fordian society is similar to what efficient totalitarianism could be in the future. In order to render persecution and oppression unnecessary the "positive" side of propaganda must be as effective as the negative one: what needs to be solved, therefore, is the problem of "making people love their servitude" (Huxley, 1958, xii). Actually, suggestion techniques, genetic manipulation, pleasure-giving drugs and, of course, *feelies* and television, dispense with the need for repression in the Fordian society.

Everyone is expected to show an expression of serene optimism to the telescreen (160) and nobody can withhold his/her attention when the plate demands it to announce military victories or magnify the results of industrial production. Reality is systematically and viciously altered: "Day and night the telescreen bruised your ears with statistics proving that people today had more food, more clothes, better houses, better recreations—that they lived longer, worked shorter hours, were bigger, healthier, stronger, happier, more intelligent, better educated, than the people of fifty years ago. Not a word of it could ever be proved or disproved" (220).

The telescreen does much more than "simply" transmit and receive, directly governing several aspects of everyday life. It acts, for example, as a siren to signal both the beginning and the end of all work shifts and as a sort of computer-data bank: by typing "back numbers," in fact, Winston is able to retrieve the *Times* issues that have to be "rectified" (189). The telescreen is also a substitute for the alarm clock, as becomes apparent when an annoying hiss interrupts Winston's dream of the Golden Country. Soon afterwards a sharp female voice urges everybody to take their morning exercise, thus demonstrating that the conditioning action of the screen is both mental and physical and that these two aspects are inseparable (183).

The first part of the work closes, as it had begun, by hinting at the telescreen: Winston is sitting in a recess of his living room, out of sight, while a patriotic song comes out of the plate (244). Later this frightening device is referred to much less frequently, only because the reader is now perfectly aware of its function and "sees" it even when it is not explicitly named. Yet, at times, the peculiar tone of a scene or of the setting are either totally or in part conveyed through the presence of the screen. *Part III* opens, for example, with the description of a cell in the Ministry of Love—itself a screen of a larger scale, a place without windows devoted to spying, inscrutable from the outside—in which four telescreens stand out, one in each wall (353). The depiction of the cell clearly alludes to the scrutiny of Winston's soul which is going to take place in that building, especially in room 101.

* * *

Though Huxley dedicates little space to it in comparison with the *feelies*, the television set, like the cinema, is integral to Fordian life and plays a relevant role in reproducing the mass character of the *Brave New World*. The TV is the most convenient device to prevent people from remaining on their own in the very few moments in which work, social activities and pastimes do not "compel" them to share their lives with others.

Bernard feels obliged to report to Lenina about the lack of television in the Hotel of the Reserve before flying there (90) and it is to TV as an instrument that guarantees "normality" that he must yield afterwards: at the end of a day marked by the utter frustration of his wish to establish a close, communicative relationship with Lenina, Bernard resigns himself to having sexual intercourse with her. Once they arrive at his place, in a most unnatural way for him but perfectly in agreement with Fordian rules, he gulps down four tablets of *soma* (the New World ecstatic drug), turns on the TV and begins to undress (83).

Linda gives in to television and *soma* as soon as she returns to her lost paradise. The drug produces such pleasant sensations as to make TV images similar to those of a *feely*. The combination of "traditional" motion pictures and drug-affected sensations, Huxley suggests, brings about the total physical involvement of the *feelies* which, from a Fordian perspective, are both a technological and a "social" advance as compared to television:

> Linda got her *soma*. Thenceforward she remained in her little room on the thirty-seventh floor of Bernard's apartment house, in bed, with the radio and television always on [ ... ] on holiday in some other world, where the music of the radio was a labyrinth of sonorous colours, a sliding, palpitating labyrinth, that led (by what beautifully inevitable windings) to a bright centre of absolute conviction; where the dancing images of the television box were the performers in some indescribably delicious all-singing feely. (139–140)

Excessive use of drug soon leads Linda to the Park Lane Hospital. When John arrives there he discovers, to his amazement, that a TV set is located at the foot of each bed, even that of a dying patient. The television is therefore shown to accompany every single moment of people's life, training them to total passivity. Linda cannot, and does not want to, do anything but watch the semifinals of a tennis tournament (181): her blank stare is a symptom of internal emptiness, the basic condition of Fordian society, a state fostered by filling the individual's mind with television images.

As we have shown, therefore, cinema, television, and *soma* construct needs and desires and cater to their fulfilment in the Brave New World, thereby providing the necessary outlet for instinctual forces and greatly helping political stability.

## Vision(s) of the (Mind's) Eyes

In *Nineteen Eighty-Four* the symbolic meaning and polysemic character of several visual metaphors cannot be ignored. The most important of them is the metaphor of the eyes, though others are worth mentioning too.

In the future society, as we have already noted, people are constantly spied upon: in addition to the telescreen, the Party's eye, Big Brother's huge face is to be found everywhere, on stamps, coins and posters in all streets and buildings. Climbing the stairs of the high-rise he lives in, on each landing Winston has to walk past "one of those pictures which are so contrived that the eyes follow you about when you move. BIG BROTHER IS WATCHING YOU, the caption beneath it ran" (157).

Orwell resorts to a well-known technique of the cinematographic language, eyes filmed in close-up as a metaphor for conscience and its values, strengthening the connection between visual metaphors and the screens in the text (Lotman 83). The eyes, in fact, are indeed the windows to the soul in Orwell's novel. They can either disclose or conceal new perspectives and are associated with positive or negative meanings according to the different characters and to Winston's capability to see "through" them. In fact, while he is able, for example, to spot the fierceness in the look of Mrs Parson's children (176) Winston completely misinterprets O'Brien's gaze at the end of the Two Minutes Hate, taking it for an expression of solidarity due to shared feelings and thoughts: "Momentarily he caught O'Brien's eye. O'Brien had stood up. He had taken off his spectacles and was in the act of re-settling them on his nose with his characteristic gesture. But there was a fraction of a second when their eyes met, and for as long as it took to happen Winston knew—yes, he *knew*!—that O'Brien was thinking the same thing as himself" (170–171).

Later, when O'Brien turns off the telescreen in his office, Winston is deceived again. He does not realize that the Inner Party Member is allowed to do that only because he leaves his *eyes* switched on, a perfect surrogate for the plate (302). The police can do much better than Winston, as shown by the fact that everybody needs to maintain an impassive look in front of the screen, because "a single flicker of the eyes could give you away" (187).

The eye metaphor tends to recur whenever the narrator portrays a character or conveys his/her state of mind. Thus, for instance, Syme's sharpness manifests itself in protruding eyeballs, which scrutinize Winston and appear to see right through him (198). On the contrary, the Ministry of Truth's employees have small eyes and wear glasses (a detail deserving attention, as we shall see). They are short-sighted, literally and figuratively, and they all "look" the same (208). In spite of all his efforts, Winston resembles them, and that is why he repeatedly proves himself unable to "see" correctly. He is scared by Julia's gaze, for instance, and deceitfully reassured by Mr Charrington's mild eyes, glasses and intellectual air (237). Different though he is, Winston possesses several of the traits that identify the members of his social group: he is an intellectual, loves reading, takes pride in his ingenuity and is often unable to see beyond appearances.

The first meeting between Winston and Julia pivots on the girl's facial expression, which conveys much more than a simple request for help (247). Winston helps Julia get up after she fakes a bad fall in a corridor of the Ministry of Truth: the contrast between the love transmitted by Julia's eyes and the inquisitive coldness of the telescreen, in front of which everything happens, is noteworthy. Later on, Winston meets the eyes of several war prisoners carried away on a truck: their intense gaze, like Julia's, reveals extreme suffering and possesses a humane quality (256–257). On this occasion, Winston shows how deep is his need for strong feelings and truthfulness, which he searches in other people's eyes, a need which contributes to his misinterpretation of the true nature of the individuals he meets.

Love broadens Winston's horizons. In and from the antiquary's room he enjoys what in Oceania's grim and repressive world are extraordinary sights, such as the spectacle of Julia wearing make-up and the artless lighthearted gesture of the huge prole woman hanging the washing out (278–279). So extraordinary is what can now be "seen" that Winston even has the opportunity to glimpse his innermost nature, in the episode of the appearance of the rat. He does not take advantage of this moment, however, as Julia inadvertently touches the most sensitive chords of his own personality, causing him deep emotional disturbance: "did you know they attack children? [ . . . ] And the nasty thing is that the brutes always—'Don't go on!'—said Winston, with his eyes tightly shut" (281). In room 101 Winston will finally face his greatest fear, the dread of rats, and the subconscious conviction of being similar to them (they assail children, just as he had done to his dying little sister by snatching her chocolate ration). Winston's terror, therefore, is the acknowledgement of his own egoistic and predatory nature. In actual fact, one might look at things from a different perspective. Given the Party's emphasis on the negation of individuality and absorption into a collective entity, Winston may not have to face his own evil nature so much as the guilt complex originating from having shown love for himself. His slow progress in seeing beyond appearances, proceeding throughout the novel, comes significantly to a stop in the episode of the rat, which is the culmination of the misunderstandings of the first part of the book.

As expected, the term "eye" is widely employed in the novel, occasionally repeated within a few lines. Orwell utilizes many other nouns and verbs belonging to the semantic field of vision. The most interesting case is that of the verb "to see," which is employed as "perceive through the eyes," "understand" and, at times, in both senses at once. When O"Brien enters his cell, for instance, Winston supposes the Inner Party Member has been captured but he is soon disenchanted: "Yes, he saw now, he had always known it" (365). Unfortunately, it"s too late: Winston"s eyes can now only watch the guard"s cudgel ready to strike.

In Oceania, it is impossible to see reality with eyes different from those of the Party. On one occasion, O"Brien"s gaze occupies Winston"s entire visual angle and then "swallows" him, thus bringing about his melting into the collective being: "He was in a cell which might have been either dark or light, because he could see nothing except a pair of *eyes*. Near at hand some kind of instrument was ticking slowly and regularly. The *eyes* grew larger and more luminous. Suddenly he floated out of his seat, dived into the *eyes* and was swallowed up" (368, emphasis added).

The physical and psychological condition of the political prisoners "cured" in the Ministry of Love can be easily detected from their eyes. The representative sample offered in *Nineteen Eighty-Four* ranges from the "troubled eyes" of Ampleforth the poet to the evasive look of the man-rodent to the disproportionately big eyes standing out of the bony face of the convict "filled with a murderous, unappeasable hatred of somebody or something" (357–361).

Needless to say, the attack on Winston"s deviant personality is also delivered through physical aggression against his eyes: during the interrogation, for instance, a glaring light is directed against them until they run with water (367). In room 101 O"Brien threatens Winston by placing the cage with the rats in front of his face and "reminds" him that "Sometimes they attack the eyes first": in this episode, the comparison between rats and Inner Party Members (or rather, intellectuals in general) is forcefully drawn (406).

The final purpose of torture is to teach prisoners to negate the "objectivity" of optical vision in order to substitute for it the subjective and changeable vision of the mind. It is not by chance that Winston"s utmost fight to preserve his own individuality takes the shape of a claim on the right to see "objectively": Orwell underlines this attempt by repeatedly employing the possessive form to refer to the protagonist"s eyes ("my eyes", "Winston"s eyes", "his eyes": 375) when O"Brien tries to make Winston "see" five fingers while showing him four.

After the ordeal of torture Winston observes his devastated body and unrecognizable face reflected in a mirror: the eyes, however, have not been utterly subdued, thus proving that the complete erasure of his individuality has yet to be achieved (393). As a matter of fact, until the final expiation, Winston's re-education remains partial and it is accomplished with great difficulty and torment.

\* \* \*

Glasses are connected with a number of negative meanings and characters in the novel, as we have already seen in regard to the antiquary. Even Winston wears them, like any other clerk of the Ministry of Truth and most members of the Inner Party, including O'Brien. Lenses are nothing but the materialization of the mental screen through which intellectuals—integrated in, and subjugated to, the system—watch reality. When Tillotson's glasses flash hostilely at him, Winston is incapable of recognizing himself as part of that very system within which he plays exactly the same role as his colleague (192). Like Tillotson, he loves his work—document "rectification"—even when, or rather especially when, altering the past becomes much more of a challenge than mere routine tasks and requires the use of one"s brains.

The link between glasses and mental labour is more explicit in *Nineteen Eighty-Four*"s Part III. Some of the officers who interrogate Winston in prison are not "ruffians in black uniforms but party intellectuals, little rotund men with quick movements and flashing spectacles" (367). *Flashing spectacles*, that is to say the kind of glasses worn by men who serve power and are nothing else than automatons, men-telescreens endowed with frames and light emission power.

One more episode is worth mentioning. During the re-education treatment, when O"Brien grants Winston permission to pose him a few questions, his glasses shine with an "ironical gleam" (383): such an anthropomorphic metaphor is further evidence that the glasses of the integrated intellectual are merged and work as one with his eyes, since "educated" eyes have the ability to filter and distort reality without making use of lenses.

\* \* \*

The meaning of dreams,[3] as with many other elements in *Nineteen Eighty-Four*, is far from univocal: dreams can be prophetic or deceiving, and they provide both an instrument for and an occasion of psychological (self) analysis. They represent one of the very few possible "personal" experiences in Oceania because they are not rationally controllable. By spying into dreams the Thought Police can understand if the heart of an individual, in addition to his/her brain, also loves and obeys Big Brother. That is why, to be completely "reclaimed," Winston "must not only think right; he must feel right, dream right" (401). On the one hand, therefore, dreams sharply contrast with the telescreen since they express and symbolize the triumph of the inner self. Yet, on the other hand, they are similar to the screen in that both supply the Police with apt tools with which to investigate the most hidden secrets of the human soul.

As has already been pointed out, the protagonist's understanding of both external reality and his subconscious nature grows slowly and laboriously along the narrative. In the beginning Winston remembers having ascribed a sense of hope and freedom to the voice that, in a dream, had promised to meet him "in the place where there is no darkness" (177), which eventually turns out to be the torture cell of the always illuminated Ministry of Love. Later however, through the oneiric experience, he is able to recollect some significant moments of his childhood and to make his own guilt feelings and fears emerge. The two apparently disjointed parts of the first dream the protagonist has in the novel are linked by their emotional intensity and both originate from strong feelings unknown to the new society. Winston does not quite grasp the meaning of the image of his mother and sister sinking in the dark water but deems himself responsible, one way or another, for the sacrifice of their life (181–182). The setting shifts then to the Golden Country and the dream becomes prophetic as Winston witnesses Julia's "political act": she undresses gracefully and nonchalantly, with a gesture "belonging to the ancient times" which reminds him of his mother's warm embrace to protect her little daughter (182–183).

In the second half of the book the veil hiding his unconscious from him is partially torn, or rather made much thinner. Waking up with a start in the antiquary's room, Winston recollects the bombing raids and the shelters where he sought refuge with his family, the dark room where he lived as a child and his chronic hunger. He also remembers one day stealing his sister's chocolate ration, fleeing and finding nobody home upon his return. In a place he perceives as his own, Winston can finally reach within himself and break free of the oppressive sensation of having killed his mother. Yet, not even this dream enables him to arrive at the heart of his unease: in fact, Winston does not realize that he feels his nature as fundamentally egoistic (294–298).

While he regains strength, waiting to confront the final decisive trial of room 101, Winston dreams several times. He finds himself in the Golden Country or in other luminous places with Julia, his mother and O'Brien. Orwell renders perfectly the conflation of different settings and the inclusion into mental activity of external elements peculiar to the oneiric reality. As a matter of fact, the brightness of the places he dreams of is nothing but the "strong light on his face" of the cell where he is sleeping (396).

The episode in which Winston wakes up from a *reverie* shouting his love for Julia is worth noting (400). Dreams are the last refuge for personal feelings but, unfortunately, the integrity of this refuge can be violated: O'Brien's presence in Winston's dreams since he first promised to meet him "in the place where there is no darkness" is indeed a proof that the Party reaches the innermost recesses of everybody's mind right from the outset.

\* \* \*

Several other screen metaphors are found in the text, but they are less pervasively present and less symbolically relevant than those we have analyzed so far. Windows are normally associated with a positive meaning, even though not systematically. Their contrast with the telescreen is established from the very beginning when Winston, looking through the panes, grasps that the real world is totally divergent from the picture of it drawn by the Party and sees it as a cold and deserted place constantly swept by Big Brother's gaze (158). Yet, just as with the telescreen, the view offered by Winston's window never changes, always showing the grim spectacle of bomb explosions and propaganda posters covering the street sides. Furthermore, through the panes, as through the screen, people can be spied upon by the Police helicopters (158).

The opening in the antiquary's room shows how "extraordinary" the view offered by a window can be. From it, in fact, Winston repeatedly enjoys the sight of a prole woman hanging the clothes out in a sunny courtyard (275, 278, 346–347). The vision of the woman, the perception of her authenticity and of her potential for instinctive rebellion, also provides Winston with the opportunity to plunge himself into the past and ponder over the present. Windows, therefore, help advance awareness of the true reality of things and show a different, better perspective which gives hope and supplies people with at least a mental way out. Is it by chance that the Ministry of Love, where room 101 is situated, lacks any opening whatsoever?

\* \* \*

In a three-sided mirror Winston observes the devastation torture has caused to his body, a destruction which reflects the condition of his soul. The mirror somewhat reproduces the illusory three-dimensional reality of the cinema, as it provides distinct perspectives of the same image and delimits a three-surfaced space whose missing side is occupied by the spectator:

> He had stopped because he was frightened. A bowed, grey-coloured, skeleton-like thing was coming towards him. Its actual appearance was frightening, and not merely the fact that he knew

it to be himself. He moved closer to the glass. The creature's face seemed to be protruded, because of its bent carriage. A forlorn, jailbird's face with a knobby forehead running back into a bald scalp, a crooked nose and battered-looking cheekbones above which the eyes were fierce and watchful. The cheeks were seamed, the mouth had a drawn-in look. [ … ] Except for his hands and a circle of his face, his body was grey all over with ancient, ingrained dirt. [ … ] But the truly frightening thing was the emaciation of his body. The barrel of the ribs was as narrow as that of a skeleton: the legs had shrunk so that the knees were thicker than the thighs. He saw now what O'Brien had meant about seeing the side view. The curvature of the spine was astonishing. The thin shoulders were hunched forward so as to make a cavity of the chest, the scraggy neck seemed to be bending double under the weight of the skull. At a guess he would have said that it was the body of a man of sixty, suffering from some malignant disease. (393)

Shortly after having looked at his external appearance, in room 101 Winston is forced to face his internal fears. The specular position of the figures illustrates the function of this much dreaded place which is nothing more, and nothing less, than a "magnifying mirror" where prisoners can, and indeed must, see what they truly (feel they) are.

*   *   *

Finally, photographs, as documents, are manipulated and used instrumentally by the regime. Aaronson, Jones and Rutherford's picture, testifying to their role as leaders of the Revolution, reappears in O'Brien's hands when he shows it to Winston only to deny its existence and to educate him to see according to the *doublethink* technique (372). The snapshots of Winston and Julia's love-making, instead, are employed more as tools of humiliation and psychological pressure than as simultaneous demonstration and negation of factual reality (398). In Oceania, the function of photographs, just as of documents in general, is not the recording and revelation of facts but the supply of "evidence" to be blatantly twisted at the service of the Party's needs.

*   *   *

Both Huxley and Orwell strongly denounce visual conditioning and the political use made of it: in fact, in the dystopic worlds described by the two authors images and screens constitute fundamental means of exercising mental and physical dominance over people. Also, their condemnation implicitly extends to the distorting power of media in non-fictional reality and to their frightening future potential.

However, there are a few noticeable differences between the two novels. In addition to watching, in Oceania an essential part of the process of repression entails being watched. In that society political indoctrination, and visual brain-washing in particular, are violent and pervasive. The members of the Inner Party do not want to daze their subjects' minds so much as to train them and bend their resistance: more than prevent from thinking, they impose *their own way* of thinking. In *Nineteen Eighty-Four* images generally possess a very negative meaning and the telescreen, whose presence is obsessively felt in the novel, is the principal instrument of totalitarian control and invasion of privacy. On the contrary, in the Fordian society conditioning mainly rests on the earlier stage of genetic engineering. Cinema, and television to some extent, produce effects comparable with those generated by *soma*, dulling people's wits and providing an outlet for their primal needs: they are, therefore, associated with pleasure, though artificial, for the majority of the members of the Brave New World. Thus, while Orwell describes the working of a repressive apparatus, Huxley portrays the annihilation of any possible residue of individual personality in the members of the superior caste (the only ones who could still have a trace of it) and the regulation of physiological needs through the dispensation of visual and/or physical pleasure, as is the case with the *feelies*. From this point of view the world depicted by Huxley is undoubtedly more 'advanced' than the one imagined by Orwell, and does not have to resort to torture to correct deviations.

The peculiar organization of the Fordian and the Big Brother societies determines the different kind of danger to which they are exposed and the methods they adopt to cope with it. In the Fordian world the disturbing elements are represented by a dissatisfied Alpha-Plus who wishes to experience the deep emotions and passions crushed by the system and by a "savage" who reads Shakespeare and leaves his confinement in the Reserve. In Oceania the threat to the system is embodied by a deviant intellectual who does not conform to the "logic" of power. The enemy to face is thus the force of Nature and Art on the one hand and intellect on the other. That is why in Oceania (visual) conditioning is aimed at affecting rationality whereas in the New World it intends to erase Culture and to control instincts by catering for them.

In conclusion it is worth remarking that, despite its relevance, in *Brave New World* the visual element is only one factor in the process of social control. Furthermore, though it is recurrent, the visual theme appears to be formed by "discrete units" and it is explicit, easily detectable on the surface of the narration. In *Nineteen Eighty-Four*, instead, the visual element has both an overt and a metaphorical character. Besides, in this work the frequent use of visual metaphors strengthens the sensation of the ubiquity of power and shows that the pervasive presence of the Party's eye in the story has also been translated into narrative technique.

## Notes

1. The Brave New World counts time from the "advent" of Ford, and employs the abbreviation A.F. instead of the familiar A.D.

2. The proles do not have telescreens in their houses or in their bars (218, 232). Their ignorance and the outlets provided by the Party (beer and pornography) make police control unnecessary.

3. The affinity between dreams and cinematographic vision has been pointed out in many contexts, from experimental psychology to psychoanalysis to film theory (see Costa 63 and 65). According to Pier Paolo Pasolini cinema is fundamentally oneiric for the elementary character of its archetypes—the habitual (and therefore unconscious) observation of the environment, mimicry, memory and dreams—and for the prevalence of the pre-grammaticality of objects as symbols of visual language (171–172).

## References

Bertinetti, Roberto, Angelo Deidda and Mario Domenichelli. *L'infondazione di Babele, l'antiutopia*. Milano: Angeli, 1983.

Costa, Antonio. *Immagine di un'immagine. Cinema e letteratura*. Torino: Utet, 1993.

Crick, Bernard. "Introduction." George Orwell. *Nineteen Eighty-Four*. Oxford: Clarendon Press, 1984. 1–153.

Firchow, Peter E. "The Satire of Huxley's *Brave New World*." *Modern Fiction Studies* 12.4 (Winter 1966–1967): 451–460.

Huxley, Aldous. *Brave New World*. London: Flamingo, 1994 (first edition 1932).

Lotman, Jurij M. *Semiotics of Cinema*. Ann Arbor: U. of Michigan P., 1976, (English translation of *Semiotika Kino i problemi Kinoestetiki*. Tallin: Eesti Raamat Edit, 1973).

Meloni, Irene. *Aldous Huxley. Stagioni d'utopia*. Pisa: ETS, 1989.

Orwell, George. *Nineteen Eighty-Four;* with a critical introduction and annotations by Bernard Crick. Oxford: Clarendon Press, 1984.

Pasolini, Pier Paolo. *Empirismo eretico*. Milano: Garzanti, 1991 (first edition 1972).

Plank, William. "Orwell and Huxley: Social Control Through Standardized Eroticism." *Recovering Literature* 12 (1984): 29–39.

BRAD BUCHANAN

# Oedipus in Dystopia: Freud and Lawrence in Aldous Huxley's Brave New World

Freud's role in Aldous Huxley's *Brave New World* has been much discussed, but little consensus has emerged, partly because of Huxley's apparent ambivalence about Freud's ideas and his growing reluctance, after he had written the novel, to admit that he had ever been in agreement with Freud's conception of human nature. In a 1960 interview, Huxley said, "I was never intoxicated by Freud as some people were, and I get less intoxicated as I go on."[1] Although some have taken this statement as an unequivocal denial of any affinity Huxley may have had for Freud,[2] it reads less as a repudiation of Freud than as a confession that Huxley was indeed "intoxicated" by Freud to a certain extent when he was younger, although he certainly never reached the stage of feverish zealotry achieved by some of his contemporaries.[3] Indeed, Huxley's half-hearted protestations against Freud have prompted insinuations about the motives behind them. For instance, Charles Holmes claims: "throughout his life Huxley rejected Freud, though the tone and intensity of his rejection varied. Given Freud's emphasis on sex and Huxley's near-obsession with it, the rejection implies unconscious resistance incompletely understood."[4] Philip Thody has undertaken to explain this "resistance" in biographical terms:

From *Journal of Modern Literature* 25, nos. 3–4 (Summer 2002): 75–89. Copyright © 2003 by Indiana University Press.

Huxley's adoration of his mother implied feelings of intense jealousy for his father, and . . . these were translated into the subconscious notion that Leonard Huxley was at least partly guilty for
his wife's death. . . . [T]he hostility which Huxley always shows
for Freud's ideas . . . [is] an indication of the fear which he had
that such a diagnosis might be true, and the fact that almost all
the fathers in Huxley's fiction are caricatures would lend weight
to this view.[5]

My concern, however, is neither to confirm nor refute such descriptions of
and speculations about Huxley's ambivalent attitude to Freud, but to show
how this attitude manifests itself in *Brave New World*, in which Freudian
ideas are plainly on display. I also suggest that any account of Huxley's reaction to Freud should take into account the probable influence on Huxley of
D.H. Lawrence, who attacked Freud's views yet whose life and work present
clear examples of many Freudian theories.

The most prominent of Freud's ideas, at least for my purposes, is his
notion of the "Oedipus complex," which, according to Freud, describes a male
child's feelings of incestuous desire for his mother and parricidal aggression towards his father. Oedipus' story is potentially every boy's, according
to Freud, because all boys see their mothers as love-objects and their fathers
as rivals.[6] This was perhaps Freud's most controversial and unpopular theory,
and one that Huxley might have been particularly eager to debunk. Yet on
24 August 1931, shortly after finishing *Brave New World*, Huxley wrote a
letter to his father in which he describes his new book as "a comic, or at least
satirical, novel about the Future . . . and adumbrating the effects on thought
and feeling of such quite possible biological inventions as the production of
children in bottles (with [the] consequent abolition of the family and all the
Freudian 'complexes' for which family relationships are responsible)."[7] This
letter shows that Huxley was willing to discuss the "Freudian 'complexes' for
which family relationships are responsible" very seriously indeed and with
his own father, no less. If Huxley had any doubts at all about the truth of the
most famous of these complexes, he would certainly have assured his father
that he harbored no such "complex," with its attendant murderous and incestuous feelings, or at least would have palliated the unpleasant thought that his
own family was to blame for imposing these emotions on him. The fact that
he did not, I propose, says a good deal about his opinion of the fundamental
truth of Freud's theory of the Oedipus complex.

This opinion is shown even more clearly in *Brave New World*, in which
the Oedipus complex is deemed such a dangerous and powerful force that it
(along with the family structure that produces it) has been eliminated from

civilized life, as far as possible. Children are no longer born to a set of parents but produced in an assembly-line process from fertilized eggs, which are then "decanted" into bottles and subjected to endless chemical alteration and conditioning.[8] By controlling all aspects of a child's birth and upbringing and by keeping adults in a condition of infantile dependency on a larger social body, Huxley's imaginary state has taken over the role of parent and robbed the child of his or her Oedipal potentialities. Indeed, it could be argued that the active suppression of the Oedipus complex is the principal tool of social stability practiced in this future. Yet this state of affairs is really just an extension of principles that have helped to form twentieth-century life, according to Freud. After all, in *Totem and Taboo* Freud postulates that the reason Oedipus' parricide and incest shock us so much is that we have constructed civilization precisely to discourage the two crimes of which Oedipus is guilty, the "only two crimes which troubled primitive society."[9] In Huxley's futuristic utopia, the prohibitions against parricide and incest are simply taken to their logical extreme, so that even the unconscious energies produced by repressing such desires are dissipated. The solution to the problem of Oedipal desire is to make everyone so infantile that he still feels as if he were in the womb/decanter. A popular song within the novel expresses this pre-Oedipal state: "Bottle of mine, it's you I've always wanted! / Bottle of mine, why was I ever decanted?" (*Brave New World*, p. 91).

Freud himself is treated as a prophet in this pseudo-paradise; indeed, he is elevated to near-divinity, along with Henry Ford (the similarity of their names comes in handy): "Our Ford—or Our Freud, as, for some inscrutable reason, he chose to call himself whenever he spoke of psychological matters—Our Freud had been the first to reveal the appalling dangers of family life" (p. 44). These dangers have to do not with incest or parricide but with "the prohibitions they were not conditioned to obey" and which force them to "feel strongly" (p. 47). Strong feelings, of course, are unpleasant enough to the denizens of the "brave new world," but the Director of London's Central "hatchery" supplements this already grim picture with the horrible thought of emotionally suffocating parents who once clung desperately to their children: "The world was full of fathers—was therefore full of misery; full of mothers—therefore of every kind of perversion from sadism to chastity" (p. 44). He sums up the plight of past generations vividly:

> home was as squalid psychically as physically. Psychically, it was a rabbit hole, a midden, hot with the frictions of tightly packed life, reeking with emotion. What suffocating intimacies, what dangerous, insane, obscene relationships between the members of the family group! Maniacally, the mother brooded over her

children . . . like a cat over its kittens; but a cat that could talk, a
cat that could say, "My baby, my baby," over and over again. "My
baby, and oh, oh, at my breast, the little hands, the hunger, and that
unspeakable, agonizing pleasure. . . ."

"Yes," said Mustapha Mond, nodding his head, "you may well
shudder." (pp. 42–43)

The people of Huxley's future have not read Freud, quite clearly, but
they have been indoctrinated with a Freud-influenced awareness of the possibility of illicit relations between mother and child. This awareness, which
manifests itself in Lenina Crowne's distaste for the "indecent" spectacle of
"two young women giving the breast to their babies," the sight of which
makes her "blush and turn away" (p. 130), is exploited to inculcate a less visceral but nonetheless strong suspicion of any private or emotionally intense
relationship between two people. Indeed, any individualized, personalized
sexual feelings are branded as essentially incestuous, and the language of
forbidden passion is essentially a disgusting outgrowth of the obsolete love-
talk between mother and child: "My baby, my mother, my only, only love"
(p. 49). An "only love" is an incestuous love, in Huxley's futuristic world,
because it tends to work against the social solidarity which is the key to
peaceful life.

Despite all this revulsion towards the very possibility of Oedipal crimes
or Oedipal urges, the mythical figure of Oedipus returns to Huxley's novel
with a vengeance, in the form of John ("the Savage"), a man who was born (in
the traditional "viviparous" way) into an Indian tribe on a reservation in New
Mexico. John's father is the Director of the London Hatchery, who leaves John
to be raised by his mother, Linda, after he has impregnated her in the once-
traditional but now unthinkable way. Like Oedipus, John grows up without
knowing who his biological father is, but finally, with the help of his mother,
he learns the truth. He also unintentionally ruins his father by embracing him
publicly, kneeling before him, and addressing him as "My father"—a scene
that no doubt functions as Huxley's satirical rendition of Oedipus' unwitting
murder of his own biological father. Yet John is more of a Freudian case study
than a reincarnation of Oedipus himself; his sensibilities have been formed
by a battered edition of Shakespeare which he finds (rather improbably) in
the squalor around him, and he identifies strongly with Hamlet's rage about
his mother's marriage to Claudius. He experiences some classically Freudian
Oedipal jealousy of the native man who sleeps with his mother, spurring his
anger with apt quotations from *Hamlet*: "He hated Popé more and more. A
man can smile and smile and be a villain" (p. 156).[10] Finally, as if to complete
the Freudian cliché, John tries to kill Popé as he is "drunk asleep" (p. 158); he

fails, but Popé is mildly impressed with his attempt and says laughingly but affectionately: "'Go, my brave Ahaiyuta'" (p. 159).

As if belatedly following this directive, John and his mother eventually leave the reservation with Bernard Marx, an insecure would-be intellectual who seeks to win approval and social status by parading them as curiosities back in London. Yet even after he has encountered the many attractive and available women there, John remains obsessed with his mother. He remembers the intimate moments between him and Linda fondly, recalling "those times when he sat on her knees and she put her arms about him and sang, over and over again, rocking him, rocking him to sleep" (p. 244). Linda's own behavior towards John has contributed heavily to his fixation on her; she has been neglectful, sentimental, abusive, and affectionate by turns towards John. For instance, when John was little, she slapped him for calling her his "mother" and then, in a matter of moments, repented and kissed him "again and again" (p. 150), as if he were a suitable replacement for the lovers whom she has lost temporarily because of other women's jealousy. John never understands the nature of his feelings towards Linda, conflating his incestuous desires and violent impulses towards Popé with the trappings of heroism (after all, both traits are found in Hamlet). The fact that such powerful attachments are not normal any longer in a world of obligatory contraception and institutionalized promiscuity simply reinforces John's sense of tragic self-importance. Direct exposure to Freud's writings might have informed John that his feelings are not symptoms of some extraordinary powers or responsibilities, that they are normal emotions (at least in Freud's mind) to be recognized and overcome. Yet as we can readily see, no one any longer reads Freud, or if people do, they fail to apply or explain his theory of the Oedipus complex to John, the one human being to whom it is still relevant.

John finds it difficult to renounce his mother or sever their emotional connection (as he shows throughout the novel), and this leads him to be extremely censorious of any lustful impulse in himself, since all of his erotic attachments seem charged with the unsatisfied desires of his childhood love for Linda. When he calls Lenina an "impudent strumpet" (p. 232), he is not only censuring her evidently promiscuous behavior (which she, ironically, seems at times to be willing to change for his sake); he is projecting his revulsion at his own lusts onto her. We get a sense of how deeply John's libido has been repressed when he attends a "feely" (a futuristic movie which allows spectators to feel as well as see the actions onscreen) which features scenes of lovemaking between "a gigantic negro and a golden-haired young brachycephalic Beta-Plus female" (p. 200). No doubt prompted by memories of Linda and Popé,[11] John is revolted by this interracial love story; he "start[s]" violently as it begins and later terms it "horrible" (p. 202), although he is struck by the similarities between it and Shakespeare's *Othello*. Long afterwards, John's desire for Lenina becomes inextricably linked to the mixture of sexual arousal and disgust that he feels while watching the "feely": "he felt her [Lenina's] lips soft against his own. So deliciously soft, so warm and electric that inevitably he found himself thinking of the embraces in *Three Weeks in a Helicopter*. Ooh! ooh! the stereoscopic blonde and aah! the more than real blackamoor. Horror, horror, horror . . . he tried to disengage himself" (p. 229).

John seems to identify with the possessive "negro" (whom he links to Shakespeare's nobler *Othello*), just as he had once identified with Popé, and yet he reacts with predictable disgust at the depiction of his own incestuous fantasies on the screen (just as he comes to hate Popé for having sexual access to Linda). Like Linda, the heroine of the "feely" is a blonde Beta who makes love to a man from a different, darker-skinned race. Lenina, who accompanies John to the "feely," is herself associated in John's mind with the "brachycephalic blonde" and, by extension, with Linda herself;[12] thus, as Freudians might well argue, he cannot imagine having sexual relations with Lenina before he has exorcised the unconscious incestuous demons that plague him and make him mistrust all sexual activity. These demons seem to determine his reactions to many of the everyday features of the world he has entered; for instance, he is outraged by the docile subservience of a group of identical Deltas awaiting their *soma*. He sees such twins as "less than human monsters," asking them why they do not want to "be free and men" and challenging them to throw off their dependence on drugged bliss: "Do you like being babies? Yes, babies. Mewling and puking" (p. 254). Here Huxley's keen sense of irony is at its most forceful: the Savage accuses the cloned workers of the same infantilism he has managed to confront only (and that partially) through his violent and unresolved "Oedipus complex." There may be more than Freudian theory at work here, however; as anthropologists have observed, twins frequently symbolize the results of incestuous activity. As René Girard writes in *Violence and the Sacred*, "Incestuous propagation leads to formless duplications, sinister repetitions, a dark mixture of unnamable things. In short, the incestuous creature exposes the community to the same danger as do twins . . . mothers of twins are often suspected of having conceived their children in incestuous fashion."[13] Thus, it may be that Huxley wants to indicate that John associates these twins with his own unfulfilled urges, which he must then repress all the more violently, or sublimate into radical activity (witness his act of throwing the Deltas' long-awaited *soma* out the window). After Linda's death, the link between her and these twins remains prominent: "he had sworn to himself he would constantly remember . . . Linda, and his own murderous unkindness to her, and those loathsome twins, swarming like lice across the mystery of her death" (pp. 296–97).

Haunted by such memories, John finally commits suicide, having failed to live up to the standards of chastity and morality which he has set for himself, yet he is not the only one who finds himself unable to live within the parameters of Huxley's imagined society. Bernard Marx and Helmholtz Watson share a sense that "they were individuals" (p. 80) and chafe against the conformity imposed on them, however pleasant its trappings may be. Like John, both of these heroes have a certain amount in common with Oedipus; both end up in exile, Bernard for his obstreperousness and Helmholtz for his refusal to live by the usual rules enforcing indulgence, promiscuity, and sociability.[14] They are friends but are conscious of a major difference between them: "whereas the physically defective Bernard had suffered all his life from the consciousness of being separate, it was only quite recently that, grown aware of his mental excess, Helmholtz Watson had also become aware of his difference from the people who surrounded him" (p. 80). While Bernard's show of resistance to the permissive status quo disappears once he has gained the self-confidence to get what he wants,[15] Helmholtz' desire to impose a measure of austerity on himself, especially with respect to his sexual relationships, is genuine.

John's and Helmholtz' moral objections to the amorous goings-on around them have long been assumed to be an expression of Huxley's own disapproval of promiscuity, and understandably so. After all, a few years before writing *Brave New World*, Huxley had claimed that "Nothing is more dreadful than a cold, unimpassioned indulgence. And love infallibly becomes cold and unimpassioned when it is too lightly made."[16] In a 1931 essay, Huxley argues that "No reasonable hedonist can consent to be a flat racer. Abolishing obstacles, he abolishes half his pleasures. And at the same time he abolishes most of his dignity as a human being. For the dignity of man consists precisely in his ability to restrain himself ... to raise obstacles in his own path."[17] This view is remarkably close to that expressed by Freud in *Civilization and its Discontents*,[18] a book translated into English and published in 1930, which Huxley may or may not have managed to read before or during the composition of *Brave New World* (from May of 1931 to August of that year). Nevertheless, Freud is certainly to be numbered among the "reformers" mentioned by Mustapha Mond in *Brave New World* when he addresses his charges: "Has any of you been compelled to live through a long time-interval between the consciousness of a desire and its fulfilment? ... And you felt a strong emotion in consequence? ... Our ancestors were so stupid and short-sighted that when the first reformers came along and offered to deliver them from those horrible emotions, they wouldn't have anything to do with them" (pp. 52–53). Yet passages such as these have caused some of Huxley's readers to lump Freud in with his supposed followers in the novel. For instance,

Philip Thody[19] argues that "In *Brave New World* it is . . . the implied ethical teachings of Freudianism that attract his scorn, the rejection of complex and mature emotions in favour of instant gratification and the pleasure principle. His disapproval is, in fact, almost Victorian in its moral intensity."[20] Nevertheless, critical opinion on this issue has been divided; Peter Firchow points out that "In *Brave New World* excessive restraint, like the Savage's, still leads to self-destruction."[21] Firchow not only contests the claim that Freud is a spokesman for libertinism in Huxley's eyes, he even goes so far as to argue (without much evidence, it must be said) that "Freud . . . is the closest the new world's science comes to having a conscience."[22]

Another, more clear-cut area in which Huxley and Freud have been deemed to disagree irreconcilably has to do with artistic creation. We know that, in Huxley's view, Freud was guilty of implying that art is (as Huxley puts it) a "happy efflorescence of sexual perversity."[23] In an article called "Formulations Regarding the Two Principles in Mental Functioning," first published in 1911, Freud did make the somewhat insulting claim that "The artist is originally a man who turns from reality because he cannot come to terms with the demand for the renunciation of instinctual satisfaction as it is first made, and who then in fantasy-life allows full play to his erotic and ambitious wishes."[24] Yet this position is a long way from the simple choice presented by Mustapha Mond (or "the Controller"), who states the official position: "'You've got to choose between happiness and what people used to call high art. We've sacrificed the high art'" (p. 264). Some have inferred that this passage means that in Huxley's mind Freud is the opponent of high art, since his theory of the "Oedipus complex" is meant to induce people to accept their lot and to be happy, rather than continue being neurotic and creative. Whatever the merits of this characterization of Freud's position, its assumption about the straightforwardness of Huxley's views does them a disservice. Huxley was deeply ambivalent about "high art," especially tragedy, which he regarded as an outdated genre. In his essay "Tragedy and the Whole Truth," Huxley argues that there is something inherently false about a tragic narrative: "To make a tragedy the artist must isolate a single element out of the totality of human experience and use that exclusively as his material. Tragedy is something that is separated from the Whole Truth, distilled from it, so to speak."[25] In this essay, Huxley uses *Othello* as an example of a tragedy which must exclude realistic details which would make it more truthful in order to achieve its dramatic effect. Of course, *Othello* is also mentioned prominently in *Brave New World*, where its interracial sexual themes resurface in the pornographic "feely" attended by John and Lenina. Mindful of John's habit of viewing everything in Shakespearean terms, Mond admonishes John that "'our world is not the same as Othello's world . . . you can't make tragedies without social instability'" (p. 263). We may infer that in Huxley's eyes the "Whole Truth" lies somewhere between tragedy and pornography and that John's tragic vision of reality is an oversimplification of what Huxley recognizes as the complexities of modern life.

Huxley even seems to endorse one element of Freud's characterization of the artistic impulse, insofar as it is related to the Oedipal energies represented by John. In *Group Psychology and the Analysis of the Ego*, a monograph published in 1923, Freud creates a scenario to explain the role of creativity, or more specifically, of epic narrative, in primitive society just after the parricidal crisis in which the famous band of brothers has slain the tyrannical father: "some individual ... may have been moved to free himself from the group and take over the [dead] father's part. He who did this was the first epic poet; and the advance was achieved in his imagination ... He invented the heroic myth."[26] This formula of original creativity is extremely tendentious, to say the least; as Richard Astle puts it in his article "Dracula as Totemic Monster: Lacan, Freud, Oedipus and History," Freud is "projecting the Oedipus onto an earlier age to explain the origin of myth and, more generally, of narrative."[27] Nevertheless, Huxley seems to endorse something rather like it in his description of Helmholtz Watson's artistic difficulties. While John has no difficulty expressing his emotions (even if only through Shakespearean tags), Helmholtz, although a would-be artist, seems to be searching for an objective correlative with which to express his sense of difference and his ambitions; he has "'a feeling that I've got something important to say and the power to say it—only I don't know what it is ... If there was some different way of writing ... Or else something else to write about'" (p. 82). He is looking for something "'important'" to say, something "'more intense'" and "'more violent'" (p. 83), but he cannot countenance John's suggestion that he look to family life for his subject matter. Helmholtz refuses to see family life as a possible source of what he lacks: "'You can't expect me to keep a straight face about fathers and mothers ... We need some other kind of madness and violence'" (p. 221). It seems clear that Helmholtz will never be a real artist, nor will he ever be able to understand his friend John, as long as he cannot accept that there is some validity to the Oedipal narrative.

Another disagreement that has been noted between Huxley and Freud has to do with their attitudes towards religion. Huxley plainly deplored Freud's implication that religion and other mystical experiences were a product of neuroses or sexual repression, yet he seems to acknowledge the reality of what Freud referred to in *Civilization and Its Discontents* as "the oceanic feeling." If Huxley had not read this book, it must stand as an extraordinary coincidence that the religious ceremonies in *Brave New World* employ much of the same vocabulary used by Freud to describe a theory propounded by

one of his correspondents (who turned out to be none other than the French
writer Romain Rolland):

> I had sent him my small book that treats religion as an illusion,
> and he answered that he entirely agreed with my judgement upon
> religion, but that he was sorry I had not properly appreciated the
> true source of religious sentiments. This, he says, consists in a
> peculiar feeling, which he himself is never without, which he finds
> confirmed by many others, and which he may suppose is present
> in millions of people. It is a feeling as of something limitless,
> unbounded—as it were, "oceanic." This feeling, he adds, is a purely
> subjective fact, not an article of faith; it brings with it no assur-
> ance of personal immortality, but it is the source of the religious
> energy which is seized upon by the various Churches and religious
> systems, directed by them into particular channels, and doubtless
> also exhausted by them. One may, he thinks, rightly call oneself
> religious on the ground of this oceanic feeling alone, even if one
> rejects every belief and every illusion.[28]

The quasi-spiritual rituals of "atonement" (p. 94) in *Brave New World* rely
heavily on imagery very close to Freud's here; one song which features in
these moments of group celebration is called a "Solidarity Hymn" and contains the lines: "'Ford, we are twelve; oh, make us one, / Like drops within
the Social River'" (p. 95). Each participant drinks from a "loving cup" of
*soma* after reciting a pledge of self-effacement—"I drink to my annihilation"
(p. 95)—in a ceremony that seems like a parody of Christian self-abnegation.

This kind of water imagery is very much a part of everyday life in Huxley's dystopia; a group of ecstatic dancers is described as if "they might have
been twin embryos gently rocking together on the waves of a bottled ocean
of blood-surrogate" (p. 91). Yet, as if to register his awareness that this kind
of mindless bobbing on the ocean's surface is not quite what Freud meant
by the "oceanic feeling," he shows Bernard contemplating the ocean after
participating in one of these liquefying moments. Bernard takes comfort in
the ocean's inhuman wholeness, and he feels that his tenuous individuality
has been strengthened somehow: "'It makes me feel as though . . . I were
more *me*, if you see what I mean. More on my own, not so completely a part
of something else. Not just a cell in the social body'" (p. 106). While Bernard's testimony of what this "oceanic feeling" means to him does not quite
fit Rolland's description of a vague spiritual awareness, it does correspond
rather well to Freud's judgment on the sources of such a feeling. Freud
writes: "we are perfectly willing to acknowledge that the 'oceanic' feeling

exists in many people, and we are inclined to trace it back to an early phase of ego-feeling."[29]

Another accusation made by Huxley against Freud is the not terribly original claim that the latter's emphasis on sexuality was "monomaniacal," as Huxley wrote in *Proper Studies*, published in 1927.[30] Yet Huxley himself reconsidered this verdict very publicly, in a newspaper article published March 11, 1933. In this brief piece, Huxley editorializes about the relative nature of Freud's insights about human nature, claiming that "It is only in the more prosperous sections of civilized urban communities that hunger loses its pre-eminence. Freud, who gives the palm to sex, worked in Vienna. . . . Love, as a wholetime job, has only been practiced by the more prosperous members of civilized societies."[31] Huxley admits that Dr. Audrey Richards is right to point out that sex does not assume the same importance in Bantu society as Freud claims it does in all human civilizations, but he goes on to say something that those who see Huxley as an unflinching anti-Freudian ought to find rather surprising: "That the psycho-analysts should be wrong about savages is not particularly important. The significant fact is that they are probably right about civilized people."[32] Huxley implies that Freud's "Pleasure Principle" is likely to triumph wherever social and technological "efficiency" prevails,[33] and he shows no signs of regarding this likelihood as anything to be lamented. In this respect, we may well wonder whether all the promiscuity which he portrays in *Brave New World* is to be regarded as the inevitable manifestation of otherwise desirable advances in human civilization.

*   *   *

Huxley was more than capable of making up his own mind about the relative merits of psychoanalysis, but around the time he began to write *Brave New World* he was still very much under the influence of D.H. Lawrence. Huxley first met Lawrence in December 1915 but did not become a close friend of his until 1926, when he and his wife, Maria, saw a good deal of the Lawrences in Italy. In 1920, Huxley had referred to Lawrence as a "slightly insane novelist" who had been "analysed for his complexes, dark and tufty ones, tangled in his mind."[34] As a result, Huxley cattily writes, "The complexes were discovered, and it is said that Lawrence has now lost, along with his slight sexual mania, all his talent as a writer."[35] Huxley soon changed his mind about Lawrence, but his conviction remained that literary talent cannot survive psychoanalytic scrutiny or successful therapy. Lawrence was a very important figure for Huxley during the years just before *Brave New World* was written;[36] Huxley visited Lawrence in Italy during the latter's final illness, and as his letters testify, he was profoundly moved by Lawrence's courage and his uncompromising (albeit frequently irrational) views about sex, social life, and the artistic vocation. Huxley was with Lawrence when he died on March 2, 1930, and witnessed his final struggles with great emotion, calling Lawrence "the most extraordinary and impressive human being I have ever known."[37] In memory of his friend, Huxley put together an edition of Lawrence's letters and even contemplated writing a biography of him, although the freshness of the memory and his own contractual obligations prevented him from writing a full-length work devoted to Lawrence.

Between the time Huxley renewed his acquaintance with Lawrence in 1926 and Lawrence's death in 1930, Huxley published *Point Counter Point*, *Proper Studies*, *Do What You Will*, and *Music at Night*, all of which contain references to Freud and/or psychoanalysis. Furthermore, while Huxley was writing *Brave New World* between May and August of 1931, he was still looking at Freud largely through Lawrentian lenses. Lawrence's deep attachment to his sensitive mother and his hostility to his crude father, the Nottinghamshire coal miner, might well have showed Huxley that at least one aspect of Freud's writing (the basic conception of the Oedipus complex) was very likely true, or at least very plausible. In any case, Lawrence's own passionate engagement with Freudianism, as well as his dogged but rather confused attempts to refute Freud's theory of the universality of the Oedipus complex,[38] certainly made an impression on Huxley. In his essay on Lawrence, Huxley addresses the question of Freud's relevance to Lawrence only once, and rather defensively: "Explanations of him [Lawrence] in terms of a Freudian hypothesis of nurture may be interesting, but they do not explain. That Lawrence was profoundly affected by his love for his mother and by her excessive love for him, is obvious to anyone who has read *Sons and Lovers*. None the less it is, to me at any rate, almost equally obvious that even if his mother had died when he was a child, Lawrence would still have been, essentially and fundamentally, Lawrence."[39] Huxley is no doubt reacting against the crudely Freudian analysis of Lawrence's writing contained in John Middleton Murry's book *Son of Woman*, which in the same essay Huxley dismisses as "destructive" and "irrelevant."[40]

Huxley deemed Lawrence "a great man,"[41] and although he found Lawrence "difficult to get on with, passionate, queer, violent,"[42] he was generally very loyal to him, and especially so after Lawrence's death.[43] In September 1931, Huxley was "making notes for a short study of [Lawrence] to serve as introduction to the letters," a study which, as Huxley says, "cannot be specifically a retort to Murry" but will "try to undo some of the mischief that slug has undoubtedly done."[44] The main symptom of Murry's mischievous "cleverness" is his exploitation of "the psycho-analytical rigamarole" where

Lawrence was concerned.[45] Addressing this aspect of Murry's book, which Huxley (showing an uncharacteristic taste for oxymorons) terms a "vindictive hagiography," he admits that Murry's insights into Lawrence's psyche are often accurate; Murry's Freudian analysis of Lawrence as a man in love with his mother and in violent rebellion against his father "is able and in parts very true."[46] *Son of Woman* was published in April 1931, and as a friend of Lawrence's as well as a man of letters, Huxley might well have read it in time for it to affect his portrayal of Freudianism in *Brave New World*. Whether this was in fact the case, we may draw several analogies between John "the Savage" and Lawrence himself, with whom Huxley was undoubtedly still preoccupied regardless of his reaction to Murry's book. As a visionary (at least in Huxley's mind) who remained true to his beliefs to the bitter end, Lawrence would have provided an excellent model for John the Savage, whose ultimately self-destructive moral absolutism is as unusual in the London which he visits as Lawrence's was in his own bohemian circle (which included the notorious womanizer Bertrand Russell, his wife, Dora, Lady Ottoline Morrell, and Gerald Heard). While John's apparent prudery seems to be fundamentally opposed to Lawrence's worship of the phallic principle and emphasis on the regenerative aspects of sexual activity, these two figures share an important common trait in Huxley's eyes: they cannot countenance sex as a meaningless form of recreation. Both are convinced that sex bears a tremendous significance and that the purely recreational, hedonistic promiscuity of people such as Lenina and Bernard is deeply obscene.

The Oedipal themes in Lawrence's own life resonate deeply with John's struggles in *Brave New World*; Huxley's decision to have John direct his parricidal aggression towards Popé, a Native American, may have been inspired by Lawrence, who (having spent many years living among the native people of America) muses in a later essay about the notion of having a "dusky-lipped tribe-father" who, "like many an old father with a changeling son ... would like to deny me."[47] Moreover, Linda's capricious yet ardent affection for John is entirely in keeping with Lawrence's pronouncements about the culpability of the mother in the development of incestuous desires in their sons. The over-affectionate mother, in Lawrence's eyes, "has not the courage to give up her hopeless insistence on love and her endless demand for love,"[48] and therefore "she provokes what she wants. Here, in her own son, who belongs to her, she seems to find the last perfect response for which she is craving. He is a medium to her, she provokes from him her own answer. So she throws herself into a last great love for her son."[49] Other familial situations found in Lawrence's work crop up in *Brave New World*; for instance, in Lawrence's *Sons and Lovers*, Paul Morel's aborted parricidal impulse seems to have been diverted and to have attached to Mrs. Morel. As her cancer worsens, Paul wishes that she would die and even goes so far as to administer a large dose of morphine to speed up the process. Huxley's John does not actually administer the gradual overdoses of *soma* that kill Linda, but, pressured by doctors, he agrees to allow her to take as much as she wants, and this leads to her demise (and to his crippling feelings of guilt).

Before he wrote *Brave New World*, Huxley denied having portrayed Lawrence in his own fiction, claiming that Mark Rampion, the Lawrence-like character in *Point Counter Point* is "just some of Lawrence's notions on legs."[50] Huxley felt that Lawrence was "incomparably queerer and more complex" than the dogmatic Rampion, whom Lawrence himself referred to as a "gas-bag."[51] Despite Huxley's diffidence about his fictional renditions of Lawrence, we cannot avoid suspecting that his portrayal of John in *Brave New World* is heavily indebted to his friend. Thus, Huxley repeatedly describes Lawrence's sense of humor as "savage," his "high spirits" are "almost terrify-ingly savage," and his "mockery" is "frighteningly savage."[52] In both cases, Huxley remarks upon Lawrence's satirical intelligence (one of Lawrence's less well-known traits) and testifies to its power; it is therefore not surprising that he chooses a Lawrence-like hero such as John to be the explicitly "savage" vehicle of his own most biting satire. Although John does not display himself a terribly sophisticated sense of humor, his naïveté, intense earnestness, and plain-spokenness make for some mordant scenes in *Brave New World*. For instance, when John falls to his knees in front of the DHC and hails the horrified bureaucrat as "My father!" (p. 180), a word which is so "comically smutty" to the onlookers that they break into "hysterical" laughter (p. 181), Huxley is making the sardonic point that traditional family-based values have been completely turned on their head in his utopia.

Furthermore, like John opposing Mond, Lawrence stands in Huxley's mind for the integrity of the artistic impulse, as for the belief that it must be permitted to express itself even if the result is disastrous; as Huxley claims, "Lawrence was always and unescapably [sic] an artist."[53] In describing the difficulties of being an artist, Huxley quotes Lawrence's complaint that "At times one is *forced to* be essentially a hermit. I don't want to be. But everything else is either a personal tussle, or a money tussle; sickening. . . . One has no real human relations—that is so devastating."[54] Huxley echoes this lament after quoting it: "One has no real human relations: it is the complaint of every artist. The artist's first duty is to his genius, his *daimon*; he cannot serve two masters."[55] Huxley's remarks here imply that there is a split between the art-ist's task and his or her "human" relationships and that the true genius must finally lose faith in the "human" social setting that others depend on. We recall that, after making the rounds in London (visiting the self-declared intellectu-als, much as Lawrence once did, to his own great disgust), the Savage tries to live as a hermit in the woods, and Helmholtz Watson decides that exile will serve his own artistic ambitions better than continuing to live in London.

Another odd detail that links Lawrence to *Brave New World* surfaces in a letter sent by Huxley to Lawrence in December 1928. Huxley describes a visit to a "night-bar ... devoted to Lesbians" in which he witnessed "a wrestling match between two gigantic female athletes."[56] In *Brave New World*, we are told that Bernard and Lenina fly to Amsterdam to witness "the Women's Heavyweight Wrestling Championship" (p. 104). In 1928, the Huxleys contemplated spending six months on Lawrence's ranch in New Mexico, the Western state which would later become the location of the "Savage Reservation" on which John is born and raised in *Brave New World*. To this circumstantial evidence we may also add the fact that Lawrence's relationship with his wife, Frieda, struck Huxley as being highly unusual, not to say disturbing. Frieda Lawrence was older than her husband and behaved in a very maternal way towards Lawrence, at least in Huxley's eyes: "Lawrence was ... in some strange way dependent on her presence, physically dependent."[57] Frieda's promiscuity came uncomfortably close to matching Linda's in *Brave New World*, just as Lawrence's possessiveness matched John's, as Huxley was well aware. He writes:

> Frieda and Lawrence had, undoubtedly, a profound and passionate love-life. But this did not prevent Frieda from having, every now and then, affairs with Prussian cavalry officers and Italian peasants ... Lawrence, for his part, was aware of these erotic excursions, got angry about them sometimes, but never made the least effort to break away from her; for he realized his own organic dependence on her.[58]

Frieda exasperated Huxley by her unreliability, indolence, and stubbornness and may have provided a model for Linda. Huxley confesses, "I like Frieda in many ways but she is incurably and incredibly stupid—the most maddening woman I think I ever came across."[59] Of course, Huxley realized that Lawrence too had his shortcomings; as he says, "I never understood his anti-intellectualism.... His dislike of science was passionate and expressed itself in the most fantastically unreasonable terms."[60] In this respect, once again, Lawrence is very like John, who dismisses the scientific and technological advances of supposedly civilized London with quotations from Shakespeare or some other irrelevancy.

Despite his sympathy for Lawrence, Huxley felt that his friend's illnesses, both physical and psychological, were "unnecessary, the result simply of the man's strange obstinacy against professional medicine."[61] Clearly, Huxley was deeply ambivalent about both Lawrence and Freud; while he felt a great loyalty towards and admiration for Lawrence, he could not suppress his feeling that Murry was in fact right about the "complex" that afflicted Lawrence and that the latter could have been happier and healthier, although not necessarily a better writer, if he had accepted Freud's insights to a greater extent. This feeling is perhaps reflected in *Brave New World*; indeed, it could well be argued that John desperately needs Freud to explain his own urges and hostilities before they destroy him. However, while Lawrence knew of Freud and disagreed strenuously (perhaps mistakenly, in Huxley's eyes) with Freud's assessment of the incestuous subtext of human sexuality, the real problem in Huxley's *Brave New World* as far as John is concerned is perhaps not that Freudianism has taken over the social structure, but that no one is any longer able properly to explain, remember, or apply Freud's theories, since the family structure that they assumed has been abolished in "civilized" circles.

Clearly, Huxley's distrust of Freud was by no means the typical antagonism felt by an artist towards a scientist who is treading on his or her toes; Huxley's own ancestry (his grandfather was T.H. Huxley, the father of so-called "Social Darwinism") made him rather more receptive to scientific principles than most novelists would be. Indeed, Huxley was often dismayed at what he took to be Freud's lack of real scientific rigor; as he once exclaimed, "How incredibly unscientific the old man [Freud] could be!"[62] Furthermore, although *Brave New World* seems to imply that the conflicts within human nature are worth preserving, since they make us interesting, heroic, and tragic, Huxley himself was committed to treating mental and emotional illness by any means necessary. He was a firm supporter of the use of drugs in psychotherapy, and despite the fact that he derided Freud's insistence on the value of his famous "talking cure,"[63] he shared Freud's urge to help individual people survive their psychological disturbances. What *Brave New World* shows us, however, is that Huxley was willing to mock his own (and Freud's) drive to limit or eliminate suffering from human existence. *Brave New World* may still be read as a parable about the difficulty of preserving anything we can recognize as "human" if and when Freud's theory of the Oedipus complex is taken seriously and acted upon by an authoritarian political system. Nevertheless, given Huxley's own documented assent to many of Freud's views on the subject of infantile desire and repression, it is difficult to disagree with Robert Baker's claim that "The Freudian family romance, despite Huxley's repeatedly expressed misgivings concerning Freud's emphasis on erotic behavior, is one of the principal satirical conventions of his social satire. *Brave New World* is no exception to this practice."[64] In other words, Huxley seems to have been using the "Oedipus complex" not as a target for mockery in *Brave New World*, but as a weapon in his satirical attack on the mores of modern life and on its utopian fantasies.

NOTES

1. Quoted in Jerome Meckier, "Our Ford, Our Freud and the Behaviorist Conspiracy in Huxley's *Brave New World*," *Thalia*, I (1978), p. 37.

2. Foremost among these scholars is Jerome Meckier, who argues that Huxley's novel is a rejection of Freud's theories. Meckier's article, while intriguing, is unsatisfactory, mainly because it dogmatically asserts that Huxley satirizes Freudianism for being part of what Meckier calls a "behaviorist conspiracy" that dominates Western thought, which Meckier deems mechanistic and materialistic (p. 41). Of course, as Peter Firchow points out, "Huxley knew very well [that] mechanistic psychologists . . . were adamantly opposed to Freud; for them, consciousness was the last refuge of the soul" (p. 47). Furthermore, as we shall see, Huxley was often more of a materialist than Freud ever was, recommending drugs and behavioral modification therapy rather than Freud's "talking cure" in cases of mental illness.

3. According to an oft-repeated anecdote, Huxley mocked these Freud-worshippers at a psychoanalysts' convention by crossing himself whenever their hero's name was mentioned.

4. Charles Holmes, *Aldous Huxley and the Way to Reality* (Indiana University Press, 1970), p. 147.

5. Philip Thody, *Huxley: A Biographical Introduction* (Charles Scribner's Sons, 1973), pp. 16–17.

6. For Freud, Oedipus (who kills his father and marries his mother) is "nothing more or less than a wish-fulfillment—the fulfillment of the wish of our childhood" (*The Basic Writings of Sigmund Freud*, James Strachey, trans. [Random House, 1938], p. 308).

7. Aldous Huxley, *Letters of Aldous Huxley*, Grover Smith, ed. (Chatto & Windus, 1969), p. 351.

8. Aldous Huxley, *Brave New World* (Harper & Row, 1946), p. 91. All subsequent parenthetical references to *Brave New World* are to this edition.

9. *The Basic Writings of Sigmund Freud*, p. 917.

10. Reading *Hamlet* intensifies and focuses John's anger towards Popé, as Huxley is at pains to indicate: "it was as though he had never really hated Popé before; never really hated him because he had never been able to say how much he hated him. . . . These words . . . gave him a reason for hating Popé; and they made his hatred more real" (p. 157). Here Huxley implies that literary examples of human behavior—for instance, the Shakespearean representation of a son's jealousy about his mother's relations with another man in *Hamlet*—anticipate the Freudian theory of the Oedipus complex. His portrait of John shows how the Oedipus complex is produced partly through natural boyish pride and jealousy and partly through John's aesthetic enjoyment of Shakespeare's language. This is no doubt a sidelong jab at Freud, and certainly adds resonance to Huxley's remark that "All that modern psychologists . . . have done is to systematize and de-beautify the vast treasures of knowledge about the human soul contained in novel, play, poem and essay" (Aldous Huxley, *Music at Night* [Chatto & Windus, 1970], p. 292).

11. John has memories of "white Linda and Popé almost black beside her, with one arm under her shoulders and the other hand dark on her breast, and one of the plaits of his long hair lying across her throat, like a black snake trying to strangle her" (p. 157).

12. The link between Lenina and Linda remains strong in John's mind, even after Linda dies from an overdose of *soma*: "He tried to think of poor Linda, breathless and dumb, with her clutching hands . . . Poor Linda whom he had sworn to remember. But it was still the presence of Lenina that haunted him. Lenina whom he had promised to forget" (p. 302). John seems to have successfully transferred his love from his mother to Lenina, but instead of congratulating himself on his more adult object-choice (as Freud would likely have told him to do) he feels guilty for forgetting Linda, especially since he still blames himself for her death. It is difficult to avoid the suspicion that reading a bit of Freud might have helped John accept his adult sexuality.

13. René Girard, *Violence and the Sacred* (Johns Hopkins University Press, 1979), p. 75.

14. Oedipus exiled himself after discovering he was guilty of incest and parricide. While Helmholtz's genius with words and metaphors seems to recall Oedipus' facility in solving the riddle of the Sphinx which depends upon a metaphorical interpretation of the word "legs," Bernard's bodily defects—he is abnormally short—bear a resemblance to Oedipus' deformed feet. Both Bernard and Oedipus are forced to make their minds their most powerful asset; as Huxley remarks of Bernard, "a physical shortcoming could produce a kind of mental excess" (p. 81).

15. Bernard claims to want to delay his own gratification, telling Lenina that he wishes that their date had not ended "with our going to bed" (p. 109), but (unlike Helmholtz) he lacks the willpower to impose real obstacles on himself.

16. Aldous Huxley, *Do What You Will* (Chatto & Windus, 1956), p. 137.

17. *Music at Night*, p. 167.

18. In *Civilization and Its Discontents*, Freud makes it quite clear that in his view all pleasure is only the release of tension, or the overcoming of obstacles and impediments; without the unpleasant uncertainty of anticipation or fear, there is no real enjoyment: "What we call happiness in the strictest sense comes from the (preferably sudden) satisfactions of needs which have been dammed up to a high degree . . . When any situation that is desired by the pleasure principle is prolonged, it only produces a feeling of mild contentment" (Sigmund Freud, *Civilization and Its Discontents*, James Strachey, trans. [W.W. Norton & Company, 1961], p. 23). There is no essential contradiction between Freud's view and that expressed by Huxley: "Love is the product of two opposed forces—of an instinctive impulsion and a social resistance acting on the individual by means of ethical imperatives justified by philosophical or religious myths. When, with the destruction of the myths, resistance is removed, the impulse wastes itself on emptiness" (*Do What You Will*, p. 137).

19. Thody is eager to make Freud the main villain of the novel, as his analysis makes plain:

> . . . in *Brave New World* it is the declared aim of the authorities to translate into the sexual behaviour of adults the total irresponsibility and immaturity which supposedly characterize a child's attitude to its own body . . . The Freudian idea that we should avoid repressions and frustrations, that the way to happiness lies in the satisfaction of those primitive, instinctual, sexual drives which previous societies have been compelled to inhibit, is thus criticized first and foremost for the effect that it has on people's emotional life. (Philip Thody, *Huxley: A Biographical Introduction* [Charles Scribner's Sons, 1973], pp. 54–55).

20. *Huxley: A Biographical Introduction*, p. 54.

21. Peter Firchow, *The End of Utopia: A Study of Huxley's Brave New World* (Associated University Presses, 1984), p. 55.

22. *The End of Utopia: A Study of Huxley's Brave New World*, p. 47.

23. Aldous Huxley, *Proper Studies* (Chatto & Windus, 1933), p. xvi.

24. Sigmund Freud, *A General Selection from the Works of Sigmund Freud*, John Rickman, ed. (Doubleday & Co. 1957), p. 44. Freud goes on to mitigate this slight against artists: "But he [the artist] finds a way of return from this world of fantasy back to reality; with his special gifts he molds his fantasies into a new kind of reality, and men concede them a justification as valuable reflections of actual life. Thus by a certain path he actually becomes the hero, king, creator, favorite he desired to be, without pursuing the circuitous path of creating real alterations in the outer world" (*Freud: A General Selection*, p. 44).

25. *Music at Night*, pp. 12–13.

26. *A General Selection from the Works of Sigmund Freud*, p. 203.

27. Richard Astle, "Dracula as Totemic Monster: Lacan, Freud, Oedipus and History," *Sub-Stance*, XXV (1980), p. 99.

28. *Civilization and Its Discontents*, p. 11.

29. *Civilization and Its Discontents*, p. 19. Characteristically, Freud denies that this feeling is truly the source of religious emotions, which he attributes directly to one's relationship (or lack thereof) with a paternal figure: "I cannot think of any need in childhood as strong as the need for a father's protection. Thus the part played by the oceanic feeling, which might seek something like the restoration of limitless narcissism, is ousted from a place in the foreground" (*Civilization and its Discontents*, p. 19).

30. *Proper Studies*, p. xix.

31. "The Bantus and Dr. Freud," quoted in *Huxley's Hearst Essays*, ed. James Sexton (Garland, 1994), p. 161.

32. *Huxley's Hearst Essays*, p. 161.

33. Huxley concludes his essay with the remark: "Men and women under high biological pressure arrange the pattern of their life in one way; under low pressure, in another way. With every increase in the efficiency of social organizations, more individuals will come to live under low biological pressure" (p. 161).

34. *Letters of Aldous Huxley*, p. 187.

35. *Letters of Aldous Huxley*, p. 187.

36. As Huxley's biographer Sybille Bedford argues, Huxley was very much under Lawrence's influence when he was writing *Do What You Will*, a collection of essays published in October of 1929: "Much of *Do What You Will* was a continuation of ideas turned up in *Point Counter Point*. Mark Rampion is talking on. The impression of the Lawrentian ship was still upon the water" (Sybille Bedford, *Aldous Huxley: A Biography* [Chatto and Windus, 1973], p. 219).

37. *Letters of Aldous Huxley*, p. 332.

38. Lawrence was convinced that Freud was wrong about incestuous desire, claiming there was in fact a natural antipathy between parents and children where sex was concerned, and that "The incest motive is a logical deduction of the human reason, which has recourse to this last extremity, to save itself" (D.H. Lawrence, *Fantasia of the Unconscious: Psychoanalysis and the Unconscious* [Penguin, 1975], p. 206).

39. Aldous Huxley, *The Olive Tree* (Harper & Brothers, 1937), p. 206.

40. *The Olive Tree*, p. 205.

41. *Letters of Aldous Huxley*, p. 88.

42. *Letters of Aldous Huxley*, p. 288.

43. After Lawrence died, Huxley visited Nottingham to see some of Lawrence's relatives, then in January of 1931 Huxley went to the coal fields in Durham, trying to understand more about Lawrence's background as the son of a miner, and researching the problem of unemployment. By 18 May 1931, he had begun writing *Brave New World*, which he at first described in a letter as a "revolt" against "the Wellsian Utopia" (*Letters of Aldous Huxley*, p. 348). The initial anti-Wellsian flavor of the book soon receded in importance and by the time he finished the book he was more concerned about its "Freudian" and "Pavlovian" themes, as we can see from the letter he wrote to his father on 24 August 1931.

44. *Letters of Aldous Huxley*, p. 355.

45. *Letters of Aldous Huxley*, p. 355.

46. *Letters of Aldous Huxley*, p. 353.

47. D.H. Lawrence, *Phoenix: The Posthumous Papers of D.H. Lawrence* volumes I and II (Viking, 1964), vol. I p. 99. Lawrence continues: "I know my derivation. I was born of no virgin, of no Holy Ghost . . . I have a dark-faced, bronze-voiced father far back in the resinous ages. My mother was no virgin" (*Phoenix* I, p. 99).

48. *Fantasia of the Unconscious: Psychoanalysis and the Unconscious*, p. 126.

49. *Fantasia of the Unconscious: Psychoanalysis and the Unconscious*, p. 122.

50. *Letters of Aldous Huxley*, p. 340.

51. *Letters of Aldous Huxley*, p. 339.

52. *The Olive Tree*, pp. 238–39.

53. *The Olive Tree*, p. 203. Huxley is clearly directing this remark at Murry, who deemed Lawrence a kind of prophetic, almost messianic figure, but refused to call him an "artist" because of the intensely personal and occasionally didactic nature of Lawrence's work.

54. Quoted in *The Olive Tree*, p. 226.

55. *The Olive Tree*, p. 226.

56. *Letters of Aldous Huxley*, p. 305. Huxley says that this contest was "ghoulishly funny," and, evidently adverting to earlier discussions with Lawrence, adds that "It was just the place for the Brewsters" (*Letters of Aldous Huxley*, p. 305), the Brewsters being Earl and Achsah Brewster, two oft-mocked admirers of Lawrence's work.

57. *Letters of Aldous Huxley*, p. 364.

58. *Letters of Aldous Huxley*, p. 831.

59. Quoted in Sybille Bedford, *Aldous Huxley: A Biography*, p. 228.

60. Quoted in *Aldous Huxley: A Biography*, p. 192.

61. Quoted in *Aldous Huxley: A Biography*, p. 215.

62. *Letters of Aldous Huxley*, p. 837.

63. Huxley enunciates his dissent from Freud on this point in no uncertain terms: "Freud—although he did himself say that finally all nervous disorders would turn out to be organic—he did say that in the meanwhile . . . we could treat them successfully by purely psychological means—I think this is absolutely *untrue*" (Bedford, p. 641). Thus in *Brave New World* Freud's verbal therapeutic technique has been replaced entirely with drugs and Pavlovian systems of punishment and reward. Interestingly enough, in 1949 Huxley wrote a letter to George Orwell, congratulating him on the publication of *Nineteen Eighty-Four*, but explaining why he felt that his own vision of dystopia was more likely to prevail than Orwell's. He writes:

"Freud's inability to hypnotize successfully . . . delayed the general application of hypnotism to psychiatry for at least forty years. But now psycho-analysis is being combined with hypnosis. . . . Within the next generation I believe that the world's rulers will discover that infant conditioning and narco-hypnosis are more efficient, as instruments of government, than clubs and prisons" (*Letters*, p. 605).

64. Robert S. Baker, *The Dark Historic Page: Social Satire and Historicism in the Novels of Aldous Huxley 1921–1939* (University of Wisconsin Press, 1982), pp. 141–42.

JEROME MECKIER

# Aldous Huxley's Americanization
# *of the* Brave New World *Typescript*

When Aldous Huxley revised the *Brave New World* typescript[1] between 27 May and 24 August 1931, he strove to Americanize his dystopia. His cleverest expedient was to ink in additional insults to Henry Ford, so that a novel that began as a satiric rendition of the future according to H. G. Wells grew increasingly anti-Fordian. With Ford as synonym and stand-in, each new uncomplimentary use of his name further condemned the World State for being America writ large. Mustapha Mond's jurisdiction forms part of an insanely rational society for which several of Huxley's finest holograph insertions blame America's archetypal technocrat.

In the choicest of emendations herein called Americanizations, Huxley writes a new paragraph of two short sentences:

> "Ford's in his flivver," murmured the D.H.C. "All's right with the world."

This paragraph becomes the last two of 15 lines on TS 49; the other 13 lines are typewritten and only lightly edited. Lives in the brave new world are "emotionally easy," Mustapha Mond boasts, because the interval "between desire and its consummation" (*BNW* 50) has been eliminated. Huxley added

From *Twentieth Century Literature* 48, no. 4 (Winter 2002): 427–60. Copyright © 2002 by Hofstra University.

95

a fervent outburst from the Director of Hatcheries and Conditioning to complete this vignette.[2]

Huxley's two-sentence autograph addition discredits its utterer, castigates Our Ford, and ridicules the brave new world. Despite the D.H.C.'s piety, all is not "right" in the World State. The opening pages of chapter 3 switch back and forth from Mond's impromptu history lesson to Lenina's conversation with Fanny Crowne about irregularities in Bernard Marx's sex life. The World Controller's speech to the D.H.C.'s new students about the splendors of the brave new world is undercut by Lenina's growing dissatisfaction with promiscuity and Bernard's penchant for solitude.

A travesty of religious sentiment, the lines about Our Ford resemble slogans such as "Everybody's happy now," one of many bromides brave new worlders use to reassure themselves that the World State is the perfect place. Given a bookless society of nonreaders, one doubts the Director knowingly makes a literary allusion. Nevertheless, Huxley reveals an embarrassing contradiction between Robert Browning's robust optimism and the new situation parodying it. Instead of God overseeing the universe from heaven, brave new worlders envision Our Ford superintending their affairs from his "flivver," a slang expression for a small, inexpensive automobile, hence a decline misrepresented as apotheosis.[3]

In Browning's closet drama *Pippa Passes* (1841), a young girl from the silk mills of Asolo hopes to improve everyone she encounters on her annual holiday. As she passes by singing "God's in his heaven—/ All's right with the world!" (Browning 15), her words confound Sebald and Ottima, an adulterous couple who have just murdered the latter's dotard husband. Stung by remorse, they atone through double suicide. Pippa's song voices Browning's "basic view" of the universe: "under an omnipotent, benevolent God, all must, at least in a cosmic sense, be right with the world," Kenneth L. Knickerbocker contends (Browning xvi). Due to the influence that Pippa's songs have on several parties during her day-long release from Ottima's husband's silk mill, "All *is* a bit righter."

This sense of augmented rightness is absent from the brave new world because standards have been lowered. Proof sheets substitute "All's well with the world" (PS 50) for "All's right," which is quoted correctly in typescript. The brave new world trivializes Browning's conception of a totally responsible God. Indifferent to questions of rightness, this supposedly utopian society only seeks wellness, "the maintenance of well-being" as Mond later defines it (*BNW* 209)—effortless comfort without the bother of a metaphysics.

TS 49 is partly blank. It could be a retyped leaf that ends at midpage "to fit a pre-existent following page" (Wilson 31). But TS 48 has only six typewritten lines, and TS 50 just nine. Fairly clean leaves such as TS 48–50 probably replaced heavily revised leaves, the evidence of prior revision disappearing forever. Yet even in a three-page portion already so heavily reworked that Huxley presumably retyped it, TS 49 exhibits an inspired afterthought.

As the counterpoint in chapter 3 becomes increasingly complicated, ever-briefer excerpts from the Director's history lesson vie with snippets of Lenina's ongoing discussion with Fanny and of Henry Foster's attempts to rile Bernard Marx. The Director explains that "We have the World State, now. And Ford Day celebrations, and Community Sings" (TS 57).[4] Huxley wrote in a brand-new one-line paragraph: "'Ford, how I hate them!' Bernard Marx was thinking." His inner fury is directed against Foster and the Assistant Predestinator, whom he overhears discussing Lenina's "pneumatic" charms as if she were "so much meat" (*BNW* 62), but thanks to a nicely ambiguous autograph insertion, Bernard also seems to be railing against Ford Day and Community Sings, perhaps abjuring the World State.[5]

Flying above the brave new world in chapter 6, Bernard Marx and Lenina Crowne discuss the advisability of cultivating strong feelings. Brave new worlders, Bernard groans, are "Adults intellectually and during working hours" but "Infants where feeling and desire are concerned" (TS 88). For Lenina's reply, Huxley inked in a new one-line paragraph from which he canceled the last two words: "'Our Ford loved infants,' said Lenina." To accommodate this observation, Huxley jotted down a participial phrase, "Ignoring the interruption," as preface to Bernard's next comment (TS 88; *BNW* 109). Lenina's remark breaks Bernard's disquisition into two parts, creating the appearance of a conversation. But she seems not to realize how foolish her rejoinder sounds. Our Ford's parodically Christlike regard is for infantility, not infants.

An addition near the conclusion of the typescript is Huxley's second-best handwritten Americanization. Self-exiled to an abandoned lighthouse, John Savage is fond of "hitting himself with a whip of knotted cords" until "trickles of blood" run "from weal to weal" (*BNW* 292). Three Delta-Minus land workers in a passing lorry stare "open-mouthed" as they count his strokes up to 12. At the bottom of the typewritten page, Huxley inked in two short paragraphs to record their astonishment:

> "Ford!" whispered the driver. And his twins were of the same opinion.
> "Fordey!" they said. (TS 236)

Due to this sighting, John is soon besieged by reporters and the Feely Corporation's movie cameras. The morning after sightseers lure him into an "orgy of atonement" (*BNW* 305), the Savage, disgusted with himself, commits suicide.

Mustapha Mond disappears from the novel 10 pages before the Delta-Minuses spy John; their awe reintroduces him. The oath swearing also connects the brave new world's foundation figure, Henry Ford, with John's suicide in the final paragraphs. In chapter 17, Mond and the Savage argue to a standoff: embracing Mond's technology-worshipping future and returning to the Savage's primitive past seem equally inadvisable. The final inked-in Americanization confirms the Savage's inability to survive in, much less overthrow, the world that Mond and his fellow Controllers administer.

The twins' colloquial-sounding oath "Fordey!" acknowledges Ford's continuing supremacy. Although the Delta-Minuses scarcely realize as much, *dey* can mean governor, ruler, pasha. Huxley had already Easternized "his fordship" (*BNW* 37) by rechristening Sir Alfred Mond, a powerful, prominent British industrialist, after a notorious seventeenth-century Turkish sultan. Mond's first name also alludes to Mustafa Kemal (Kemal Atatürk), president of Turkey since 1923. H. G. Wells preferred a disinterested scientific oligarchy such as the samurai in *A Modern Utopia* (1905); Lawrence yearned for the preindustrial theocracy that Don Ramon and Cipriano establish in Mexico in *The Plumed Serpent* (1926); but Huxley feared a worldwide dystopia governed by sophisticated Western dictators wielding greater power than an oriental despot.

Two of the four inked-in emendations just mentioned appear to be very late embellishments. Huxley uses the anti-Ford paragraphs on TS 49 and 236 to bracket his novel. Unlike some emendations, which have faded, both paragraphs are written in bright blue ink—the first on a page probably retyped late in the revision process, the second in the novel's final sequence, itself not part of Huxley's original plan. Paragraphs on TS 49 and 236 are finishing touches in the Americanization of the typescript.

\* \* \*

Few explicit references to Our Ford or America can be found in the first 27 pages of the *Brave New World* typescript. This suggests that the first chapter of the novel was completed before Huxley fused Henry Ford's America with H. G. Wells's worldwide Utopia as his novel's target. Once he did so, *Brave New World* became increasingly anti-Fordian: one definite and two possible references in chapter 1 increase to five in chapter 2; the count rises to 19 by the third chapter, where the D.H.C.'s allusion to Ford in his flivver is the ninth reference.

During the D.H.C.'s lecture in chapter 1, Ford is never mentioned by name. The unidentified narrator tries to guess the Director's age "in this year of stability, A.F. 632" (*BNW* 3), but these numbers and letters probably meant little to Huxley's first readers. Similarly, when Mr. Forster explains "the system of labeling" bottle babies—"a T for the males, a circle for the females" (*BNW* 13)—the connection between the male symbol and Ford's T-Model would not have been automatic.

An indirect yet unmistakable allusion to Ford occurs on TS 6. The "problem" of "staffing" the brave new world with "identical workers" will be solved, the unnamed narrator anticipates, by producing "Millions of identical twins": "The principles of mass production at last applied to biology." This may be the hint that Huxley took when he resolved to expand America's nefarious influence. Brave new worlders inhabit a factory-like society whose workers are mass produced in A.F. 632 more proficiently than Detroit turned out cars in the 1920s. Huxley reduced "principles" to "principle" (PS 7, *BNW* 7) to suggest that Ford lacked a full-fledged philosophy.

On the other hand, the brave new world's solution to its labor problem satirizes Wells as severely as Ford. In *Anticipations* (1901), Wells relied on "procreation" by those with "beautiful and strong bodies, clear and powerful minds," to populate the "future world-state" (167–68). But the brave new world has heeded Wells's subsequent prediction in *A Modern Utopia*: "There appears no limit to the invasion of life by the machine" (98). In the brave new world, machinery does the work of procreation. The workforce consists of machine-made products: "standard Gammas, unvarying Deltas, uniform Epsilons" (*BNW* 6).

Not until TS 27, the bottom half of a sheet whose top has been torn off, does Huxley refer directly to the brave new world's guiding light. The Director relates how sleep teaching was discovered "while Our Ford was still on earth" (*BNW* 25). The implied parallel between Ford's career and Christ's ministry reveals the technocrat's godlike importance for the first time. On TS 29, one learns further that the first documented instance of hypnopaedia "occurred only twenty-three years after Our Ford's first T-Model was put on the market," which begins to explain the significance of the letters "A.F." Divulging these crucial facts, the Director "made a sign of the T on his stomach and all the students followed suit" (*BNW* 27).[6] This absurd gesture confirms Ford's divine status, but the primacy of stomach over head and heart implies a faith premised on consumer satisfaction rather than spiritual fulfillment.

Much of the Americanization of the World State depends on Huxley's clever uses of Henry Ford's name. Prominent places and famous landmarks, such as Charing Cross Tower ("Charing-T Tower" [*BNW* 68]) and Big Ben ("Big Henry" [99]), have been renamed for Ford; the highest religious and temporal authority, Mustapha Mond, is addressed respectfully by Fordian titles, namely, "Our Ford" or "his fordship" (35, 37). In 306 pages, one counts at least 110 references to Ford and things Fordian.

In chapter 3, with a total of 19 allusions to Ford, they come in clusters—on pages 60, 62, and 63, for example. In chapter 5, which has no fewer than 21 references to Ford, eight occur on pages 91–92. Chapter 4, which makes only one reference to Ford, may have been written earlier, before chapters 3 and 5. When Bernard discusses with Lenina their trip to New Mexico, she asks if it will start from "the Charing-T Tower" (68).

After chapter 5, the number of references to Ford per chapter evens out: seven in both 6 and 7, four apiece in 9 and 10, five in 11 and 12, four in 13, seven in 15, eight in 16, and seven again in the final chapter. But there is only one reference to Ford in chapter 8 and just two in 17, a good indication that materials in these chapters belong to an early stage in the writing process. After no more than several weeks of composition, Huxley began to complicate his parody of Wells by stepping up the attack on Ford, peppering the typescript with short phrases to invoke the American industrialist as the World State's be-all and end-all. Although three of Huxley's first six chapters (1, 2, and 4) have a grand total of nine references to Ford and thus may antedate the decision to link Ford and Wells as coevils, the first third of *Brave New World* still makes no less than 56 such references, compared to 28 in the second third (chapters 7–11) and 26 in the final third (chapters 13–18).[7]

Huxley caricatured H. G. Wells and Sir Alfred Mond in the composite figure of Mustapha Mond because he considered both men proponents of antihumanistic rationalization—the reorganization of society on an allegedly more scientific, more efficient, more technological basis. Such a reorganization might reverse the economic slump that had crippled Europe since 1929, but Huxley feared it was more likely to reduce human beings to machines by destroying freedom and individuality. Instead of the utopia that Wells touted in fantasies such as *Men Like Gods* (1923), the rationalized future would resemble Joseph Lucas's magneto plant or Imperial Chemical Industries (ICI), Sir Alfred Mond's industrial complex.

When Huxley visited Lucas's factory that made electrical equipment for cars at Acock's Green in Birmingham, he witnessed mass production on British soil. He had also toured Mond's Billingham plant for producing sodium and synthetic ammonia. Both visits are described in "Sight-Seeing in Alien Englands."[8] Huxley's premise is that factory and plant are foreign countries to middle-class English intellectuals such as himself. "Sight-Seeing" appeared in June 1931, when Huxley was in the throes of a massive reconsideration of the *Brave New World* typescript.

At the Lucas factory, Huxley saw

forty or fifty girls sitting at a long table. In front of them an endless band slowly crawled along, carrying on its surface the constituent parts of an electrical machine. Each girl had her special function— to insert a rod, to tighten so many screws, to make fast certain wires. When the last girl had done her job, yet another magneto was ready to be fitted to yet another car. (74)

Girls were used because they could be paid less than skilled mechanics; each worker performed "one small and specialized task" without having to understand "how a magneto worked" (74).

This experience found its way into *Brave New World* as the "small factory of lighting-sets for helicopters" that John Savage tours in chapter 11. Mass-produced Gamma-Plus dwarfs are mass-producing helicopter lights:

In the assembling room, the dynamos were being put together by two sets of Gamma-Plus dwarfs. The two low worktables faced one another; between them crawled the conveyor with its load of separate parts; forty-seven blond heads were confronted by forty-seven brown ones. (*BNW* 188)

The factory's "Human Element Manager" boasts that the workers never cause trouble. Nevertheless, John, breaking away from Bernard, is heard "violently retching behind a clump of laurels" (189).

Huxley suddenly realized that he had mistaken the national scene for the international; he was creating a modern British dystopia instead of a universally frightening one in which Ford's factories were the prototype for Lucas's plant and Sir Alfred's conglomerate. "Fifteen racks" in the Social Predestination Room, conveyors covering "Two thousand one hundred and thirty-six metres in all" (*BNW* 11–12), connote Ford, not Lucas; but with so few specific references to Ford in chapters 1 and 2, the novel's opening, if not the earliest draft generally, failed to underline the devilish partnership Huxley foresaw between Wellsian utopian fantasizing on one hand and Ford's know-how, his managerial expertise, on the other.

Wells's ideal of a rationalized society run by scientifically trained bureaucrats and Ford's confidence in the organizational skills that produce a well-run factory went together as ends and means. To universalize his antiutopia, Huxley realized, was to Americanize it, to become blatantly anti-Fordian.[9] In satisfying most of Wells's criteria for a "modern utopia," the brave new world shows how such a phenomenon could turn out differently from Wells's predictions. "London will be the first Utopian city centre we shall see," Wells promised (*Modern Utopia* 238). Huxley's focal point is also London, but one Americanized by a dramatic rise from three anti-Ford references in chapter 1 to 15 in chapter 3.

In *Point Counter Point* (1928), Huxley's spokesperson, Mark Rampion, condemns "Americanization" as the deification of "Machinery and Alfred Mond or Henry Ford . . . in the name of society, progress, and human happiness" (415–16). Initially, Huxley believed his archvillain in *Brave New World* could be a caricature of either Sir Alfred Mond or Henry Ford, hence the choice of the former's surname for the World Controller's. However, by the time Mustapha Mond enters the novel in chapter 3, he is hailed as "his fordship" (*BNW* 37), Henry Ford's disciple and successor—not "Alfred Mond or Henry Ford" but both. The current Resident Controller for Western Europe is named for a figure familiar to British readers, but the position he occupies relates to an American industrialist, known the world over, who had made businesses such as Sir Alfred's possible. Mond continues a parodic papal succession that makes the Ford factory and the Wellsian scientific utopia extensions of each other.[10]

*   *   *

Perhaps *Brave New World* did not begin in the Central London Hatchery and Conditioning Centre but in Malpais. TS 120–28, which provide material for chapter 8, are among the oldest surviving pages of the typescript. Unlike surrounding leaves, these pages—heavily edited, faded, some with frayed edges—were typed with a black ribbon, a telltale sign of antecedence. For most of the typescript, Huxley used purple ribbons of varying shades, the lighter or more faded the type, the older the page.[11] Between TS 120 and 128, Huxley recounts a visit from one of Linda's admirers (120–21) and dramatizes the beating she receives from the pueblo women (122–23). Linda tells her son stories about the "Other Place," the brave new world (125–26), and John is tormented by Indian boys (127).

The earliest draft of *Brave New World* may have started with these reservation scenes. TS 120–28 reveal that Nina, Huxley's original name for Linda, has been left behind by Bernard, not by Thomas, the D.H.C. She has had a son but remains an outcast because the Indian women object to her promiscuity. The canceled lower half of TS 122 is enclosed in a box with lines drawn through it; Nina's whine, "Oh, why did I ever think of going with Bernard?" remains legible.

One suspects that Bernard and his son John originally were to be reunited for insurrectionary purposes. Together, this duo of malcontents would disrupt the Wellsian world order. On TS A1, the rejected but saved version of TS 169 that follows TS 248 in the typescript, it is the morning after John's refusal to make an appearance at Bernard's party. John urges a despondent Bernard to reform, forsake soma, and "Play the man. Haven't you often said that you only wanted the opportunity? Well here it is. Take it." Bernard promises, "I'll do it." This could have been the start of a subversionary clique. On TS 169 (*BNW* 211), the version Huxley decided on after opting for a novel without a hero, a "deflated" Bernard is "bitterly" unhappy to have lost his prestige as the Savage's exhibitor.

Having settled on ignominious defeat for the Savage, Huxley struck a passage in which John hints at enlisting confederates. At the end of their debate, Mond recites a long list of human miseries banished from the brave new world (old age, impotence, syphilis, cancer) and John declares, "I claim them all" (*BNW* 283). Mond's succinct reply, "You're welcome," originally read: "You won't find many other claimants," to which Huxley typed in and crossed out John's response: "That's where I believe you're wrong" (TS 230).

Americanizations of the typescript suggest that *Brave New World* was transformed from a fairly conventional antiutopia into an "amused, Pyrrhonic" aesthete's parody of one.[12] The original plan was to show heretics revolting against an insufferable Wellsian system, as happens in Zamyatin's *We*, where dissidents disturb the One State, a regimented society run with maximum efficiency by the Benefactor and a cadre of guardians.[13] Instead, Huxley tells a thoroughly ironic tale in which three malcontents—John Savage, Bernard Marx, and Helmholtz Watson—fail to dislodge Mustapha Mond, one of the World State's Controllers, or even to shake his confidence.

Initially, Huxley appears to have imagined *Brave New World* as a pro-Lawrencian tract; it would resemble Zamyatin's *We*, upend Wells's *Men Like Gods*, and corroborate Lawrence's *The Plumed Serpent*. In Lawrence's utopia, Cipriano, an Oxford-educated Indian, helps Don Ramon Carrasco, a descendant of Spanish conquerors, transform Mexico into a pre-Christian society predicated on "the old blood-and-vertebrate consciousness" (455). Similarly, a noble savage from Lawrence's beloved American Southwest, spouting a preference for God, freedom, and poetry, was to pose a formidable challenge to the ascendancy of technology and material comfort in the brave new world's deceptively blissful society.

By the time Huxley penned the Savage's suicide, however, Lawrence's influence, waning steadily since his death, had faded almost completely. Lawrence's excessive admiration for America may have been the last straw. Doubtless, Lawrence was sincere in declaring that New Mexico had "liberated [him] from the present era of civilization, the great era of material and mechanical development" (*Phoenix* 42). But Huxley foresaw no such liberation. The more he reconsidered, the more ineffectual New Mexico seemed, an eminently ignorable appendage to the real America that Ford and his ilk not only epitomized but were exporting worldwide.

Lawrence believed in America's destiny, its salvationary mission to revivify civilization. He exhorted America to "pick up the life-thread where the mysterious Red race let it fall" (*Phoenix* 90).[14] In a world given over to industry and machines, Lawrence continued, America must reanimate "the spirit of her own dark, aboriginal continent"; only America could quicken life's "pulse" from where "the Red Indian, the Aztec, the Maya, the Inca left it off." To Huxley, pronouncements of this sort sounded more like madness than hubris.

Recalling Lawrence in New Mexico—on the fringe, that is, of an expanding industrial state indifferent to his appeals to its "aboriginal" past—Huxley predicted his former mentor's increasingly marginal significance as a social prophet. Whether John is in Malpais or Fordian London, he never fits in, much less sparks a general renewal. On the reservation, the Savage is resented as an anomaly; transported to London, he becomes a novelty, not the World State's redeemer but its latest curiosity.

Huxley resolved not to let New Mexico furnish a Lawrencian alternative to the Wellsian future; he condemned Wells's prescription and Lawrence's antidote. In Huxley's mind, the Savage metamorphosed from courageous crusader against the World State into a ruthless caricature of Lawrence's naive overconfidence in preindustrial cultures.[15] Through John, Lawrence is Americanized pejoratively, his so-called blood philosophy emanating from Santa Fe instead of Nottingham.[16] Besides decrying the onset of a world-wide Americanization along Fordian guidelines, Huxley ridiculed Lawrence's New Mexican primitivism as a particularly pointless variation; it was an Americanization as misguided as the brave new world's, only smaller, weaker, impossibly reactionary—a ludicrous counterstroke. Once Huxley added Ford to Wells, Malpais became an even wickeder parody of Lawrence's vital community. "Pulsing with the indefatigable movement of blood" (*BNW* 125), it seemed certain to be an anachronism by A.F. 632 if not already an absurd impossibility in 1932.

Declining to champion Lawrence dovetailed nicely with Huxley's determination to indict Ford as the primary villain behind both Wells and Sir Alfred Mond. Huxley made both madhouses in *Brave New World* fundamentally American. As he Americanized London and Lawrence, the former grew more Fordian while New Mexico became Lawrencian. Huxley damned two equally unacceptable alternatives, Fordian London and Lawrencian Malpais, as contrapuntal opposites, satiric versions of the same theme, namely, aberration—a choice, as Huxley later put it, between "lunacy" and "insanity" (Foreword viii).[17]

*  *  *

Conceivably, TS 120 contains the first paragraph of the novel that Huxley originally planned to write:

> It was very hot. They had eaten a lot of tortillas and sweet corn. Nina said: "Come and lie down, Baby." They lay down together in the big bed. "Sing," he said. Nina sang. "Streptococo-Gee to Banbury T," and "Bye Baby Banting, soon you'll need decanting." And then he went to sleep. There was a loud noise and he woke up with a start. A man was standing by the bed . . .

In the typescript, the first five lines (up to "he woke up") plus three words in line six ("with a start") have been boxed in and crossed out.

Done with purple ribbon and essentially free of emendations, TS 119 stops three quarters of the way down the page once it has overlapped the lines crossed out on the much older TS 120. Bernard asks John to tell him all about his life "as far back as you can remember," and the Savage recalls that

> It was very hot. They had eaten a lot of tortillas and sweet corn. Linda said, "Come and lie down, Baby." They lay down together in the big bed. "Sing," and Linda sang. Sang "Streptocock Gee to Banbury-T" and "Bye, Baby Banting, soon you'll need decanting." Her voice got fainter and fainter . . .
>
> There was a loud noise and he woke up with a start.

"Baby" is a survival of John's original name throughout TS 120–28 when these pages may have begun the novel.[18]

Admittedly, the first seven paragraphs of chapter 8 appear on both TS 119 and TS 120. But they give the impression of a bridge devised to connect the reservation scenes to preceding material actually written later. When Huxley no longer wanted to begin with Malpais, he needed a frame for John's recollections: he transformed them from the novel's opening episode into a story within a story, a flashback that contains some of the novel's earliest events. If one ignores the first seven paragraphs, chapter 8 reverts to a straightforward narrative of formative developments in the Savage's life from infancy through age "sixteen" (*BNW* 160). The story of the Savage's early years is told from John's perspective in the third person by an unnamed omniscient narrator whose comments can also be heard throughout the rest of the novel.

Huxley did not tour Mexico until 1934; he did not visit the American Southwest around Taos until 1937. For chapter 7 in the typescript, he relied on *The Plumed Serpent* and Lawrence's essays in *Mornings in Mexico* (1927).

Bernard and Lenina witness a mixture of Zuni and Hopi rituals that provide a contrapuntal variation on the Solidarity Service Bernard attends in chapter 6. As parodies of each other, Malpais and the brave new world exhibit variant forms of barbaric behavior. John's recollections, the bulk of chapter 8, make sense with or without Bernard's request for them. As John begins to remember, the narrative moves inside his mind; thanks to indirect discourse, the Savage does not speak his reverie aloud to Bernard.

Instead of reuniting Nina's son John with Bernard, his father, Huxley made John the D.H.C.'s son. Instead of providing a confrontation between a son and a father who is also potentially a confederate, Bernard facilitates John's translation to Fordian London, where he and Linda discombobulate the D.H.C. His threats to exile Bernard (chapter 6) may be another late addition,[19] Huxley's way of motivating Bernard's interest in John once the latter was no longer his progeny. The Savage gives Bernard an opportunity to take revenge on his boss and avoid being sent to Iceland. However, after John has called the D.H.C. "My Father" (*BNW* 178), he forgets him entirely, spending the rest of his days in the brave new world under Bernard's tutelage, a carryover from their previous connection as father and son.

Bernard Marx requests John Savage's life story in order to "reconstruct" the past. He and John, Bernard points out, have been "living on different planets in different centuries" (*BNW* 144). The request sounds reasonable. If they are father and son, Bernard wants to narrow the distance between them; or else he hopes to reconcile opposites—the pueblo and the World State, "a mother, . . . dirt, and gods, and old age, and disease with bottle babies and perfect health until sixty." But Linda's pregnancy remains difficult to explain. She does not have a child as a direct consequence of getting lost and being abandoned on the reservation; she must have been pregnant before the catastrophe and despite having taken the usual precautions. "I still don't know how it happened, seeing that I did all the Malthusian drill," she complains to Bernard and Lenina (*BNW* 139–40). Linda's protestations smooth over a rough spot in Huxley's plot: he needed a natural childbirth for which Linda's getting lost cannot fully account.

When Huxley pushed back the original opening, he inked in "Linda" over "Nina" throughout what became TS 120–28. Three overlooked instances were caught between typescript and proof. "Lenina" was reserved as the name for Bernard's companion and John's femme fatale. Huxley also altered the name of "the anxious-looking little girl" whom a howling small boy refuses "to join in the ordinary erotic play": "Lenina Crown" (no *e*) became "Polly Trotsky" (TS 34). Bernard's Lenina first appears toward the end of chapter 1, when Henry Foster greets her by first name in the Hatchery's Embryo Store (*BNW* 17), but she is not seen again until chapter 3, several paragraphs after the Polly Trotsky passage (37), by which time "Nina" presumably had been changed to "Linda."

Even in the printed version, Lenina and Nina-Linda remain similar in more than name. Both are Betas. Linda informs Lenina that she worked in the Fertilizing Room, but she tells John that her "job was always with the embryos" (154), as is Lenina's. "Was our Linda originally the Savage's mother?" Wilson pondered (40). The D.H.C. recalls that the girl with whom he visited the reservation was "particularly pneumatic" (*BNW* 112). To make things less complicated, Huxley invented Bernard's contretemps with his boss, substituting the D.H.C.'s paternity for Bernard's and separating Bernard's Lenina from John's Nina by altering the latter's name to Linda. The scene in which the D.H.C. confides in Bernard about his disastrous excursion to the New Mexican reservation, during which he lost his Beta-Minus girlfriend, smacks of contrivance. "'I really don't know why I bored you with this trivial anecdote,'" he concludes, "furious with himself for having given away a discreditable secret" (*BNW* 113).

The D.H.C. says he took his New Mexico trip "twenty-five" years ago, when he was Bernard's age (*BNW* 111). Because brave new worlders do not age visibly, the unnamed narrator finds it "hard" to pinpoint the D.H.C.'s age—"Thirty? fifty? fifty-five?" (3). If one assumes the Director is in his fifties, having abandoned Linda a quarter of a century ago, John and Bernard are both roughly 25. In Huxley's original conception, a less comical, potentially more heroic Bernard would have been the Director's age, that is, twice John's.

Instead of a 50-year-old Bernard returning to the reservation, this time with Lenina, to find Nina, whom he had lost there 25 years earlier, Bernard is the same age as Lenina and John. He need make only one trip to New Mexico, where he discovers Linda and the D.H.C.'s son. Lenina can infatuate Bernard and attempt to seduce John; this seduction would have been impossible if she and Nina were identical, and it would have been confusing if John had a mother named Nina and a love interest named Lenina.

Bernard and Lenina meet John 12 pages into chapter 7; he introduces them to Linda six pages from its end. Although Bernard finds the D.H.C.'s son instead of his own, this is still a useful discovery. Spying Lenina, Linda, who is all "flabbiness" and "wrinkles" with "sagging cheeks" and "purplish blotches" (138), confronts her former self. Part of a contrast in miniature between Malpais and Fordian London, Linda personifies the primitive past that John will be compelled to embrace in the novel's climactic debate. No brighter than Linda but shuddering with disgust at the sight of her, Lenina represents Mond's antiseptic alternative.

Section 3 of chapter 6 (the last eight pages) is also typed with black ribbon and may be as old, or nearly so, as TS 120–28. Beginning "The journey was uneventful" ("quite uneventful" on PS 116), these pages bring Bernard and Lenina to Santa Fe. Perhaps they formed part of the reservation episodes starting on TS 120 or were devised as preparation for them after Huxley changed his mind about commencing in New Mexico. If he considered starting the novel with section 3, the first seven paragraphs of chapter 8, in which Bernard solicits John's life story, became necessary immediately. All of chapter 7 describing Bernard and Lenina's reactions to Malpais, TS 94–119, are typed in purple ribbon and probably were written later than section 3, on which they elaborate without Lawrence's enthusiasm for Indian rites and rituals.

When Bernard telephones Helmholtz Watson from New Mexico, he learns that the D.H.C. is planning to follow through on his threat to send him to Iceland. Huxley worked into chapter 6 two preparations for Bernard's discovery of the D.H.C.'s son instead of his own: the Director's earlier threat to exile Bernard—it occurs in section 2, right after the D.H.C.'s revelation of his own trip to the reservation (*BNW* 114)—and the phone call to Watson. Of the seven references to Ford in chapter 6, two appear during Bernard's interview with the D.H.C. and another two are part of the telephone call. A fifth—"Our Ford loved infants" (*BNW* 109)—is one of the four holograph emendations discussed earlier.

The sole reference to Henry Ford in chapter 8 occurs in proof, not typescript, which is additional evidence for the primacy of TS 120–28. When the Savage asks Bernard if he is married to Lenina, the latter responds: "Ford, no!" (*BNW* 165). Surprisingly, Huxley's correspondence never refers to his work in progress by its Shakespearean title. Not until February 1932, a month after publication, did Huxley tell Mrs. Flora Strousse how "glad" he was that she "liked *Brave New World*" (*Letters* 358). Typescript for PS 163–65, wherein Bernard invites the Savage to London, and the latter, overcome, replies by quoting Miranda's line from *The Tempest*, "O brave new world" (PS 164; *BNW* 165), is missing. It seems incredible that these important pages were added between typescript and proof sheets. But in the pro-Lawrencian dystopia that Huxley originally started to write, jokes at John's expense were not a priority. The Savage may have been brought to London without speaking the novel's ironic title.[20]

*   *   *

An antiutopia that begins with John leaving the reservation for the brave new world better fits Huxley's account of how *Brave New World* "started out"—"as a parody of H. G. Wells's *Men Like Gods*" that "got out of hand and turned into something different from what I'd originally intended" (Interview 198). Prior to the Americanization of the typescript, Huxley's major model for the brave new world was the future society in Wells's 1923 fantasy. Several Earthlings are accidentally transported through time from the Maidenhead Road near Windsor Castle into another world thousands of years more advanced. One hears an echo of this in Bernard's remarks about living on a different planet in a different century from John (*BNW* 144).

One of Wells's Earthlings, Mr. Barnstaple, finds himself enamored of the new society, calling it Utopia, "the world of his dreams" (264). Through a series of conferences, Earthlings are taught how Utopia came about. After "nearly five centuries" of struggle (71), science and education prevailed. Wells's Utopians travel by airplane, communicate telepathically, and have solved the population problem. For the competitive instinct, they substitute creative service. Having outgrown the need for government, they go about naked, enjoying complete sexual freedom in a technologically proficient, disease-free society; eugenics guarantee there are "few dull and no really defective people" (73).

Surprisingly, Barnstaple's fellow Earthlings fail to perceive Utopia's superiority. When they plan a coup, he warns the Utopians. Nevertheless, this future society has no need for retardants. Barnstaple is the first to be sent back to his own time, a misfortune that leaves him "bitterly sorrowful" (296) yet physically and psychologically refreshed. A vacation in the Wellsian future has made him optimistic about the future of the human race.

John Savage's sojourn in the brave new world is the reverse of Barnstaple's in Wells's allegedly perfect society. The Savage's disappointment and death mock Barnstaple's heartfelt praise and reinvigorated sense of purpose. Instead of "demi-gods," males like "Apollos" for example (*Men Like Gods* 264, 26), the technologically oriented future of A.F. 632 deluges the Savage with regimented, pug-faced identical twins, such as the Gamma Plus dwarfs in chapter 11. When Huxley interpolated the riot at the Park Lane Hospital, khaki-clad Deltas swarm maggot-like around John's dying mother—"Twin after twin, twin after twin" (*BNW* 238). John fights to undo Huxley's version of the Wellsian future, not to preserve it. Having failed, he pleads to be sent away, but Mond vetoes his request.

Several of the opening typescript pages—TS 10, 11, and 13, for example—are typed with black ribbon and appear worn, frayed, and as faded as TS 120–28. This suggests that some form of the lecture scene was composed about the same time as John's account of life on the reservation. Huxley began either with the reservation or with the lecture, perhaps juxtapositioning two equally disturbing upbringings—the brave new worlders' in the Central London Hatchery's Fertilizing Room and Infant Nurseries and John's schooling by Linda, Popé, and Old Mitsima in New Mexico. The Savage may have been translated to London in time for the D.H.C.'s talk, much as Barnstaple attends explanatory conferences about Utopia in *Men Like Gods*.

In effect, Huxley began *Brave New World* twice. Both beginnings remain visible. Originally, the novel started on the reservation, then proceeded with John's London misadventures. When Huxley began the reorganized typescript with the D.H.C.'s lecture, the novel commenced in a Wellsian London that grows increasingly Fordian by chapter 3. *Brave New World* seems to begin a second time when the Savage arrives from the reservation. Readers are shown the brave new world through the eyes of the students on the lecture tour and again through John's as Bernard takes him around. Instruction is mandatory for Mr. Barnstaple and his fellow Earthlings, given their ignorance. With the Savage's London appearance reserved for chapter 10, Huxley had to pretend that the D.H.C.'s students, native brave new worlders, need orientation.

Jointly, lecture and history lesson parody the conferences in which Wells's Utopians outline their society for Mr. Barnstaple and his companions. They recall "The Great Confusion" from which "the universal scientific state" emerged after "nearly five centuries" (*Men Like Gods* 71). The brave new world has taken an equivalent time to reach perfection. Mond recounts absurdly gruesome highlights from the "Nine Years War" that began in A.F. 141; together with "the Great Economic Collapse," it ushered in Fordism, the World State. Particularly reprehensible atrocities include the use of anthrax bombs, the "Russian technique for infecting water supplies," machine-gunning "Eight Hundred Simple Lifers," the British Museum Massacre, and "the blowing up of historical monuments" (*BNW* 54–59).

"The reading of *Men Like Gods*," Huxley recalled in a 1962 lecture,

> evoked in me an almost pathological reaction in the direction of cynical anti-idealism. So much so that, before I finished the book, I had resolved to write a derisive parody of this most optimistic of Wells's utopias. But when I addressed myself to the problem of creating a negative Nowhere, a Utopia in reverse, I found the subject so fascinatingly pregnant with so many kinds of literary and psychological possibilities that I quite forgot *Men Like Gods* and addressed myself in all seriousness to the task of writing a book that was later to be known as *Brave New World*. ("Utopias" 1)

Nevertheless, the first two chapters and the history lesson in chapter 3 still read best as a point-by-point repudiation of the Utopia Mr. Barnstaple admires.

\* \* \*

Huxley supposedly preferred "constant piecemeal revision" (Wilson 30–31). That is, he produced "successive versions of typed pages," all of which he "revised by autograph emendations" (Watt 368). The novel allegedly grew by "insertions of short passages" typed or in ink or between lines, and by inclusion of "longer ink passages in 'balloons'"; rarely does one find expansions of "cancelled sections" or "whole new pages" (Wilson 35). But Huxley's letters in spring and summer 1931 suggest a major rethinking; they indicate that he undertook at least one massive overhaul of the *Brave New World* typescript. The modern literary masterpiece known as *Brave New World* is the result of this large-scale revision, much of it an Americanization.

According to Grover Smith's chronology, Huxley wrote *Brave New World* in just four months, "May–August 1931" (14), a remarkable achievement.[21] To Mrs. Kethevan Roberts, Huxley divulged on 18 May that his next novel would concentrate "on the horrors of the Wellsian Utopia and a revolt against it" (*Letters* 348). This sounds like the straightforward parody of *Men Like Gods* in which the Savage is brought from the reservation and, unlike Mr. Barnstaple, rebels against the supposedly utopian society to which he is exposed.

One can outline this Zamyatin-like, anti-Wellsian *Brave New World*. A Lawrencian Savage grows up on the reservation. Revealed to be Bernard's son, John is transported to a Utopia the reverse of the world state Mr. Barnstaple finds so attractive in *Men Like Gods*. Perhaps he arrives in time for the lecture explaining how this perfect society operates. Bernard shows the Savage the sights, such as the Bombay Green Rocket that fails to impress him in chapter 11. After about a fortnight, Bernard conducts the Savage to Mustapha Mond, and John delivers an unfavorable verdict. During this interview, the Savage raises the prospect of a serious revolt.

Huxley may have done most of this in the first three and a half weeks of May. That is, he had written chapter 8, chapter 1 and possibly 2, and chapter 17. Maybe he also had on hand Bernard and Lenina's flight to Malpais (part of chapter 6), John's tour of the brave new world with Bernard (chapter 11), and Lenina's abortive seduction of John (chapter 13). Chapters 1, 2, 8, and 17 contain only 11 references to Henry Ford, of which five appear in chapter 2.

By 27 May, however, serious complications had developed. Alarmed to be headed in new directions, Huxley confided to his brother Julian that a "literary catastrophe" had befallen him, due to which the past month's work "won't do"; it would have to be written "in quite another way" (*Letters* 348–49).[22] This refers, one supposes, to Huxley's decision not to begin on the reservation. With the force of an epiphany, he perceived a more ambitious project: condemning the future more broadly by enlarging the parody of H. G. Wells into a full-fledged anti-Fordian polemic. Instead of employing the Savage to discredit a Wellsian Mond in a dystopia that recalled Zamyatin's *We*, he would write as a total skeptic and dismiss Lawrence as well.

Extensive revisions were still under way a month later when Huxley informed Sidney Schiff that he was "rewriting large chunks" of typescript he had thought "definitively done" (Robert 73). "Large chunks" is a far cry from "successive revisions" of individual typescript pages (Wilson 31; Watt 368). Uncertain whether this revision would be "final," Huxley felt daunted by "great deserts of the yet unwritten" (Robert 73), including, one presumes, Linda's death scene and the hospital riot, a bigger role for Helmholtz Watson as beginning poet and aspiring mystic, and John's suicide.

Nearly three months after the missive to Mrs. Roberts, Huxley completed an enormous redoing. In a letter to his father late in August, he sighed with relief at having "got rid of" a "satirical novel about the Future" (*Letters* 351).[23] Between 27 May and 24 August 1931, Huxley transformed *Brave New World* from a burlesque of "the Wellsian Utopia" into a modern "satirical novel" of ideas about "the Future" in general. His quarrel was with the oncoming situation and all who were bringing it about.

The précis in Huxley's late-August letter to his father describes *Brave New World* as

> a comic, or at least satirical novel about the Future, showing the appallingness (at any rate by our standards) of Utopia and adumbrating the effects on thought and feeling of such quite possible biological inventions as the production of children in bottles (with consequent abolition of the family and all the Freudian "complexes" for which family relationships are responsible), the prolongation of youth, the devising of some harmless but effective substitute for alcohol, cocaine, opium etc:—and also the effects of such sociological reforms as Pavlovian conditioning of all children from birth and before birth, universal peace, security and stability. (351)

The reference to "Utopia" with a capital *U* connotes Wells; "production" is a code word alluding to Ford. The appalling society results from a synthesis of bad ideas. Fordian expertise supplies the common denominator: a mechanical conception of human nature. To achieve the unity, stability, and identity that Wells's universal utopia requires, brave new worlders are invested with Freudian formative experiences in Neo-Pavlovian Conditioning Rooms. Ford's principle of mass production is applied to impart identical traumas, those involving books and flowers, for example, in conditioning centers that follow the same procedures the world over.[24]

* * *

An early version of the novel's climax, the Savage's debate with Mustapha Mond, survives as TS B1–B9 in light, faded, purple type. This simpler affair is conducted without Bernard Marx and Helmholtz Watson. Part of the initial draft of *Brave New World*, it contains only two references to Henry Ford: Mond's resolution to keep "God in the safe and Ford on the shelves" and his exclamation "Ford forbid" when the Savage asks why brave new worlders are not allowed to do things "on their own" (*BNW* 272, 279). Chapter 16, the preliminary skirmish between Mond and the Savage with Marx and Watson involved, probably was written later than the climactic debate. It makes no fewer than six references to Ford, including the only mention of his autobiography: skimming *My Life and Work*, John concludes that Ford's life story "didn't interest him" (*BNW* 257).

On C1 and C2, which follow TS B1–B9 and may have been written when they were, the Savage invites Bernard to live with him in the country. "Linda died this afternoon," he tells Bernard, but does not say how. The earliest version of *Brave New World* did not dramatize Linda's death or the disturbance her distraught son causes at the Park Lane Hospital. Bernard declares himself willing to accompany John, provided he can get time off, a reply that reduces the Savage to violent laughter. If C1 and C2 originally followed John's interview with Mond, John's derision may have provoked Bernard to sterner measures.

Huxley demoted Bernard from virile protagonist to farcical antihero, a process that coincided with the Savage's decline from Lawrencian standard-bearer to futile alternative. Huxley transformed Marx into a smallish man with a large inferiority complex; he transferred Bernard's original physique and potential for rebellion to Helmholtz Watson. No longer intent on making Bernard and John father and son, Huxley chose Watson, not Bernard, for John's closest friend. In chapter 13, John has "made up his mind to talk to Helmholtz about Lenina" (*BNW* 222); his confidant in the typescript was "Bernard" (TS 179). When the Savage instigates a riot, Helmholtz plunges in while Marx hesitates on the sidelines.

Initially a minor figure, Watson is twice described as "little" (TS 95, 97). Huxley crossed out the first reference in typescript and omitted the second (Bernard's reference to "poor little Helmholtz Watson") between typescript and proof. He shrank Bernard instead. Three allusions to the excessive amount of alcohol in Bernard's blood surrogate, allegedly the reason for his smallness, are inked-in insertions (TS 83, 89, 114). Late in the composition process, Huxley bolstered Watson's role with a balloon-enclosed insertion of more than 50 inked-in words. Helmholtz declares himself "profoundly happy" with the extra latent power he feels welling up inside him (TS 172), a sign of poetic inspiration and mystical influx.

Originally, as Bernard's contemporary, Watson too would have been old enough to be John's father. In the revised typescript, where he is the 25-year-old Bernard's closest friend, Watson still gives the impression of being an older, maturer person; as his enlightenment begins, he experiences a secondary adolescence, a supplementary growth or rebirth. Although Huxley conceived Watson's expanded role late, he managed to make his importance clear by chapters 15–17, the confrontation with Mond. In contrast, Huxley compromised Bernard Marx by inserting two handwritten paragraphs in which he invites Miss Keate to one of his parties to meet the Savage. Huxley also typed in the advances Bernard makes to Eton's headmistress during the showing of the *Penitentes* film (TS 152–54). Before Bernard became popular as the Savage's guide, he frowned on casual sex.

Huxley wrote Linda's death scene by hand on 11 pages (TS 189–99, both sides of the pages as 189, 189$^2$, and so on). The absence of references to Henry Ford is not a factor. Huxley inserted this episode as chapter 14 to motivate John's attack on the Park Lane Hospital's menial staff; the attack is also a late addition but probably written prior to Linda's death scene. More of a skirmish than a full-scale uprising, the ill-fated soma riot is not the "revolt" against the Wellsian Utopia promised in Huxley's original plan (*Letters* 348). Huxley wrote the earliest version of the Mond–Savage debate without Linda's death scene as the pretext for the riot, probably without the riot itself. The earliest draft of the debate does not mention Linda's demise; nor is John's left hand, "bitten" (*BNW* 255) in the riot, bandaged. One concludes that the "revolt" was to be a consequence of the meeting between Mond and the Savage, not its cause.

Because Watson and Marx take part in the Savage's attempt to rouse the Deltas, they are brought before Mond along with John. On TS 208–11, Huxley incorporated them both into the opening stages of John's argument with Mond (*BNW* 256–61). But only Mond and the Savage talk on TS 212–14, which was surely written before TS 208–11. For TS 215–18 Huxley involved Watson and Marx again, breaking up the conversation with the latter's hysterical collapse (*BNW* 266–70). The order of composition for chapter 16 was most likely TS 212–14 (light, faded type with just Mond and the Savage), then TS 208–11 (dark purple type with Marx and Watson present), and then 215–18 (dark type with Marx and Watson included) (*BNW* 262–65, 256–61, 266–70). In chapter 17, where the type is light purple and faded throughout, the core interview pits John directly against Mond with no else present (TS 219–30; *BNW* 271–83). This scene perpetuates Huxley's earliest inspiration for a debate between opposing value systems.

Huxley probably added John's suicide (chapter 18) about the time he dramatized Linda's death and introduced Marx and Watson into chapter 16.

TS 200–07, 208–11, 215–18, and 231–48—the soma riot, the two parts of the Mond interview with Watson and Marx present, and John's suicide at the lighthouse—are all in dark purple type. TS 177–88, which relate Lenina's attempt to seduce John much as I–330 sidetracks D–503 in Zamyatin's *We*, are in faded purple type; this episode must have been written about the same time as the earliest version of the Mond–Savage debate and may have led directly to it.

Building on the riot and John's arrest, Huxley energized the climactic debate with Mustapha Mond so that it became one of the finest discussion scenes the novelist of ideas ever wrote. A moderately dramatic encounter in which a D. H. Lawrence figure was to embarrass a Wellsian spokesperson was transformed into a highly charged exchange between champions of opposed and equally repellent philosophies: the revisionary world according to simple-lifers such as Lawrence on one side, the future world being concocted by Ford and Wells on the other. Instead of one alternative rebelling against another, Huxley staged the debate as a clash of inadequate perspectives the reader cannot resolve: Lawrencian primitivism versus Fordism—that is, Malpais versus the World State, life in a pueblo in the American Southwest versus life in an enormous factory.

Early and late, Huxley kept three cornerstones in mind: reservation scenes, introductory lecture on the brave new world, and the Mond–Savage confrontation. Each changed substantially as *Brave New World* became less a traditional antiutopia and more a satirical novel of ideas. John's experiences in Malpais do not open the final draft; nor does he turn out to be the brave new world's Lawrencian liberator. The D.H.C.'s introduction to a funny yet frightening scientific utopia is not just a parody of rationalization in the Wellsian World State; it expands into Mond's full-fledged history lesson on the Fordian world order. The argument between John Savage and Mustapha Mond becomes the novel's climactic dead end: instead of a revolution, two incomplete philosophies collide, neither able to defeat or accommodate the other.

\*   \*   \*

Huxley traveled across America on the final leg of his round-the-globe journey in 1925–26. Summing up this trip in "The Outlook for American Culture," he declared that America had shown him the "immediately coming civilization" (1). During spring and summer 1931, events of the last decade coalesced for him. Huxley connected his negative vision of America in 1926 with his mounting disbelief in the utopian possibilities of Mexico and the American Southwest as they had been set forth in *The Plumed Serpent* (1926) and *Mornings in Mexico* (1927). He brought this vision of Fordian America and his increasing disdain for Lawrence's Southwest to bear on the contempt he had felt for Wells's *Men Like Gods* (1923).

*Brave New World* fulfills the string of prophecies in the opening paragraph of "The Outlook for American Culture." Huxley predicted that "the future of America" would be "the future of the world." Speculating on this American future, Huxley insisted, was tantamount to "speculating on the future of civilized man" (1). The world to come, America universalized, would be ruined by the "standardization of ideas"; "imbecility" will "flourish and vulgarity cover the earth" (9), which has happened by A.F. 632.[25] "The contemporary environment . . . is everywhere becoming more and more American," Huxley lamented; "it seems that the world must be Americanized" (1). Between May and August 1931, so too was the *Brave New World* typescript.

## Notes

1. The signed typescript, 260 pages in three blue folders, is the centerpiece of the Aldous Huxley Collection in the Harry Ransom Humanities Research Center at the University of Texas, Austin. After pages 1–248 come 12 supplementary leaves: A1, an earlier version of 169; B1–B9, a rejected version of 208–17; and C1–C2 (in Huxley's handwriting), a rejected version of text missing between 230 and 231. The typescript was "disarranged" when the research center acquired it in 1958 as part of the T. E. Hanley Collection (Wilson 28). Pages have been numbered based on internal evidence and their order of appearance in the published novel. However, material found in the printed text is missing from the typescript between pages 81 and 82, 93 and 94, 131 and 132, 132 and 133, and 230 and 231. Pages 26 and 27 are half sheets, material on the torn-off top of one leaf leading to material on the torn-off bottom of the other. Donald Watt called the typescript a "conflation" of an "early" with a "later . . . but by no means final version"—in short, "a patchwork of Huxley's first draft and subsequent revisions before he put together fair copy for his publishers" (369). This echoes Robert H. Wilson's conclusion that "there was only one later manuscript version, a fair copy for the printer, very likely by a professional typist" (29). On page 1 of the typescript, signed "Aldous Huxley," what follows is described as "Corrected typescript—the nearest approach to a manuscript version."

The research center also houses a bound volume of "Authors Corrected Proof-Sheets 1932." For "alterations not marked on [Huxley's] proof," Wilson "suspects the work of an editor" between proof and first edition (30). But discrepancies between proof and first edition, as well as between typescript and proof, suggest that Huxley could not resist revising the fair copy intended for his publishers; he may even have made changes on a second set of proof sheets now lost.

Hereafter TS refers to the typescript, PS refers to the proof sheets, and *BNW* refers to the first edition of the novel, published by Chatto & Windus in 1932.

2. Ford narrowed the interval "between desire and its gratification" (*BNW* 50) by making car ownership possible for everyone.

3. Helmholtz Watson's oath "Ford in Flivver!" (*BNW* 250) when he is summoned to the riot the Savage has started at the Park Lane Hospital appears to be a variation. But if the holograph addition to chapter 3 was made when (or even after) Huxley wrote chapter 15, it may be said to embroider Watson's oath, the brave new

world's substitute for "God in Heaven!" Our Ford, it has been noted, rhymes with Our Lord (Baker 25).

4. PS 62 and the first edition have no comma after "State." The period after "Sings" has changed to a comma, after which Huxley added "and Solidarity Services."

5. TS 57 is a busy page that also boasts a minor autograph insertion and a successful rearrangement of Fordian material. To the Controller's statement that "Two thousand pharmacologists and biochemists were subsidized," Huxley appends "in A.F. 178." "Six years later," the brave new world was producing soma commercially, so this narcotic, which came on the market in A.F. 184, is nearly 450 years old. Supplying dates for the discovery and production of soma connects Henry Ford with the doping of an entire society. Originally, Huxley typed: "There was a thing called Christianity. The new and happier era. All crosses had their tops sawn off and became T's." After crossing out the last two sentences, Huxley amended the remaining one-sentence paragraph between typescript and proofs: "There was a thing, as I've said before, called Christianity" (PS 61). Further down TS 57, Huxley reinstated the sawed-off crosses for greater effect. His autograph insertion opens a three-sentence paragraph, of which the other two sentences, the original paragraph, are typewritten: "All crosses had their tops cut off & became T's. Gradually suppressed; but not before adequate substitutes had been prepared. There was a thing called God." Huxley crossed out the two middle sentences, inserting "also" after "was" in the last line. Between proof sheet and first edition, "off" was eliminated from "cut off." Changes to the sentence about the fate of the world's crosses—cancellation, reinsertion to start a subsequent paragraph—produce a more dramatic impression of God's overthrow. The revised typescript portrays Christianity's demise and the death of God as separate, sequential events. Mutilation of the world's crosses into *T*s is a consequence of Christianity's demise in the earlier paragraph and the signal to abolish God in the later one. Two succinct paragraphs—the first with only one sentence, the second with two—emerge from what was originally five sentences of material. In the autograph emendation, crosses have their tops "cut off" instead of "sawn off" in the typed version of this sentence (TS 57). Huxley suggests execution, worldwide decapitations to exterminate Christianity in favor of the new religion from America. Altering "cut off" to "cut" weakens this suggestion; on the other hand, it connotes throat cutting, if not castration. That *T*s, the brave new world's religious emblem, can be salvaged from crosses, the emblem they displace, is a tribute to efficiency, a Henry Ford hallmark. Crosses remind one of Christ's sacrifice; *T*s venerate a secular success: the engineering, mass producing, and triumphant marketing of a commercial product. Ford's T-Model symbolizes a quintessentially American materialism. Making "the sign of the T," brave new worlders worship the person and process, both American, behind the auto's creation. Ford's technological know-how and the mass distribution of consumer goods it facilitates acquire a religious aura.

6. In the first edition, Huxley closes a parenthesis he never opened. Later, when the D.H.C is poised to banish Bernard to Iceland, PS 175 delivers a parenthetical stage direction: "(here the Director made the sign of the T)." Ironically, he makes this sign just before Linda and John burst in and destroy his career (*BNW* 179).

7. Anti-Ford references constitute a defamatory thread running through the text of *Brave New World* the way a poet weaves a pattern of imagery into a poem. Five references in chapter 2: "while Our Ford was still on earth" (25); "Our Ford's

first T-Model"; "a sign of the T"; "A.F. 214" (27); "Oh, Ford!" (32). Nineteen references in chapter 3: "in Our Ford's day" (33); "the time of Our Ford" (35); "his fordship"; "His fordship" (37); "from the mouth of Ford himself"; "inspired saying of Our Ford's" (38); "Ford knew what" (39); "Our Ford—or Our Freud" (48); "Ford's in his flivver" (50); "his fordship"; "Oh, Ford, Ford, Ford" (52); "A.F. 141" (54); "A.F. 150"; "Our Ford's first T-Model" (60); "Ford's Day celebrations"; "Ford, how I hate them!" (62); "A.F. 178"; "Ford, I should like to kill him" (63); "his fordship" (66). One reference in chapter 4: "the Charing-T Tower" (68). Twenty-one in chapter 5: "Fordson Community Singery" (91); "an immense T" (91–92); two references to "Big Henry"; "Ford . . . Ford, Ford, Ford"; "Ford's Day"; "Thank Ford"; "Ford!" (92); "Ford!" three times (93); "sign of the T"; "another sign of the T"; "Ford, we are twelve"; "the shining Flivver" (94); "Oh, Ford, Ford, Ford"; "Ford!" twice (96); two references to "Ford and fun" (98); "Big Henry" (99). Chapter 6 contains seven references: "Oh, for Ford's sake" (104); "Thank Ford" (107); "Our Ford loved infants" (109); "Ford-speed" (110); "Ford knows" (112); "thank Ford"; "Ford!" (120). Chapter 7 also has seven references: "the Charing-T Tower" (126); "cleanliness is next to fordliness"; "Our Ford" (127); "Ford's Day" (131); "Ford! Ford!"; "Ford!" (138); "Oh, Ford, Ford, Ford!" (142). One reference in chapter 8: "Ford, no!" (168). Chapter 9 has four: "your fordship"; "Your fordship" (167); "his fordship" twice (168). Four also in chapter 10: "the teachings of Our Ford"; "the sign of the T" (175); "unfordly" (176); "Oh Ford, oh Ford" (178). Five occur in chapter 11: "(Ford!)" (180); "your fordship's" (187); "statue of Our Ford" (189); "Young Women's Fordian Association"; "Ford Chief-Justice" (195). Five again in chapter 12: "Ford's Day Celebrations" (206); "in the form of a T"; "the sign of the T" (207); "the golden T" (210); "Ford!" (213). Four in chapter 13: "for Ford's sake"; "My Ford" (220); "For Ford's sake" (225); "golden T" (227). No references in chapter 14, but seven in 15: "Ford!" (249); "Ford in Flivver!" (250); "Ford help him!"; "Ford helps those who help themselves" (252); "Ford be praised!" (253); "Ford keep you!" twice (254). Eight references in chapter 16: "large golden T's"; "his fordship" (256); "OUR FORD"; "Society for the Propagation of Fordian Knowledge" (257); "flivvers" (260); "A.F. 473" (263); "Our Ford" twice (269). There are only two references in chapter 17: "Ford on the shelves" (272); "Ford forbid" (270), but seven in chapter 18: "the Charing-T Tower" (289); "Ford!"; "Fordey!"; "*Fordian Science Monitor*" three times (295–96); "by Ford" (299).

    8. In "Sight-Seeing in Alien Englands," Huxley called Sir Alfred Mond's Billingham factory "one of those ordered universes that exist as anomalous oases of pure logic in the midst of the larger world of planless incoherence" (67–68), which is not as complimentary to the rationalization of society as it sounds. Huxley implies a counterpoint between "planless incoherence" and "pure logic," two equally unsatisfactory conditions. His 1927 essay "The Outlook for American Culture" contains this classic understatement: "Mass production is an admirable thing when applied to material objects but applied to things of the spirit, it is not so good" (7–8). Toward the end of "Sight-Seeing," Huxley rejected Ford's contention that the monotony of work under mass-production conditions exists not "in the shops" but "in the minds of . . . bookish reformers" such as the sightseeing essayist (74).

    9. For an account of Huxley's shift from fascination with Ford in 1925–26 to profound contempt by 1932, see Meckier, "Debunking Our Ford." Having defined rationalization and weighed its negative impact on *Brave New World*, James Sexton dubbed Alfred Mond "the single Henry Ford at the head of Western Europe."

Mustapha Mond allegedly resembles Sir Alfred physically (92–93). In "The Victory of Art over Humanity," Huxley accused Ford of wanting to turn the workforce into robots. Huxley observed that English "motor factories are not so completely rationalized as the corresponding thing in America," but any motor factory—no matter what "faultless, logical process" it is "the embodiment of"—struck him as a "pretty depressing" workplace (77).

10. Ford's frame of mind is blamed for every untoward development in modern urban industrial society—technological, psychological, sociological—since the advent of the T-Model. Ford's last name serves as the brave new world's most powerful prayer and heartiest curse. When the girl on Bernard's left at a Solidarity Service asks whether he has been playing obstacle golf or electromagnetic, Huxley originally typed: "Bernard blushed and had to admit that he had been playing neither" (TS 80). Retyped on TS 81, the last nine words of this sentence remain unaltered, but Huxley eliminated the first two words before redoing the opening half of the sentence in ink to read: "Bernard looked at her (Ford! it was Morganna Rothschild) and, blushing, had to admit he had been playing neither." On PS 92–93, there is no comma after "and"; instead of "blushing," Huxley opts for "blushingly."

Huxley moves "for Ford's sake" from last place to first when Lenina replies to Henry Foster's crude inquiries about her love life since her trip to Mexico. Crossing out "Oh, shut up," Huxley inked in "Oh for Ford's sake" while reinstating "Shut up!" at the end of the sentence, where he also crossed out the original "For Ford's sake." The result was more effective: "'Oh, for Ford's sake,' said Lenina, breaking her stubborn silence, 'Shut up!'" (TS 177). The first edition has a lowercase *s*: "'shut up!'" (*BNW* 220).

Spying Lenina at Malpais, Linda is so overjoyed that she hugs and kisses her. Huxley amplifies Lenina's disgust from "—oh, Ford!" to the double expletive "Ford! Ford!" (TS 114). Actually, he crossed out "oh," then wrote the new oath in the right-hand margin; the second "Ford!" begins the next typewritten line. In proof, thanks to an added conjunction, the distressed Lenina's thoughts run: "and—Ford! Ford! it was too revolting" (PS 138). Brave new worlders share Lenina's revulsion. Abandoned for years among reservation Indians, Linda has grown "Fat," with "bad teeth and a blotched complexion, and that figure (Ford!)—you simply couldn't look at her without feeling sick" (TS 145). The parenthetical expression of disgust is an autograph insertion. The first edition puts a comma after "teeth" (*BNW* 180).

Whenever Huxley crossed out a phrase that Americanizes the brave new world, a superior reference to the Fordian future already exists on the typescript page, or Huxley had a cleverer reference in mind. After Mond shows the Savage his collection of "pornographic books"—"books about God"—John asks why the Controller refuses to release *The Imitation of Christ* and *The Varieties of Religious Experience* for general consumption. For Mond's response, Huxley originally typed "they're old; they're about God hundreds of years ago, before Our Ford" (TS 220). Scratching out the last three words, Huxley replaced the comma after "years ago" with a full stop. He wanted to stress that ideas about God in philosophers such as William James are hopelessly outdated, not that they antedate Our Ford. Earlier on the page, Mond says that he prefers "God in the safe and Ford on the shelves" (TS 220; *BNW* 272). Huxley sacrificed the phrase "before Our Ford" because he had already done better: hypocritically, Mond privately savors texts that he restricts publicly. When Bernard Marx and Helmholtz Watson cannot find the Savage, they sense a crisis developing. "Where in Ford's name can he have got to?" Watson demands before Huxley cancels "in Ford's name" in favor of Watson's subsequent outcry upon receiving a call that John has instigated a riot: "'Ford in Flivver!' he swore, 'I'll come at once'" (TS 203; *BNW* 250). Huxley chooses the sharper oath. The statement that "There was the famous Cyprus Experiment of A.F. 475" has a line drawn through the date. Three lines further down the typescript page, this experiment is mentioned again: "It began in A.F. 473" (TS B6; *BNW* 263). Originally, having quoted Ford's "beautiful and inspired saying" that "History is bunk," Mond went on to celebrate a bunkless society: brave new worlders, he boasted, "have now given practical effect to what was, when Our Ford first uttered it, a counsel of perfection. The Past, the stupid unnecessary past, has been abolished" (TS 38). Huxley deleted this self-congratulatory elaboration, more than 25 words altogether. Instead, the satirist shows Ford's dismissive precept at work: waving his hand as if it were "an invisible feather whisk," Mond obliterates Ur of the Chaldees, Thebes, Babylon, Cnossus and Mycenae, Odysseus, Gotama, and King Lear—"all were gone" (*BNW* 38). Demonstration, Huxley felt, was more damning than explanation. When the Assistant Predestinator opines that Fanny Crowne is "Not so pneumatic as Lenina. Oh, not nearly" (TS 55), 13 words have been eliminated. Initially, Huxley followed this observation with a new paragraph consisting of an incomplete sentence: "A man called Napoleon at the beginning of the second century before Ford . . ." (TS 55). This sentence subordinates Ford when the point of the entire section is to regret the ideas and individuals that the American industrialist rendered obsolete—God and Shakespeare, for example.

On TS 217, Mustapha Mond pinpoints Ford's lifetime as the period when the brave new world altered the direction of scientific research: "Our Ford himself did a great deal to shift the emphasis from truth and beauty to comfort and happiness." On TS 219, a messier leaf, Huxley wrote in by hand, in the upper right-hand corner, the first 11 words of the sentence just quoted from TS 217. TS 219 (in chapter 17) probably was written before TS 217 (in chapter 16). When Huxley expanded the confrontation between Mond and the Savage to include a preliminary discussion involving Helmholtz Watson as well as John, he may have introduced the remarks atop TS 219 as part of Mond's conversation with Helmholtz. Ford's promotion of "comfort and happiness" also appears, typed, on TS B9, an earlier version of TS 217.

11. Wilson conjectured that "most of the typing is identifiable as Huxley's own" (28) but singled out no page typed by someone else. There are no black pages "written unmistakably later than nearby purple ones," he added (31). Having designated black pages "a kind of stratum in the history of the novel," he pointed to TS 120–28 as a sequence containing "information about the Savage's mother which is earlier than found anywhere else" (32). Yet Wilson feared that some purple typing may be older than black, whereas "differences in darkness of the purple ribbon are hard to interpret as evidence of age" (32). Nevertheless, Watt based his reconstruction of the composition process for chapters 15 through 18 largely on the different darknesses of purple ink pages (379–80), an approach implicit in his observation that pages "with the typeface bold and clear" and with few "holograph revisions" contrast with pages of "faded typeface" containing "numerous" changes both handwritten and typed (369). I base this essay on three assumptions: (1) All the typing most likely is Huxley's. (2) Black type characterizes the oldest leaves, but in some cases these are virtually synchronous with pages in faded purple. (3) Few if any bright purple sheets predate those in faded purple.

12. In the 1946 foreword to *Brave New World*, Huxley characterized "the author of the fable" as an "amused, Pyrrhonic aesthete" (viii).

13. Huxley denied having read Zamyatin but seems to know *We* very well. In *We*, for example, R-13 summarizes Adam and Eve's choice in paradise: "happiness without freedom, or freedom without happiness. There was no third alternative" (61). The brave new world solves "the happiness problem" by "making people love their servitude" (Foreword xiv). The question that Mond and the Savage debate is not just whether one can have freedom and happiness but which is preferable. Huxley regretted offering John "only two alternatives" (Foreword vii).

14. "Mexico" and "America, Listen to Your Own" are the titles of Lawrence's essays in *Phoenix*. If Huxley did not know these essays, he was familiar with their sentiments.

15. Donald Watt suggests a two-stage process: "Huxley at first thought of Bernard as the novel's hero, then switched to John as more fitting for the hero's role" (375). Actually, Huxley planned to unite a redeemer from without with a rebel from within.

16. "My great religion is a belief in the blood," Lawrence wrote to Ernest Collings on 17 January 1913, "the flesh as being wiser than the intellect. We can go wrong in our minds. But what our blood feels and believes and says, is always true (*Letters* 96).

17. "At the time the book was written," Huxley lamented, he found the idea "that human beings are given free will in order to choose between insanity . . . and lunacy . . . amusing and . . . quite possibly true" (Foreword viii).

18. The first edition has a hyphen after "Streptocock" and commas after "Bye" and "noise" (144–45).

19. See Watt 380n10.

20. Also missing are typescript pages for most of the Solidarity Service (*BNW* 94–99) and for John's discussion of soma with Dr. Shaw at the start of chapter 11.

21. Of course, Huxley spent most of the twenties, especially the last years of that decade, schooling himself to write a dystopia. In the preface he contributed to J. H. Burns's *A Vision of Education* (1929), his skepticism regarding a genuinely benevolent system of eugenics and education is already manifest. See Meckier, "A Neglected Huxley Preface" and "Prepping for *Brave New World*."

22. In this letter, Aldous canceled a trip to Russia with Julian because of difficulties with *Brave New World*. The need to "re-write," he informs his brother, "throws me right back in my work and as I must, if humanly possible, get my book done before the autumn I see no alternative but to renounce the Russian scheme altogether" (349).

23. David Bradshaw concluded that *Brave New World* proved "problematic" for Huxley because he was "unsure" whether he was writing "a satire, a prophecy or a blueprint" (Introduction vii). Actually, the completed novel may be read as all three simultaneously, the result of intentional irony rather than indecision. Bradshaw views the post-1929 Huxley as a supporter of government by men of rational foresight ("Open Conspirators"). But Huxley's response to Wells and Sir Alfred Mond is at best a preference for rationalization over chaos—for Mond and Wells rather than Karl Marx and communism—as the way out of an ever-worsening economic slump. When John Savage is offered a choice between "lunacy" and "insanity," Huxley imbues *Brave New World* with his sense of the early thirties as a dystopian time of impossible choices. In the finished novel, the alternatives become happiness

or freedom, Mond (Wells) or the Savage (Lawrence), instead of rationalization or communism. Huxley saw Marx and Wells as proponents of happiness and enemies of freedom. Marx survives in the typescript as Bernard's last name.

24. See Meckier, "Our Ford, Our Freud" (35–42).

25. "In the United States," Peter Firchow argues, Huxley "recognized that what confronted him" was "the future of mankind." The "next step," Huxley predicted, would be "the Fordian (that is, American) world" (128–29).

> I examined typescript and the proof sheets on a Mellon grant from the Harry Ransom Humanities Research Center in February 1999. I quote from both with the center's permission. Earlier versions of this essay were delivered as a lecture at the Centre for Aldous Huxley Studies in Münster (June 2000) and as the keynote address to the International Huxley Symposium in Singapore (December–January 2000–01).

## WORKS CITED

Baker, Robert S. Brave New World: *History, Science, and Dystopia*. Boston: Twayne, 1990.

Bradshaw, David, ed. *The Hidden Huxley*. London: Faber, 1994.

———. Introduction. *Brave New World*. By Huxley. London: Flamingo, 1994. i–x.

———. "Open Conspirators: Huxley and H. G. Wells 1927–35." Bradshaw, *Hidden Huxley* 31–43.

Browning, Robert. *Selected Poetry of Robert Browning*. Ed. Kenneth L. Knickerbocker. New York: Modern Library, 1951.

Firchow, Peter. *Aldous Huxley: Satirist and Novelist*. Minneapolis: U of Minnesota P, 1972.

Huxley, Aldous. *Brave New World*. Typescript, 260 pages. 1931. Aldous Huxley Collection. Harry Ransom Humanities Research Center, University of Texas, Austin.

———. *Brave New World*. Proof sheets. 1932. Aldous Huxley Collection. Harry Ransom Humanities Research Center, University of Texas, Austin.

———. *Brave New World*. London: Chatto, 1932.

———. Foreword. 1946. *Brave New World*. London: Chatto, 1950. vii–xv.

———. Interview *Writers at Work: The Paris Review Interviews*. 2nd series. New York: Viking, 1963. 195–214.

———. *Letters of Aldous Huxley*. Ed. Grover Smith. London: Chatto, 1969.

———. "The Outlook for American Culture: Some Reflections in a Machine Age." *Harper's Magazine* Aug. 1927: 265–70. Rpt. as *America and the Future*. Austin: Jenkins, 1970.

———. *Point Counter Point*. London: Chatto, 1928.

———. "Sight-Seeing in Alien Englands." *Nash's Pall Mall Magazine* June 1931: 50–53, 118. Rpt. in Bradshaw, *Hidden Huxley* 65–76.

———. "Utopias Positive and Negative." 1963. Ed. James Sexton. *Aldous Huxley Annual* 1 (2000): 1–9.

———. "The Victory of Art over Humanity." *Nash's Pall Mall Magazine* (July 1931): 46–49. Rpt. in Bradshaw, *Hidden Huxley* 77–86.

Lawrence, D. H. *The Letters of D. H. Lawrence*. Ed. Aldous Huxley. London: Heinemann, 1932.

———. *Phoenix: The Posthumous Papers*. 1936. Ed. Edward McDonald. New York: Viking, 1968.

———. *The Plumed Serpent*. 1926. New York: Vintage, 1951.

Meckier, Jerome. "Debunking Our Ford: *My Life and Work* and *Brave New World*." *South Atlantic Quarterly* 78 (Autumn 1979): 448–59.

———. "A Neglected Huxley Preface: His Earliest Synopsis of *Brave New World*." Twentieth Century Literature 25 (Spring 1979): 1–20.

———. "Our Ford, Our Freud, and the Behaviorist Conspiracy in Huxley's Brave New World." *Thalia* 1 (Spring 1978): 35–59.

———. "Prepping for *Brave New World*: Aldous Huxley's Essays of the 1920s." *Utopian Studies* 12 (2001): 234–45.

Robert, Clementine. *Aldous Huxley, Exhumations: Correspondence inedité avec Sydney Schiff 1925–1937*. Paris: Didier, 1976.

Sexton, James. *"Brave New World* and the Rationalization of Industry." *Critical Essays on Aldous Huxley*. Ed. Jerome Meckier. New York: Hall, 1996. 88–102.

Smith, Grover. Chronology. *Letters of Aldous Huxley*. Ed. Grover Smith. London: Chatto, 1969. 11–20.

Watt, Donald. "The Manuscript Revisions of *Brave New World*." *Journal of English and Germanic Philology* 77 (July 1978): 367–82.

Wells, H. G. *Anticipations*. 1901. Minneola: Dover, 1999.

———. *Men Like Gods*. London: Cassell, 1923.

———. *A Modern Utopia*. 1905. Lincoln: U of Nebraska P, 1969.

Wilson, Robert H. "Versions of Brave New World." *The Library Chronicle of the University of Texas* 8 (Spring 1968): 28–41.

Zamyatin, Yevgeny. *We*. Trans. Mirra Ginsburg. New York: Bantam, 1972.

LAURA FROST

## Huxley's Feelies: The Cinema of Sensation in Brave New World

"I have just been, for the first time, to see and hear a picture talk," Aldous Huxley writes in a 1929 essay called "Silence Is Golden" (*Essays* 2: 19). "A little late in the day," he imagines his "up-to-date" reader remarking "with a patronizing and contemptuous smile." After all, the film that introduces Huxley to the world of sound cinema, *The Jazz Singer*, had been released two years earlier. The "gigantically enlarged" (21) images on the screen spouting noise send Huxley into paroxysms of scorn and fury; he is especially horri-fied by the scene in which Al Jolson sings "Mammy" in blackface:

> My flesh crept as the loud-speaker poured out those sodden words, that greasy, sagging melody. I felt ashamed of myself for listening to such things, for even being a member of the species to which such things are addressed. (23)

While only half feigning his reactionary pose, Huxley condemns the talkies as "the latest and most frightful creation-saving device for the production of standardized amusement" (20).

Huxley's violent response to *The Jazz Singer* is a window onto a key moment in the history of cinema, when articles such as "Silence Is Golden," "Why 'Talkies' Are Unsound" (Betts), "Ordeal by 'Talkie'" (Betts), and "The

From *Twentieth Century Literature* 52, no. 4 (Winter 2006): 443–73. Copyright © 2006 by Hofstra University.

Movies Commit Suicide" (Seldes) contended with equally impassioned defenses of sound film.[1] The crisis occasioned by the coming of sound now appears as an overblown objection to a transition that in hindsight seems inevitable. But just as the cinema itself was often perceived as revolutionary—George Bernard Shaw remarked in 1914 that "The cinema is going to form the mind of England. . . . The cinema is a much more momentous invention than the printing press" (9)[2]—the coming of sound was greeted by many as a watershed moment. Beyond the changes in the industry (the retirement of actors who had unpleasant voices, for example), the talkies raised more philosophical questions about the social, moral, and even physical effects of moving and talking images.

Cinema history would not be accurately represented by a chronicle of technical development from, say, Muybridge to the present. Such a history would miss a crucial component of the story of cinema: spectatorship. Accounts from the period such as Huxley's and Iris Barry's *Let's Go to the Pictures* emphasize not just what happens on the screen, but how the audience responds. Those responses are strikingly different from how we now think of cinema spectatorship, and this is particularly true of the reception of the talkies. Recently critics such as Tom Gunning, Miriam Hansen, Jonathan Crary, and Ben Singer, following the early lead of Walter Benjamin[3] and Siegfried Kracauer, have moved away from the psychoanalytic approach that dominated film criticism in the 1980s to a more historical and sociological model that addresses how visual modernity in general and cinema spectatorship in particular are bodily, visceral experiences. Cinema is not merely a screen for psychic identifications but is experienced by an embodied, somatically affected spectator. While the story of Lumière's train sending confused audiences screaming from the screen in 1895 has been debunked,[4] writing from the time of "Silence Is Golden" demonstrates Kracauer's assertion that film was thought of as influencing "the spectator's senses, engaging him physiologically before he is in a position to respond intellectually" (*Theory* 158). Gunning's description of the earliest filmmaking as a "cinema of attractions" (121) striving more for spectacle than telling a story and Singer's examination of early "blood and thunder" melodramas, among other work, suggest that modern technologies of vision were experienced as mobilizing the body and actively producing what Hansen calls "a new sensorium" (70). Different stages of cinematic development produced different modes of spectatorship and perception, and this was especially true of the transition to sound.

Huxley's disgust at *The Jazz Singer* reflects an impassioned assessment of the talkies that brings him into dialogue with Shaw, Barry, Charlie Chaplin, Kracauer, and other contemporaries. Among all his writing on cinema over five decades, the most illuminating appears in an unlikely source: his

best-known novel, *Brave New World*. His 1932 dystopic fiction provides
unexpected insight into a time when cinema's technological innovations were
not just observed but were truly felt.[5] Huxley's response to early cinema—and
especially the transition to sound—was far-reaching in its implications, recognizing cinema's stimulation of the body as well as the mind and imagining
cinema's potential to be either an instrument of social and political reform or
a medium of cultural degeneracy.

In some ways, the reception of early film (the "youngest" art, as Virginia
Woolf put it in her 1926 essay "The Cinema" [272]) is very much in keeping with that of mass culture in general. In the twenties and thirties, from
Kracauer's "distraction factories" (*Mass Ornament* 75–76) to Q. D. Leavis's
descriptions of popular reading as masturbatory (136) or a drug habit (31),
mass culture consumption was described as intoxication, addiction, deluded
reverie, and gluttony. All of these tropes were applied to cinema, but the specific circumstances of cinema-going were also thought to produce a distinctive
reaction in the viewer. In a 1925 *Vanity Fair* essay called "Where Are the Movies Moving?" Huxley writes that "the darkness of the theater, the monotonous
music" induce in the audience "a kind of hypnotic state" (*Essays* 1:176).[6] In
an article for *Close Up*, Bryher describes a stupefied film audience: "To watch
hypnotically something which has become a habit and which is not recorded
as it happens by the brain, differs little from the drugtaker's point of view" (qtd.
in Richards, 199).[7] Both hypnosis and intoxication influence mind and body,
suggesting that the cinema spectator is vulnerable on two fronts.

The reception of film had its roots in responses to mass culture such
as amusement parks, radio, and other leisure technologies that appealed to
the body in new ways. Film was already conceived of as a bodily experience
when it was silent, but the addition of sound made the connection more
pronounced. In 1930 Charlie Chaplin maintained: "I shall never speak in
a film. I hate the talkies and will not produce talking films.... My shadow
appears on the screen as in a dream, and dreams do not speak" (qtd. in Crafton 374). For Chaplin, the cinematic experience of ephemeral, mute dream-
ing was shattered by the talkies, which forced a new kind of embodiment
on the medium. Many remarked on the physical difficulties that the new
technologies presented to the audience. In "The Cinema" Virginia Woolf
writes of film spectatorship: "The eye licks it all up instantaneously, and the
brain, agreeably titillated, settles down to watch things happening without
beseeching itself to think.... Eye and brain are torn ruthlessly as they try
vainly to work in couples" (269). This sense of dislocation is supported by Iris
Barry's contemporaneous observation that "Every habitual cinemagoer must
have been struck at some time or another by the comparative slowness of
perception and understanding of a person not accustomed to the pictures: the

newcomer always misses half of what occurs" (13). The idea of a population divided between those who had been initiated into the new physical practice of cinema spectatorship and those who had not marked a unique and brief moment in film history.

Huxley presents himself as such a newcomer in "Silence Is Golden," but despite his pose of being wilfully out of date, he had a music and theater column in the *Weekly Westminster Gazette*, and he wrote on a wide range of cultural topics for mass-market journals including *Vanity Fair* and *Esquire*. Yet he seems to join other interwar critics who conflate all forms of mass or popular culture. In a 1927 article for *Harper's* called "The Outlook for American Culture: Some Reflections in a Machine Age," he writes:

> The rotary press, the process block, the cinema, the radio, the phonograph, are used not, as they might so easily be used, to propagate culture, but its opposite. All the resources of science are applied in order that imbecility may flourish and vulgarity cover the whole earth. (*Essays* 2: 9)

The cinema is one in a series of horrors here, but elsewhere Huxley singles it out as especially pernicious. In a 1923 essay on popular culture called "Pleasures," he writes:

> Of all the various poisons which modern civilization, by a process of auto-intoxication, brews quietly up within its own bowels, few, it seems to me, are more deadly (while none appears more harmless) than that curious and appalling thing that is technically known as "pleasure." "Pleasure" (I place the word between inverted commas to show that I mean, not real pleasure, but the organized activities officially known by the same name) "pleasure"—what nightmare visions the word evokes! ... The horrors of modern "pleasure" arise from the fact that every kind of organized distraction tends to become progressively more and more imbecile.... In place of the old pleasures demanding intelligence and personal initiative, we have vast organizations that provide us with ready-made distractions—distractions which demand from pleasure-seekers no personal participation and no intellectual effort of any sort. To the interminable democracies of the world a million cinemas bring the same balderdash.... Countless audiences soak passively in the tepid bath of nonsense. No mental effort is demanded of them, no participation; they need only sit and keep their eyes open. (*Essays* 1: 355–56)

Huxley juxtaposes "old" pleasure—"real pleasure" that is individualized and intellectually demanding—with "ready made," collective pleasures. When Huxley warns about pleasures that "demand ... no personal participation," he pinpoints those that are particularly corporeal. His example is telling. The scene of lazy cinema audiences in "Pleasures" is one that recurs throughout Huxley's writing, such as the people "sitting at the picture palace passively accepting ready-made day-dreams from Hollywood" in *Eyeless in Gaza* (355).[8] For Huxley, far from being a technological advancement, cinema is symptomatic of cultural degeneration, and the introduction of sound was a particularly alarming development because of its implications for bodily pleasure.

All of Huxley's writings on cinema are arranged around the dichotomy presented in "Pleasures."[9] It is integral to his vision of futurity in *Brave New World*. London in the Year A. F. (After Ford) 632 is a culture of genetic and psychological control; individuals are decanted into a state whose motto is "Community, Identity, Stability" (3). Huxley's novel is famous for its bottled babies, color-coded classes, hypnopaedic conditioning, and the pharmacological marvel soma. As much as it is a nightmare of a totalitarian, genetically engineered future, though, *Brave New World* is also a cautionary tale about a world in which artifacts of high culture are held under lock and key while the populace is supplied with "imbecile" entertainment. The denizens of Brave New World follow a prescribed routine of "standardized amusement" summarized by the Resident World Controller for Western Europe, Mustapha Mond, as "Seven and a half hours of mild, unexhausting labour, and then the *soma* ration and games and unrestricted copulation and the feelies" (224).

The "feelies," a cinema of titillating, pansensual stimulation, are clearly a response to the "talkies," as Huxley extends the innovation of synchronized sound to include all the senses. The most intense vehicle of mass pleasure in *Brave New World*, the feelies have a special status insofar as they are artistic productions: Mond describes them as "works of art out of practically nothing but pure sensation" (221). In a central scene, John the Savage, newly exported from the Malpais Indian Reservation, attends a feely called *Three Weeks in a Helicopter*. Billed as "AN ALL-SUPER-SINGING, SYNTHETIC-TALKING, COLOURED, STEREOSCOPIC FEELY WITH SYNCHRONIZED SCENT-ORGAN ACCOMPANIMENT" (167), a parody of the 1920s cinema slogan, "All-Talking, All-Singing, All-Dancing,"[10] *Three Weeks in a Helicopter* is three-dimensional and scented, with tactile sensations produced by metal knobs embedded in the cinema chairs. The "almost intolerable galvanic pleasure" that the feely transmits provokes in John a rage at its sensual indulgence (168)—a rage similar to Huxley's at the cheap emotion and audio excess of *The Jazz Singer*.

Mond explains to John that in the Brave New World there is "no leisure from pleasure, not a moment to sit down and think" (55). Pleasure has become a full-time job. Here Huxley would seem to fit the old stereotype of the modernist elitist who shores up what Huyssen calls the "great divide," although his relationship to modernism itself is complicated. While his work, for the most part, is not formally innovative enough to qualify as modernist according to a typical definition, his conflicting responses to cinema do bear out recent revaluations of the great divide paradigm such as David Chinitz's and Michael North's.[11] One of the cultural ironies of Huxley's fate in twentieth-century culture is the way he has been taken up by the popular culture he claims to despise (the title of his most famous novel has become a catchphrase) and in his absence from most critical discussions of modernism. His responses to popular culture and the cinema in particular suggest both why it is difficult to make a full-fledged modernist out of Huxley and how he exemplifies the more recent critical paradigms of modernism.

*Brave New World* has typically been read as "the classic denunciation of mass culture in the interwar years" (Carey 86). Certainly, associated with mass culture, pleasure is not characteristically ascribed to modernism, where alienation, anomie, and crisis typically overshadow moments of sweetness and light;[12] still less is pleasure typically associated with dystopic texts. Accordingly, Theodor Adorno argues that Huxley in *Brave New World* is "inwardly an enemy of intoxication":

> [T]he regularly occurring communal orgies and the prescribed short-term change of partners are logical consequences of the jaded official sexual routine that turns pleasure to fun and denies it by granting it. But precisely in the impossibility of looking pleasure in the eye, of making use of reflection in abandoning one's whole self to pleasure, the ancient prohibition for which Huxley prematurely mourns continues in force. (104–05)

Yet despite the broad satire of the feelies' idiocy, Huxley does not portray them as lacking in attraction—like the mechanistic Tiller Girls, for example, whom Kracauer characterizes as "sexless bodies in bathing suits" (*Mass Ornament* 67)—and his opposition to intoxication is not uniform: John's rejection of the feelies and other sensual pleasures is represented as a puritanical hysteria of which Huxley is as critical as he is of thoughtless consumption of the feelies, soma, and orgy porgy. Indeed, Adorno's observation about Lenina (whose characteristics—sensual, female, modern—code her as an embodiment of mass culture) applies equally to the feelies: "Lenina's artificial charm and cellophane shamelessness produce by no means the unerotic effect Huxley intended, but rather a highly seductive one, to which even the infuriated cultural savage succumbs at the end of the novel" (105–06). This ambivalence about the power of cinema is expressed through the complex allusions around which Huxley constructs *Three Weeks in a Helicopter*. Representing the confusion of sound and image in early cinema and the association of the filmgoer with the drugged, unconscious, or bestial body, the feelies provide both a cautionary tale and a vision of cinema's social possibilities.

### Every Hair of the Bear

Although the feelies are pap for the public, their institutional structure indicates their importance in *Brave New World*. (While the movies were increasingly thought of as an American product, Huxley portrays the feelies themselves as a markedly British industry.) The "Feeling Picture" headquarters comprise 22 floors of the Bureau of Propaganda in London (66), the "buildings of the Hounslow Feely Studio" sprawl over "seven and a half hectares" (62), and the College of Emotional Engineering includes on its faculty "professors of feelies," a title of considerable status (67). John is escorted to the feelies by the "pneumatic" Lenina Crowne, to whose attractive physique, good-natured promiscuity, and provocative clothes (hot pants, boots, and zippered lingerie) Huxley calls considerable attention. *Three Weeks in a Helicopter* is apparently a very good feely. In the opening pages of the novel, the Assistant Predestinator tells Henry Foster, "I hear the new [feely] at the Alhambra is first-rate. There's a love scene on a bearskin rug; they say it's marvellous. Every hair of the bear reproduced. The most amazing tactual effects" (35).

Huxley's choice of venue for *Three Weeks in a Helicopter*, the Alhambra, evokes a rich history of British popular entertainment. Built on Leicester Square in 1854 and known initially as the Royal Panopticon of Science and Art, the Alhambra's first of many subsequent incarnations was as a Victorian shrine to scientific exhibitions, a combination of intellectual curiosity and industry that would fall into Huxley's category of "real" pleasure. In 1858 it became the Alhambra Circus and then, in 1864, the Alhambra Music Hall. The building was demolished in 1936 to clear room for a cinema, the Odeon, as if fulfilling T. S. Eliot's apocalyptic prophecy about the passing of music hall culture and the rise of "the cheap and rapid-breeding cinema" (*Prose* 174). The transformations of the Alhambra to accommodate the evolution of popular pleasure embody what Huxley and others saw as cultural degeneration, and hence is a fitting forum for the feelies.

Huxley's feelies reach backward to cinema's music hall origins and forward to the imagination of technologies such as virtual reality. *Three Weeks in a Helicopter* is preceded by a performance inspired by music hall "turns" that were a feature of early cinema presentations and had more in common with vaudeville than today's "coming attractions." The performances preceding films in the twenties were a varied roster of "shorts" that included humorous acts, newsreels, cartoons, travel and nature films, and musical performances. *Three Weeks in a Helicopter* begins with an overture by a scent-organ that plays

> a delightfully refreshing Herbal Capriccio—rippling arpeggios of thyme and lavender, of rosemary, basil, myrtle, tarragon; a series of daring modulations through the spice keys into amber-gris; and a slow return through sandalwood, camphor, cedar and new-mown hay (with occasional subtle touches of discord—a whiff of kidney pudding, the faintest suspicion of pig's dung). . . . Sunk in their pneumatic stalls, Lenina and the Savage sniffed and listened. (166–67)

The novelty of the scent-organ is its synesthetic effects that are strongly reminiscent of the instrument in Huysman's *À Rebours*, in which sounds correspond to smells and flavors. Max Nordau's notorious critique of Huysman's decadent Des Esseintes—"a parasite of the lowest grade of atavism" (309)—is specifically connected to the synesthetic effect of symbolist art, which Nordau calls

> a retrogression to the very beginning of organic development. It is a descent from the height of human perfection to the low level of the mollusc. To raise the combination, transposition and confusion of the perceptions of sound and sight to the rank of a principle of art, to see futurity in this principle, is to designate as progress the return from the consciousness of man to that of the oyster. (142)

The "confusion" of sound and sight that characterized the talkies was a sign of cultural regression for Huxley, as it was for many critics. "The soul of the film," Ernest Betts opined, "its eloquence and vital silence," is, with the addition of sound, "destroyed. The film now returns to the circus from whence it came, among the freaks and fat ladies" (*Heraclitus* 88).

Beyond the complaints about poorly executed sound films, there was a more far-reaching philosophical/aesthetic argument against the talkies: the contention that each art should stay within and develop according to its own limits, and that images rather than sound "must be/are the primary carriers of the film's meaning and structure" (Altman, Introduction 14). Rudolf Arnheim's essay "A New Laocoön: Artistic Composites and the Talking Film" is the classic statement of this point, one reiterated by many others, including Charlie Chaplin:

> People blather of "talking films" and coloured films and stereoscopic films. I can't abide coloured etchings, and on the stage we already have a perfect three dimensions. Why, we lose half our quality if we lose our limitations. Motion, two planes, and a suggestion of depth: that is our chaos from which we will fashion our universe. (82)

Huxley makes a similar argument in "Where Are the Movies Moving?" He delightedly describes a silent sequence in which his "favorite dramatic hero, Felix the Cat," is shown singing, as indicated by "little black notes" issuing from his mouth. The cartoon cat "reaches up, catches a few handfuls" of notes and makes a scooter out of them on which he rides off. "Seen on the screen," Huxley marvels, "this conversion of song into scooters seems the most natural, simple, and logical thing in the world" (*Essays* 1:175). This example, for Huxley,

> indicates very clearly what are the most pregnant potentialities of the cinema; it shows how cinematography differs from literature and the spoken drama and how it may be developed into something entirely new. What the cinema can do better than literature is to be fantastic.

The defense of sound was most famously articulated by Sergei Eisenstein, W. I. Pudovkin, and G. V. Alexandrov in their 1928 "Statement on Sound," which advocates montage and "the creation of a new orchestral counterpoint of sight-images and sound-images" (86). Still more radically, in an essay called "Synchronization of Senses," Eisenstein describes how a "single, unifying sound-picture image" might be developed as a "polyphonic structure" that "achieves its total effect through the composite sensation of all the pieces as a whole" (*Film Sense* 77). Pointing to examples of synesthetic art including Rimbaud's "'color' sonnet" and James NcNeill Whistler's "color symphonies" (87), Eisenstein proposes that such effects could be achieved in cinema. "To remove the barriers between sight and sound, between the seen world and the heard world," he rhapsodizes, "To bring about a unity and a harmonious relationship between these two opposite spheres. What an absorbing task! The Greeks and Diderot, Wagner and Scriabin—who has not dreamt of this ideal?" It is the ideal of the *Gesamtkunstwerk*, the "total work of art" that synthesizes multiple media: precisely the reverse of the Laocoön argument, which Huxley seems to advocate. With the feelies, Huxley (who found Wagner "vulgarly emotional" [*Essays* 1: 207]) imagines a superb parody of *Gesamtkunstwerk* inspired by the talkies' "unnatural" addition of sound to image. Film alone among forms of mass culture has this fearsome potential to expand indefinitely, both aesthetically and socially, to Huxley.[13]

Huxley's feelies link cultural degeneration and artistic decadence. The posture of the audience, "sunk in their pneumatic stalls" (a word evocative of both the music hall and the barnyard as well as Eliot's Grishkin, whose "friendly bust / Gives promises of pneumatic bliss" [31]) suggests a submissive absorption of stimuli. The scent organ transports its audience through a gamut of sensations that are but a preamble to the main attraction, *Three Weeks in a Helicopter*:

> Suddenly, dazzling and incomparably more solid-looking than they would have seemed in actual flesh and blood, far more real than reality, there stood the stereoscopic images, locked in one another's arms, of a gigantic negro and a golden-haired young brachycephalic Beta-Plus female. The stereoscopic lips came together ... and ... the facial erogenous zones of the six thousand spectators in the Alhambra tingled with almost intolerable galvanic pleasure. (168)

The plot, like the pornographic films it resembles, is "extremely simple" (168). The characters sing a duet and make "a little love ... on that famous bearskin, every hair of which ... could be separately and distinctly felt." The "negro" develops "an exclusive and maniacal passion" for "the Beta blonde" and "ravished [her] away into the sky and kept [her] there, hovering, for three weeks in a wildly anti-social tête-à-tête" (168–69). She is rescued by

> three handsome young Alphas ... and the film ended happily and decorously, with the Beta blonde becoming the mistress of all her three rescuers. ... Then the bearskin made a final appearance and, amid a blare of sexophones, the last stereoscopic kiss faded into darkness, the last electric titillation died on the lips like a dying moth that quivers, quivers, ever more feebly, ever more faintly, and at last is quiet, quite still. (169)

While Lenina's "flushed" arousal by the feely is appropriate to her conditioning, John is "pale, pained, desiring, and ashamed of his desire." He tells Lenina, "I don't think you ought to see things like that. ... It was base ... ignoble" (169). The feelies and the shallow, promiscuous culture they represent drive the Savage to retreat to the countryside, where he mortifies his

body. Darwin Bonaparte, "the Feely Corporation's most expert big game photographer," stalks and films John's acts:

> He kept his telescopic cameras carefully aimed—glued to their
> moving objective; clapped on a higher power to get a close-up of
> the frantic and distorted face (admirable!); switched over, for half a
> minute, to slow motion (an exquisitely comical effect, he promised
> himself); listened in, meanwhile, to the blows, the groans, the wild
> and raving words that were being recorded on the sound-track at
> the edge of his film, tried the effect of a little amplification (yes,
> that was decidedly better)... When they had put in the feely
> effects at the studio, it would be a wonderful film. (253)

Bonaparte's efforts culminate in a hit feely feature called *The Savage of Surrey*
that "could be seen, heard and felt in every first-class feely-palace in Western Europe" (254). With its alliterative play on Robert Flaherty's popular
1922 film *Nanook of the North*, *The Savage of Surrey* perversely assimilates
John to the form of mass culture most foul to him, and the ensuing publicity contributes to his suicide. The novel's concluding scene presents John's
dangling feet cinematically:

> Slowly, very slowly, like two unhurried compass needles, the feet
> turned towards the right; north, north-east, east, south-east, south,
> south-south-west; then paused, and, after a few seconds, turned as
> unhurriedly back towards the left. South-south-west, south, south-
> east, east. . . .

With John's death, the last chance for culture perishes. Horrified by what he
sees as the animalistic amorality of the Brave New World and hunted and
framed as an animal himself in *The Savage of Surrey*, John is a casualty of
popular culture: death by feelies.

## Goats and Monkeys

The particular feely Huxley describes in *Brave New World* is a composite of
parody and allusion that draws together even more specific debates about
the implications of sound cinema. While *Three Weeks in a Helicopter* seems to
be an assemblage of random stupidity subordinated to its more spectacular
effects, it is in fact a strategic amalgamation of the two kinds of pleasure
Huxley delineates in "Pleasures" as "old" and "modern." The feely's title and
its most memorable "tactual effect" allude to a 1907 bestselling romance
novel called *Three Weeks* by one of the most prolific genre writers of the era,

Elinor Glyn. Glyn is best known now for her novel *It* and the silent film adaptation that launched Clara Bow's career as the "It Girl." After Glyn's debut as an extra in a Cecil B. DeMille film, she wrote over a dozen screenplays for major studios. To skeptics such as Huxley, Glyn represented the nadir of both contemporary fiction and popular cinema. Robert Graves and Alan Hodge observe that in the teens and twenties, "Glyn was the reigning queen of popular love literature and considered 'very hot stuff' among the 'low-brow public'" (42).[14] In *Fiction and the Reading Public*, Q. D. Leavis caustically remarks that "famous authors of bestsellers are run as limited companies with a factory called 'Edgar Rice Burroughs, Inc.' or 'Elinor Glyn Ltd'" (50). In Huxley's scheme of old and new pleasures, he chooses Glyn, Hollywood doyenne, to epitomize debased modern amusement.

    *Three Weeks* tells the story of an affair between Paul, a listless upper-class British man, and the queen of an unnamed Eastern European nation. She tells Paul, "You must help to stem the tide of your nation's decadence, and be a strong man" (199).[15] But decadence of an order that would have enraged Max Nordau is exactly what follows. In the climactic scene of the novel, Paul finds the queen reclining on a magnificent tigerskin rug, gripping a *fleur du mal* in her teeth. She writhes around ("like a snake," Glyn writes, no less than four times [86, 87, 88, 134]), and the tactile stimuli—slithery snakeskin and soft fur—are as confused as Glyn's mixed metaphors: "She purred as a tiger might have done while she undulated like a snake" (134). Nature takes its course, and Paul impregnates her. Several critics have read *Three Weeks* as a eugenics novel, a theme that would have overlapped with Huxley's interests in *Brave New World*.[16] However, it is the more sensational features of Glyn's novel that inspired *Three Weeks in a Helicopter*.

    Glyn's novel became an instant success in Britain and was filmed twice, in 1915 and 1924.[17] Glyn played up the tigerskin scene by posing with just such a rug in publicity photographs, and this prop is rendered absurd in Huxley's novel, with the characters exclaiming about the feely's simulation of the bearskin rug. Rebecca West commented that Glyn represented an "appalling . . . school of fiction . . . that imagines that by cataloging stimuli one can produce a feeling of stimulation" (73), implying that such fiction is essentially pornographic—an apt description of the feelies, whose purpose is precisely to "produce a feeling of stimulation." In this respect, the feelies resemble the early "cinema of attractions," which, Gunning argues, appealed to an audience more interested in the display of spectacle and the "act of looking" than the development of a particular narrative (121).

    In a 1915 letter in which he discusses D. H. Lawrence's censorship problems with *The Rainbow*, Huxley writes, "It is always the serious books that get sat on—how much better to suppress Mrs. Glyn" (*Letters* 85). In

Huxley's oppositional equation, Glyn and the feelies represent the popular pleasures that "mean a lot of agreeable sensations to the audience"; "the serious books" are represented by Lawrence here, and by the second intertext of *Three Weeks in a Helicopter, Othello*.

Throughout *Brave New World*, Huxley juxtaposes the feelies with Shakespeare. After John returns from his trip to the feelies, he turns to *The Complete Works of Shakespeare*, which he has smuggled in from the Indian Reservation. He "turned with religious care its stained and crumbled pages, and began to read *Othello*. Othello, he remembered, was like the hero of *Three Weeks in a Helicopter*—a black man" (171).[18] Visiting Eton, John asks "Do they read Shakespeare?" He is told that the library "contains only books of reference. If our young people need distraction, they can get it at the feelies. We don't encourage them to indulge in any solitary amusements" (163). In *Brave New World* Shakespeare's work has been severed from its theatricality, as Huxley figures it not in its enacted form but in the more threatening private experience of reading.

Its title acidly deploying a Shakespearean phrase, *Brave New World* has Shakespeare represent the lost values of what Huxley sees as civilization and culture. On another level, Huxley's choice of Shakespeare as the foil for Glyn and the feelies reflects the central role Shakespeare played in early cinema history. The silent film industry frequently turned to Shakespeare for its adaptations—from Herbert Tree's *King John* (1899) onward, including Buchowetzki's *Othello* (1922)[19]—in an effort to elevate the medium's status. Such productions introduced the irony of "silent Shakespeare" and led to vigorous debates about the relationship between cinema and theater. "As soon as the new art" (cinema), writes Rick Altman, "found the leisure to contemplate its own position it felt compelled to differentiate itself from its renowned parent, the theater" (Introduction 13). The competition became much more intense once sound film began to challenge what had previously been thought to be the stage's advantage (words); in this discussion, Shakespeare is constantly invoked as the best that theater has to offer and the best that British culture offers against the onslaught of popular culture that was increasingly identified as American.[20]

When Mond and John discuss Shakespeare in *Brave New World*, John laments the passing of "old things" such as books because

> "the new ones are so stupid and horrible. Those plays, where there's nothing but helicopters flying about and you *feel* the people kissing." He made a grimace. "Goats and monkeys!" Only in *Othello*'s words could he find an adequate vehicle for his contempt and hatred. (219)

The words refer to Iago's speech about trying to obtain visual proof of Desdemona's infidelity: "It is impossible you should see this, / Were they as prime as goats, as hot as monkeys" (3.3.402–03). For John, the feelies promote voyeurism, showing publicly and en masse what should be intimate, individual experience. He insists to Mond that

> "*Othello*'s good. . . . *Othello*'s better than those feelies."
> "Of course it is," the Controller agreed. "But that's the price we have to pay for stability. You've got to choose between happiness and what people used to call high art. We've sacrificed the high art. We have the feelies and the scent organ instead."
> "But they don't mean anything."
> "They mean themselves; they mean a lot of agreeable sensations to the audience."
> "But they're . . . they're told by an idiot." (220–21)

This discussion reiterates Huxley's formulations in "Pleasures" and goes even further in articulating the cultural divide between new popular amusements and Shakespeare. When John mistakenly calls the feelies "plays," expecting them to have "meaning," and Mond corrects him that their importance is not their content but rather their "agreeable sensations," Huxley opposes meaning to sensation and pleasure. Culture can have either meaning or it can deliver "agreeable sensations to the audience," but not both.[21] Hence Mond describes the pleasure of the feelies as a tautology: "they mean themselves." Again, Gunning's concept of the "cinema of attractions" is apt here as Huxley suggests that the cheap desire for stimulation remains cinema's (and the popular novel's) main appeal, while more refined forms of literature such as Shakespeare offer more dignified and valuable pleasures of narrative significance and complexity.

The feelies empty *Othello* of its driving emotion—passion—in order to serve the needs of a culture that prescribes periodic "Violent Passion Substitutes" to keep people properly subdued. Vicarious, mediated activities such as the feelies "ensure that the release of pent-up sexuality in leisure . . . never gets out of control, never becomes impassioned" (Wollen 58). *Othello* is played here for its most sensational elements and expunged of its linguistic beauty and philosophical weight. Even for John, the echoes of *Othello* in *Three Weeks in a Helicopter* are mainly somatic. When Lenina tries to seduce him, "inevitably he found himself thinking of the embraces in *Three Weeks in a Helicopter*. Ooh! ooh! the stereoscopic blonde and ahh! the more than real blackamoor" (192).[22]

The feely focuses on taboo: free love (against which the maniacal monogamy of the "blackamoor" is cast) and miscegenation, the latter being more complicated. Huxley was not alone in associating cinema with racial otherness and blackness in particular. In 1929, the British film journal *Close Up* devoted a special issue to "The Negro in Film" from which, Jane Gaines observes, "one receives the impression that the Negro was in vogue in London for the first time" (1). The editor of *Close Up*, Kenneth Macpherson, "lament[ed] the passing of the silent film: he concurred with others that the only consolation was that the talkies now made it possible to *hear* the Negro for the first time" (Gaines 1). The blackamoor in the feely and Al Jolson's blackface in *The Jazz Singer* associate blackness with a kind of fashionable exoticism, with simultaneous modernity (jazz, cinema) and primitivism, with physicality and with the talkies. "Again and again," Miriam Hansen observes, "writings on the American cinema of the interwar period stress the new physicality, the exterior surface or 'outer skin' of things" (70). This is certainly true of *Three Weeks in a Helicopter*, with its fetishistic emphasis on the "blackamoor" and the bearskin rug.

There is a curious congruence of racial mixing and the talkies throughout Huxley's work. Both "Silence Is Golden" and *Three Weeks in a Helicopter* showcase racial masquerade and miscegenation. Al Jolson's famous "Mammy" scene, to which Huxley calls such attention, has another "racial" layer beyond the image of the white man in blackface. Al Jolson's character is from an orthodox Jewish family; as he puts on his black make-up and prepares for an opening-night performance on Broadway that will keep him from honoring his father's dying wish that he sing Kol Nidre in the synagogue, he describes his hesitations to his love interest, Mary (a shiksa whose status worries Jolson's character's mother, adding another "racial" tension to the film's story): "There's something, after all, in my heart—maybe it is the call of the ages—the cry—of my race." "Race" is a "special effect" in *The Jazz Singer*, an identity that can be painted on. The black-and-white film stock of the early teens and twenties was animated by contrast: the less subtle the better. While Huxley does not comment overtly on the racial dimensions of *The Jazz Singer* in "Silence Is Golden," his concentration on Al Jolson's blackface performance suggests that it drew his attention, and the film's preoccupation with racial and ethnic contrast does appear in Huxley's description of how the members of the band in *The Jazz Singer* "belong to two contrasted races—dark and polished Hebrews and chubby young Nordics [with faces like] undercooked muffins" (55). Here "race" is read precisely as the "outer skin of things," as color and the consistency of flesh on the screen. But race went deeper for Huxley. Throughout his writings on cinema, he expresses anti-Semitic paranoia about Hollywood, which he feared was run by "Jews with money."[23] His association of cinema with both blackness and Jewishness, and more generally with racial promiscuity, resembles nothing so much as the fearful rhetoric of "degeneration," with its anxiety that certain forms of culture have a corrosive social influence.

At the same time, as with the debased but seductive Lenina, Huxley himself plays on the excitement of these taboo representations in the feelies. Here *Three Weeks in a Helicopter* seems to evoke another intertext: white slavery films.[24] This genre of "vice films," especially popular in the teens, told melodramatic stories of young girls being kidnapped and forced into "slavery," a code name for prostitution. Shelley Stamp argues that films such as *White Slave Traffic* and *Traffic in Souls* responded to anxiety about young women's new urban recreation culture, and particularly cinema as one of those pursuits. "Cinemas were described by many observers as arenas of particular carnal license, where women were alternately preyed upon by salacious men . . . and themselves tempted to engage in untoward conduct" (47). The beta blonde's sexualized "enslavement" to the blackamoor plays on what Judith Walkowitz has described as a sensational, even pornographic, excitement underpinning the white slavery scare at the turn of the century as well as the fantasy of miscegenation. Huxley reaffirms racial stereotypes and anxieties even as he mocks contemporary films that exploited these stereotypes.

The representation of black sexuality in films of the twenties was vexed, whether in *Birth of a Nation*, with its scene of a black man chasing a white woman, or "race films" like Oscar Micheaux's. In *Three Weeks in a Helicopter* Huxley exploits the persistent fantasy of black male sexuality threatening white womanhood in a scene that would have been banned under the explicit direction of the Motion Picture Production Code of 1930, better known as the Hays Code, that "Miscegenation (sex relationships between the White and Black races) is forbidden" (qtd. in Leff and Simmons 288).[25] Indeed, everything about the feely, from the kisses to the interracial romp on the bearskin, would have been unrepresentable in mainstream cinema in 1932.

The tigerskin and bearskin, the goats and monkeys, the pig's dung and the feelies' stalls, and the "big game photographer" Darwin Bonaparte tracking John all contribute to a strong sense of bestiality and mindlessness surrounding the feelies, of physical transgression and cultural regression that Huxley associates with film and especially with the talkies. He presents cinematic progress as at a crossroads between new and old pleasures, between the serious, thoughtful world of *Othello* and the decadent, sybaritic world of Glyn. The talkies, he suggests, are moving cinema toward dangerous, even animalistic, pleasures: a proposition that is strengthened but also complicated by a further cinematic allusion in *Three Weeks in a Helicopter*.

## The Savage of Surrey

John's feely epitaph, *The Savage of Surrey*, along with other feelies mentioned in *Brave New World*—"the famous all-howling stereoscopic feely of the gorillas' wedding" (253) and *The Sperm Whale's Love-Life*, which

Darwin Bonaparte considers the gold standard in feelatography—indicate that Huxley had a particular kind of film in mind when he invented the feelies: documentary. While the coyly titled films seem ludicrously far-fetched, they are not far off from the titles of real ethnographic and nature documentaries that were hugely popular in Britain in the twenties. The foremost among these was a series called *Secrets of Nature*, sponsored by British Instructional from 1922 to 1933. In her history of British cinema, Rachel Low notes:

> The excellence and popular success of the *Secrets of Nature* films was one of the few bright features of the British film industry during the twenties. . . . They were liked by both ordinary audiences and highbrows. (*1918–1929* 130–31)

Screened before feature-length films, *Secrets of Nature* focused on topics such as the habits of the cuckoo or plant growth: *Romance in a Pond*, for example, investigates the life cycle of newts. In their 1933 book *Secrets of Nature*, Mary Field ("the only Englishwoman at present directing talking pictures" [4]) and Percy Smith ("an expert on micro-cinematography") remark that when *Secrets of Nature* "went talky," it faced the same obstacles that other kinds of films did:

> Experiments have shown that the majority of cinema-goers cannot both look and listen. When they go to the pictures they have the tendency to look, for had they wished to listen, they would have stayed at home and turned on the wireless. (214)

According to David King Dunaway, these documentaries were Huxley's favorite kind of film, and "in particular his favorite [was] *The Sex Life of Lobsters*" (350). Huxley's brother Julian, who was active in the popularization of biology, narrated and directed an Oscar-winning film called *The Private Life of the Gannets* (1935). Although both titles sound like feelies, Huxley often praised documentary film.[26] In 1929 he writes that he is "personally . . . very fond" of "the documentary film which shows me places I have never visited, strange animals, odd people, queer trades. . . . *Nanook* and *Chang* and *Moana* are delightful, imaginative liberations for those who have undergone long slavery in the world of adult interest" (*Essays* 3: 13–14).

Huxley was always fascinated by educational systems, whether examining social conditioning in *Brave New World* or, in 1929, exploring the pedagogical potential of film in *Vanity Fair* ("The Critic in the Crib," *Essays* 3: 10–14), an interest shared by many other critics. As early as 1914, Shaw wrote:

> The cinematograph begins educating people when the projec-
> tion lantern begins clicking, and does not stop until it leaves off.
> Whether it is shewing you what the South Polar ice barrier is like
> through the films of Mr Ponting [*90 Degrees South* (1911–1912)],
> or making you silly and sentimental by pictorial novelets, it is
> educating you all the time. (7)

Indeed, he adds, the cinema "is educating you far more effectively when you
think it is only amusing you than when it is avowedly instructing you in the
habits of lobsters."[27] Of course, Huxley's version of educational film in *Brave
New World* is far from exemplary. John visits the Eton "Beta-Minus geography room," where the students are watching an ethnographic film about
the Penitentes of the Savage Reservation beating themselves. The students
roar with laughter while Bernard takes advantage of "the cinematographical
twilight" to make a pass at the Head Mistress. John, meanwhile, is "pained"
and "bewildered" (162–63). This distorted scene of cinema as education in
*Brave New World* reflects real discussions among some early film critics. In
1924 the British film journal *Bioscope* ran a column by Leonard Donaldson
arguing that the cinema could be used to "prepare the scholar for the workshop and factory" and, by "portray[ing] various industrial processes," could
"promote the general welfare and safety of the worker" (51), a view that seems
parodied in films such as Chaplin's *Modern Times*. As a mass medium, cinema could "form the mind of England" as Shaw predicted, but it could also
*de*form the mind of England as it does in *Brave New World*. In one of his
earliest responses to film, Huxley wrote in 1916 that *Birth of a Nation*

> is said to mark quite a new epoch in cinematographic art. In time,
> no doubt, we shall have cinemas being bought up by the political
> parties for propagandist work, in which they will soon excel even
> the newspapers. The effect of them in China is said to be prodi-
> gious, while Rumania is described as a Cinematocracy. (*Letters*
> 94–95)

While Huxley briefly remarks on the art of DeMille's racially inflammatory
epic, he is far more interested in the propagandistic implications of cinema
than its aesthetic possibilities.

One way Huxley's concern about the possible sociopolitical function of
the talkies emerges in *Brave New World* is as a sly joke. The sleep-teaching
that impresses the values of Our Ford is said to have been discovered by
Reuben Rabinovitch, "the child of Polish-speaking parents" (23), who was
put to bed while the radio was left on and awoke "repeating word for word

a long lecture by that curious old writer ... George Bernard Shaw, who was speaking, according to a well-authenticated tradition, about his own genius" (24). Shaw's reputation as a social reformer and didact made him a natural target for Huxley, and the details of the scene are drawn from a web of associations linking Shaw to cinema history. After the coming of sound, Shaw stood by his earlier statement about the importance of film; he was garrulous on the subject of the talkies, as for instance in his 1930 article "GBS—'Talkie Prophet'" (70–71). In 1936 he wrote, "The silent film was no use to me. . . . When movies became talkies my turn came" (qtd. in Dukore xviii). Huxley seems to have perceived Shaw, the most famous living British playwright, taking up the mantle of "Talkie Prophet" as an alarming sign, and Reuben Rabinovitch's subliminal Shavian lesson is connected to the talkies through *The Jazz Singer*, whose hero is called Jakie Rabinowitz. Arguably the most famous mouthpiece of the talkies, he delivers the first recorded, nonsung words of the film: "Wait a minute, you ain't heard nothin' yet!" Huxley uses this Rabinowitz /Rabinovitch character to draw the familiar analogy between the talkies and hypnosis. Casting Shaw in the role of droning hypnotist, Huxley knocks GBS from what Huxley perceived as a smug pedestal of self-regard and also insinuates that talkies' effects could be as insidious as radio, which, with print media, was the main vehicle of propaganda at this time. The talkies could surpass both newspapers and radio by mobilizing words and images, and the feelies portend an even more intrusive, manipulative future for film.

Shortly after the publication of *Brave New World*, in a 1935 *Daily Express* article, Huxley made a series of predictions about how life would look in 1960. He devotes considerable space to prophecies about the cinema. "As for the talkies ... they took to color in the early forties and become stereoscopic about nine years later" (*Essays* 3: 424). He forecasts that actors began "having themselves fitted with synthetic voices" and that politicians followed suit:

> Ministries of Propaganda found that it was possible to supply dictators, monarchs, and even democratic Prime Ministers with a brand of synthetic eloquence incomparably more moving than that of the greatest orators of previous epochs. (3: 424)

Here, as with the feelies, Huxley builds on the commonplace association of the talkies with sensual experience to imagine cinema as a bodily apparatus that is also inevitably a political instrument. While many of his contemporaries found the talkies excessive or confusing, Huxley expands on those reactions to explore the social and political implications of sound film. If the feelies suggest that Huxley was one of the great naysayers about cinematic development, they also suggest that few took the talkies more seriously.

## Huxley and Hollywood

In a development not anticipated by his early writings on film, in 1938 Huxley moved to Hollywood, the home of "standardized amusement" and "Elinor Glyn Ltd.," and spent the rest of his life there. His friendships with figures such as Charlie Chaplin and Anita Loos allowed him access to the inner circles of Hollywood. Along with other expatriates including Evelyn Waugh, Huxley worked as a scriptwriter for the major studios. Most of the projects with which he was involved were adaptations of literary classics—*Pride and Prejudice* (1940) and *Jane Eyre* (1944)—or similarly "highbrow" projects such as *Madame Curie* (1943). These were commercially successful examples of entertainment combining "old" and "new" pleasures, a combination that had seemed elusive to Huxley in the twenties. While he continued to write about cinema satirically in *After Many a Summer Dies the Swan* (1939) and *Ape and Essence* (1948), his participation in a developing industry that produced films such as *Citizen Kane* changed his perception of film's possibilities.[28]

Huxley made two attempts to adapt *Brave New World* to visual forms. In a 1945 letter to Loos, he proposes a film that would "revolve around the person of a very clever but physically unattractive scientist, desperately trying to make a gorgeous blonde, who is repelled by his pimples but fascinated by the intelligence of his conversation" (535). This figure, who seems to be a stand-in for Lenina (or perhaps the Beta blonde of *Three Weeks in a Helicopter*), sounds suspiciously like Loos's most famous heroine, Lorelei Lei of *Gentlemen Prefer Blondes* (1925). "In the end," Huxley continues, the scientist "makes violent passes at the blonde, gets his face slapped and is left disconsolate among the white mice and the rabbit ova—an emblem of personal frustration who is yet the most revolutionary and subversive force in the modern world." The project never got off the ground because RKO owned the dramatic rights to the novel and would not allow it to be produced (Clark 62).

More startling is Huxley's subsequent attempt, in 1956, to adapt *Brave New World* to perhaps the least likely genre. He writes in several letters that he is at work on

> a musical comedy version of *Brave New World*—for everyone tells me that science fiction can never succeed on the stage as a straight play, but that it will be accepted when the medium ceases to be realistic and makes use of music and lyrics. (*Letters* 808)

The exchange between film and literature became more fluid in the forties and fifties, the golden age of Broadway musicals such as *Oklahoma!* (1943), *South Pacific* (1949), *Guys and Dolls* (1950), *Candide* (1956), *West Side Story*

(1957), and Loos's own *Gentlemen Prefer Blondes* (1949). Jerome Meckier speculates that "Perhaps Huxley conceived of musical comedy—the musical comedy of ideas—as the ideal form for bridging the ever-widening gap between high seriousness and popular entertainment" (106). Huxley's musical adaptation of *Brave New World* came shortly after MGM's *Singin' in the Rain* (1952), with its comic treatment of the talkies. With the turn to the musical, shaped around song and dance numbers, film was, in some senses, turning back toward its roots in the music hall. This comes across strongly in Huxley's three-act musical version of *Brave New World*, which contains nine bizarre songs and several equally odd dances, including a kinetic "Death Conditioning" ballet and a soft-shoe shuffle involving workers in the hatchery singing "Everybody's Happy Now." At another point, Huxley revisits precisely the scene that so horrified him in *The Jazz Singer*—a scene straight from the music hall—and replays it as pure absurdity: a character "falls on one knee, in the attitude of Al Jolson," and sings not "Mammy" but "Bottle of Mine," an ode to the bottle from which he was "decanted" (44). As theater becomes more like film, film becomes, once again, more like the stage, suggesting that the strict boundaries for artistic forms that Huxley advocated earlier, as a means of keeping the talkies at bay, had crumbled by the mid-fifties.

Huxley gave his script to several readers, including Chaplin and Leonard Bernstein, but he never managed to find someone to write the score, and the musical was never produced. While it is a weak derivative of the novel, the musical does show Huxley reconfiguring and solving some of the problems that preoccupied him in the novel. The most striking change is the character of Lenina, who is less sexually aggressive and much more intelligent than she is in the novel. She joins John in reading *The Complete Works of Shakespeare*, and in the conclusion of the musical—where Huxley takes the "third alternative" (ix) he mentions in his 1946 foreword to *Brave New World*—Lenina and John depart to join a community of like-minded exiles in Tahiti. In Lenina's transformation, Huxley has traded in *Othello* for *The Tempest* and, of course, *My Fair Lady*.

Huxley's treatment of the feelies in the musical is similarly lighter than in the novel. In act 1, Joe, a Beta Minus, steals and gobbles up some of Lenina's soma and makes a pass at her: "Listen, Baby. Let's you and I go to the feelies tonight. I hear there's a wonderful show at the Piccadilly Palace." She turns him down "with dignity": "Nothing doing, I think your behavior is lousy and unethical." Joe persists: "Boy meets pneumatic girl on a foam rubber mattress with a chinchilla slip cover. You can feel that fur all over you—every single hair of it. They say it's terrific" (41). Riffing again on Glyn's tigerskin, now a chinchilla, Huxley has made the feelies tawdrier, but they remain a verbal reference—more like a dirty joke than a major sign of cultural decline, as they are in the novel. Significantly, Huxley chooses not to stage the feelies.[29] By the early 1950s, sound film was fully assimilated and cinema did not take on any more sensual properties (other than becoming colorized). Still, what would it have meant to represent the feelies on film or on stage? One imagines a *mise-en-abime* effect, or something like the "pleasure organ" in *Barbarella*, or John Waters's Odorama cards. It seems fitting that the feelies never made it to the big screen, for any effort to depict them cinematically would necessarily dilute their polysensual dimensions. Almost 75 years after *Brave New World* was published, the movies are still not "stereoscopic," and commercial films are still incapable of making an audience feel the hairs on a tigerskin rug. The irony is that the feelies, an incarnation of pure physical experience in *Brave New World*, cannot themselves be embodied or represented visually. Despite Huxley's anxious predictions about cinema bringing on the end of real culture, his own most fearsome representation of cinema's future, the feelies, only exists through the written word. Literature, not film, remains the medium most capable of imagining and representing the most spectacular of pleasures.

## Notes

1. See "Spectrum of Opinion, 1928–1929" in Harry Geduld's *The Birth of the Talkies*.
2. Shaw's thoughts on the cinema were not always out of step with Huxley's. When Shaw saw D. W. Griffith's *Intolerance* in 1917, he wrote, "it was the most damnable entertainment and the wickedest waste of money within my experience. It was like turning over the leaves of a badly illustrated Bible (in monthly parts) for three hours that were like three years" (23). In a 1914 *New Statesman* interview he remarked:

> The cinema tells its story to the illiterate as well as to the literate; and it keeps its victim (if you like to call him so) not only awake but fascinated as if by a serpent's eye. And that is why the cinema is going to produce effects that all the cheap books in the world could never produce. (9)

3. See Benjamin's "The Work of Art in the Age of Mechanical Reproduction" and "On Some Motifs in Baudelaire" in *Illuminations*.
4. See Loiperdinger.
5. There is some irony in Huxley's fascination with cinema: he was rendered nearly blind from an illness when he was 16. He had to sit in the front row of films, and one wonders how well he saw even then.
6. Cinema shares many of these features with theater, but critics typically maintained that there is a "striking difference between [the filmgoer] and the theatergoer" (Kracauer, *Theory* 159).
7. In her generally enthusiastic *Let's Go to the Movies*, Barry flatly states that "The cinema is a drug" (53). As Kracauer notes, "from the twenties to the present

day, the devotees of film and its opponents alike have compared the medium to a sort of drug and have drawn attention to its stupefying effects," suggesting that "the cinema has its habitués who frequent it out of an all but physiological urge" (*Theory* 159).

8. Even when traveling in Malaysia Huxley manages to find a film screening to excoriate, here as an instrument of colonial modernity:

> The violent imbecilities of the story flickered in silence against the background of the equatorial night. In silence the Javanese looked on. What were they thinking? What were their private comments on this exhibition of Western civilization? . . . The world into which the cinema introduces the subject peoples is a world of silliness and criminality. (*Jesting Pilate* 224–25)

9. That cinematic pleasures are the product of "interminable democracies" is an insight into Huxley's politics of the 1930s. For an account of his politics at this point—his conflicted feeling about democracy and his interest in eugenics even as he writes *Brave New World*—see David Bradshaw.

10. The 1929 film *Broadway Melody* first used this slogan, which was mocked by Ernest Betts in 1930 as "All-talking, all-singing, all-nothing."

11. Since the 1980s many critics have demonstrated that the relationship between modernism and mass or popular culture is much more complex than one of simple opposition, entailing local histories and significances that elude the dichotomy of a great divide. Modernism defines itself against popular culture but also enjoys and exploits it. See for example the anthologies on modernism and popular culture edited by James Naremore and Patrick Brantlinger and by Maria Di Battista and Lucy McDiarmid. See also Michael North's *Reading 1922*, which reconsiders Huyssen's paradigm, David Chinitz's and Barry J. Faulk's articles on Eliot's ambivalent relationship to popular culture, and Allison Pease's work on modernism and pornography.

12. Certainly there are representations of pleasure in modernism, but they are never far from a kind of manic, desperate energy. In a 1963 essay called "The Fate of Pleasure," Lionel Trilling contends that "at some point in modern history, the principle of pleasure came to be regarded with . . . ambivalence" (434), which develops fully into a "repudiation of pleasure" (439) with modernists, who regard conventional pleasures as a false consolation, a "specious good" (441), and this, along with a desire to destroy "the habits, manners, and 'values' of the bourgeois world" (442), results in a "devaluation of the pleasure principle" (443–44). While this reading of modernism has been questioned by critics such as Perry Meisel, others continue to write about pleasure as a "problem" for modernism not just thematically and ideologically but also formally. Leonard Diepeveen argues that modernists redefined the nature of readerly pleasure to include the struggle with difficulty (150); Richard Poirier writes that "Modernism happened when reading got to be grim" (105). These observations suggest that modernists seek not just to repudiate pleasure but also to put in its place a kind of anhedonia.

13. In 1936 Huxley reported on his recent visit to "a gigantic new movie palace" in Margate. "Its name implied a whole social program, a complete theory of art; it was called 'Dreamland'" (*Essays* 4:25). Huxley describes this forerunner of cineplexes as a totalitarian order like *Brave New World*.

14. Graves and Hodge assert that Glyn was "not read by the more discriminating," yet many modernists reference her work. Nigel Brooks explores Fitzgerald's reworking of *Three Weeks* in *The Great Gatsby*. Virginia Woolf wrote about Glyn in a 1917 diary entry: "Expecting life & smartness at least I spent 8d upon a Magazine with Mrs Asquith's love letters, & they're as flat & feeble & vulgar & illiterate as a provincial Mrs Glyn might be" (71).

15. Frank Kermode considers *Three Weeks* as an exploration of national identity and masculinity.

16. See David Trotter, George Robb, and Chris Waters for sociopolitical readings of Glyn's novel.

17. The 1924 film was titled *Romance of a Queen* (Goldwyn).

18. This slip—the blackamoor is the hero and not the villain?—is unexplained.

19. See Robert Ball, John Collick, John P. McCombe, and Roberta E. Pearson on early adaptations of Shakespeare for the screen.

20. Asked in a 1915 interview "What the Films May Do to the Drama," Shaw replied:

> When they can see and hear Forbes-Robertson's *Hamlet* equally well produced, it will be possible for our young people to grow up in healthy remoteness from the crowded masses and slums of big cities without also growing up as savages. (18)

This is a rare vision of cinema as harmonious rather than competitive with theater and not inextricably linked to modernity. Its unusual optimism is perhaps attributable to the date, well before the talkies were a realizable technological prospect. Huxley's pessimistic view in *Brave New World* is more representative: it is the "savage" who most appreciates Shakespeare.

21. Huxley's distaste for the "agreeable sensations" produced by cinema, his preference for content over form, and his interest in social meaning over aesthetics all indicate the ways in which he is difficult to classify as a modernist in the conventional sense of the term.

22. James Sexton has pointed out that the theme of sexual jealousy in the feely is central to *Othello* and to the Savage's tormented relationship with Lenina Crowne.

23. See, for example, Huxley's 1926 letter to Percy Smith, 266.

24. Thanks to Celia Marshik for pointing out this connection to me.

25. See also Linda Williams and Lucy Bland.

26. In "Silence Is Golden" Huxley lauds the "Fascinating Events of The Week" newsreels (*Essays* 2: 28). In *Heaven and Hell* he praises colored documentaries as "a notable new form of popular visionary art" and explicitly mentions Disney's *The Living Desert*, with "the immensely magnified cactus blossoms, into which . . . the spectator finds himself sinking" (168).

27. Low notes that in 1934

> the first group of classroom films to be issued in Britain were *Shakespeare*, a one-reeler . . . about Shakespeare's biographical and historical background, and three physiology one-reelers, *Breathing*, *The Blood*, and *Circulation*. (*1929–1939* 26)

These are two of Huxley's favorite subjects, Shakespeare and documentary.

28. Alongside this transformation, Huxley's views of drugs changed radically. Not only did he find value in the intelligent use of drugs such as LSD, but he also proposed that drugs could serve socially useful purposes, expanding consciousness and creativity.

29. Huxley does, however, represent the newer visual technology, television, in the musical, and it plays a role similar to that in Orwell's *1984*, as mass media have encroached even further into the lives of citizens, making their way out of the feely palace and into the private home.

## Works Cited

Adorno, Theodor. "Aldous Huxley and Utopia." *Prisms*. Tr. Samuel Weber and Shierry Weber. Cambridge: MIT Press, 1967. 97–117.

Altman, Rick. Introduction. *Cinema/Sound*. Spec. issue of *Yale Cinema Studies* 60 (1980): 3–15.

———. *Sound Theory/Sound Practice*. London: Routledge, 1992.

Arnheim, Rudolf. *Film as Art*. Berkeley: U of California P, 1971.

Ball, Robert. *Shakespeare on Silent Film*. New York: Theatre Arts, 1968.

Barry, Iris. *Let's Go to the Movies*. New York: Arno, 1972. Originally published as *Let's Go to the Pictures*. London: Chatto, 1926.

Benjamin, Walter. *Illuminations*. Ed. Hannah Arendt. New York: Schocken, 1968. Betts, Ernest. "All-talking, all-singing, all-nothing." *Close Up* June 1930: 449–54.

———. *Heraclitus or The Future of Film*. London: Kegan Paul, 1928.

———. "Ordeal by 'Talkie.'" *Saturday Review* (London) 6 July 1929: 7–8.

———. "Why 'Talkies' Are Unsound." *Close Up* April 1919: 22–24.

Bland, Lucy. "White Women and Men of Colour: Miscegenation Fears in Britain After the Great War." *Gender History* 17.1: 29–61.

Bradshaw, David. *The Hidden Huxley: Contempt and Compassion for the Masses, 1920–36*. London: Faber, 1994.

Brooks, Nigel. "Fitzgerald's *The Great Gatsby* and Glyn's *Three Weeks*." *The Explicator* 54 (1996): 233–36.

Carey, John. *The Intellectuals and the Masses: Pride and Prejudice Among the Literary Intelligentsia 1880–1939*. London: Faber, 1992.

Chaplin, Charlie. *Charlie Chaplin: Interviews*. Ed. Kevin J. Hayes. U of Mississippi P, 2005.

Chinitz, David. "T. S. Eliot and the Cultural Divide." *PMLA* 10 (1995): 236–47.

Clark, Virginia M. *Aldous Huxley and Film*. Metuchen: Scarecrow, 1987.

Collick, John. *Shakespeare, Cinema, and Society*. Manchester: Manchester UP, 1989.

Crafton, Donald. *The Talkies: American Cinema's Transition to Sound, 1926–1931*. Berkeley: U of California P, 1999.

Crary, Jonathan. "Modernizing Vision." *Viewing Positions*. Ed. Linda Williams. New Brunswick: Rutgers UP, 1994. 23–35.

DeCherney, Peter. *Hollywood and the Culture Elite: How the Movies Became American*. New York: Columbia UP, 2005.

Di Battista, Maria, and Lucy McDiarmid, eds. *High and Low Moderns: Literature and Culture, 1889–1939*. New York: Oxford UP, 1996.

Diepeveen, Leonard. *The Difficulties of Modernism*. New York: Routledge, 2002.

Donald, James, Anne Friedberg, and Laura Marcus, eds. *Close Up: 1927–1933*. Princeton: Princeton UP, 1999.

Donaldson, Leonard. "The Cinema in Education and Industry." *Bioscope* 3 Jan. 1924:
    51–52.

Dukore, Bernard F. Introduction. Shaw xi–xxvi.

Dunaway, David King. *Huxley in Hollywood*. New York: Harper, 1989.

Eisenstein, Sergei Mikhailovich. *The Film Sense*. Tr. Jay Leyda. New York: Harcourt, 1947.

Eisenstein, Sergei, W. I. Pudovkin, and G. V. Alexandrov. "Statement on Sound." *Close Up:
    1927–1933*. Eds. James Donald, Anne Friedberg, and Laura Marcus. Princeton: Princ-
    eton UP, 1999. 83–86.

Eliot, T. S. *Poems*. New York: Knopf, 1930.

———. *Selected Prose of T. S. Eliot*. New York: Harvest, 1975.

Faulk, Barry J. "Modernism and the Popular: Eliot's Music Halls." *Modernism/Modernity 8*
    (2001): 603–21.

Field, Mary, and Percy Smith. *Secrets of Nature*. London: Faber, 1933.

Gaines, Jane. *Fire and Desire: Mixed-Race Movies in the Silent Era*. Chicago: U of Chicago
    P, 2001.

Geduld, Harry M. *The Birth of the Talkies: From Edison to Jolson*. Bloomington: Indiana UP,
    1975.

Glyn, Elinor. Papers. TC.

———. *Three Weeks*. London, Virago, 1996.

Graves, Robert, and Alan Hodge. *The Long Week End: A Social History of Great Britain,
    1918–1939*. New York: Macmillan, 1941.

Gunning, Tom. "An Aesthetics of Astonishment: Early Film and the (In)credulous Spec-
    tator." *Viewing Positions*. Ed. Linda Williams. New Brunswick: Rutgers UP, 1994.
    114–33.

Hansen, Miriam. "The Mass Production of the Senses: Classical Cinema as Vernacular Mod-
    ernism." *Modernism/Modernity 6.2* (1999): 59–77.

Huxley, Aldous. *After Many a Summer Dies the Swan*. New York: Harper, 1939.

———. *Ape and Essence*. New York: Harper, 1948.

———. *Brave New World*. New York: Harper, 1998. Includes Huxley's 1946 foreword,
    vii–xvii.

———. *Brave New World: A Musical Comedy*. 1956. Ed. Bernfried Nugle. *Aldous Huxley
    Annual* 3 (2003): 33–128.

———. *Complete Essays*. Eds. Robert S. Baker and James Sexton. 6 vols. Chicago: Dee,
    2000.

———. *Eyeless in Gaza*. New York: Harper, 1936.

———. *Heaven and Hell*. New York: Harper, 1956.

———. *Jesting Pilate: Travels through India, Burma, Malaya, Japan, China, and America*. New
    York: Paragon, 1991.

———. *Letters of Aldous Huxley*. Ed. Grover Smith. London: Chatto, 1969.

Huyssen, Andreas. *After the Great Divide: Modernism, Mass Culture, Postmodernism*. Indiana
    UP, 1987.

*The Jazz Singer*. Dir. Alan Crosland. Warner Bros., 1927.

Kermode, Frank. "The English Novel, circa 1907." *Essays on Fiction 1971–82*. London: Rout-
    ledge, 1983. 45–56.

Kracauer, Siegfried. *The Mass Ornament: Weimar Essays*. Tr. Thomas Y. Levin. 3rd ed. Cam-
    bridge: Harvard UP, 1995.

———. *Theory of Film: The Redemption of Physical Reality*. Princeton: Princeton UP, 1960.

Leavis, Q. D. *Fiction and the Reading Public*. London: Penguin, 1979.

Leff, Leonard J., and Jerold L. Simmons. *The Dame in the Kimono: Hollywood, Censorship, and the Production Code*. Lexington: UP of Kentucky, 2001.

Loiperdinger, Martin. "Lumière's Arrival of the Train: Cinema's Founding Myth." *The Moving Image* Spring 2004: 89–118.

Low, Rachael, *The History of the British Film, 1918–1929*. London: Allen & Unwin, 1971.

———. *The History of the British Film: 1929–1939*. London:Allen & Unwin, 1985.

McCombe, John P. "'Suiting the Action to the Word': The Clarendon *Tempest* and the Evolution of a Narrative Silent Shakespeare." *Literature Film Quarterly* 33 (2005): 142–55.

Meckier, Jerome. Afterword. Huxley, *Brave New World: A Musical Comedy*. 105–28.

Meisel, Perry. *The Myth of The Modern: A Study in British Literature and Criticism After 1850*. New Haven: Yale UP, 1987.

Naremore, James, and Patrick Brantlinger, eds. *Modernity and Mass Culture*. Bloomington: Indiana UP, 1991.

Nordau, Max. *Degeneration*. Tr. George L. Mosse. New York: Fertig, 1968.

North, Michael. *Reading 1922: A Return to the Scene of the Modern*. New York: Oxford, 1999.

Pearson, Roberta E. "Shakespeare's Country: The National Poet, English Identity, and British Silent Cinema." *Young and Innocent? The Cinema in Britain 1896–1930*. Ed. Andrew Higson. Exeter: U of Exeter P, 2002: 176–90.

Pease, Allison. *Modernism, Mass Culture, and the Aesthetics of Obscenity*. Cambridge: Cambridge UP, 2000.

Poirier, Richard. "The Difficulties of Modernism and the Modernism of Difficulty." *Critical Essays on American Modernism*. Eds. Michael J. Hoffman and Patrick D. Murphy. New York: Hall, 1992. 104–14.

Richards, Jeffrey. "Modernism and the People: The View from the Cinema Stalls." *Rewriting the Thirties: Modernism and After*. Eds. K. Williams and S. Matthews. Longman, 1997. 182–201.

Robb, George. "The Way of All Flesh: Degeneration, Eugenics, and the Gospel of Free Love." *Journal of the History of Sexuality* 6.4 (April 1996): 589–603.

Seldes, Gilbert. "The Movies Commit Suicide." *Harper's* Nov. 1928: 706–08.

Sexton, James. "*Brave New World*, the Feelies, and Elinor Glyn." *English Language Notes* 35 (1997): 35–38.

Shaw, George Bernard. *Bernard Shaw on Cinema*. Ed. Bernard F. Dukore. Carbondale: Southern Illinois UP, 1997.

Singer, Ben. *Melodrama and Modernity: Early Sensational Cinema and Its Contexts*. New York: Columbia UP, 2001.

Stamp, Shelley. *Movie-Struck Girls: Women and Motion Picture Culture after the Nickelodeon*. Princeton: Princeton UP, 2000.

Trilling, Lionel. "The Fate of Pleasure." *The Moral Obligation to Be Intelligent: Selected Essays*. Ed. Leon Wieseltier. New York: Farrar, 2001. 426–49.

Trotter, David. *The English Novel in History, 1895–1920*. London: Routledge, 1993.

Walkowitz, Judith R. *City of Dreadful Delight: Narratives of Sexual Danger in Late-Victorian London*. Chicago: U of Chicago P, 1992.

Waters, Chris. "New Women and Eugenic Fictions." *History Workshop Journal* 60 (Autumn 2005): 232–38.

West, Rebecca. *The Young Rebecca: Selected Essays of Rebecca West, 1911–1917*. Ed. Jane Marcus. London: 1982.

Williams, Linda. *Playing the Race Card: Melodramas of Black and White from Uncle Tom to O. J. Simpson*. Princeton: Princeton UP, 2002.

Wollen, Peter. "Cinema/Americanism/the Robot." *Modernity and Mass Culture*. Eds. James
    Naremore and Patrick Brantlinger. Bloomington: Indiana UP, 1991. 42–69.
Woolf, Virginia. "The Cinema." 1926. *Collected Essays*. Vol. 2. London: Hogarth, 1966.
    268–72.
———. *The Diaries of Virginia Woolf*. Ed. Anne Olivier Bell. Vol. 1. New York: Harcourt,
    1979.

CAREY SNYDER

# "When the Indian Was in Vogue": D. H. Lawrence, Aldous Huxley, and Ethnological Tourism in the Southwest

The southwest is the great playground of the White American. The desert isn't good for anything else. But it does make a fine national playground. And the Indian, with his long hair and his bits of pottery and blankets and clumsy home-made trinkets, he's a wonderful live toy to play with.

D. H. Lawrence, "Just Back from the Snake-Dance—Tired Out"

"I had the same idea as you," the Director was saying. "Wanted to have a look at the savages. Got a permit for New Mexico and went there for my summer holiday."

Aldous Huxley, *Brave New World*

In her 1934 classic *Patterns of Culture*, the anthropologist Ruth Benedict asserts that no one has written a better description of "the form and spirit of Pueblo dances" than D. H. Lawrence (93). Although contemporary studies have examined the ethnocentrism of Lawrence's representations of indigenous people,[1] scholars surprisingly continue to praise Lawrence for his "extraordinary effort to get *inside* Indian culture" (Kinkead-Weekes 27) and for his "true engagement with the primitive" (Storch 50–51). Reading Lawrence in this way misses a more interesting element of his Southwest writings: they are illuminating not only because they shed light on specific cultural practices, but because they also (at times, inadvertently) illuminate

From *Modern Fiction Studies* 53, no. 4 (Winter 2007): 662–96. Copyright © 2007 by Johns Hopkins University Press for the Purdue Research Foundation.

the practice of cultural observation itself—which takes this writer into terrain traversed by ethnologists and tourists alike.

As made clear in his 1929 essay entitled "New Mexico," the diverse tribes of the Southwest were remarkable for Lawrence insofar as they preserved their "tribal integrity" amidst the rush of modernization. Threatening to overwhelm this tribal integrity was the already extensive commercialization of the region, epitomized for Lawrence by the figure of "the Indian who sells you baskets on Albuquerque station or who slinks around Taos plaza"—two popular venues for sightseeing and buying souvenirs. In seeking to avoid modernized Indians and commune with "a remnant of the most deeply religious race still living," Lawrence emulates the protocol of professional anthropologists like Benedict ("New Mexico" 144).

The construction of the Southwest as a site of threatened authenticity relies on a notion of cultural purity that has been complicated in recent years by James Clifford and others.[2] Yet even within its historical and ideological context, what makes this claim of discovering an unaltered indigenous culture dubious is the picture Lawrence himself paints of the region: choked with thousands of tourists crowding its plazas and pueblos, the Southwest emerges in Lawrence's derisive description as the trendy, "picturesque reservation and playground of the eastern states" ("New Mexico" 141), and Southwest Indians as "wonderful live toy[s] to play with" (*Letters* 609). In essays like "The Hopi Snake Dance"—in which three thousand tourists amusedly regard a native ceremony as if it were a "circus performance" (138)—Lawrence elaborates the process by which tribal customs and ceremonies are converted into the stuff of ethnological spectacle.[3] With the figure of "the Indian who sells you baskets on Albuquerque Station," Lawrence suggests that the star attractions of the region, its "befeathered and bedaubed darling[s]" ("Indians and Entertainment" 101), sometimes participate in their own touristification. It is hard to imagine the ideal of unchanged tribal life coexisting with the aggressive commercialization of native culture Lawrence describes. As vividly depicted in Lawrence's essays and his novella, *St. Mawr*, the reservations and pueblos of the Southwest served in the interwar period as a kind of ethnological theme park. Adapting Langston Hughes's phrase, one could say that in the 1920s and 1930s, the Indian was in vogue.[4]

Joining Lawrence in his satirical treatment of Southwest tourism is Aldous Huxley, whose depiction of the Southwest and its inhabitants is in fact indebted to Lawrence's essays and letters, the latter of which he had just finished editing for a posthumous collection when he began writing *Brave New World* (1932).[5] Although Huxley's dystopia has not been read as a novel about tourism, *Brave New World* echoes Lawrence's critique of the hype surrounding Southwest Indians by representing a New Mexican Savage

Reservation as the destination for a pair of English tourists, and, conversely, charting the trajectory of John the Savage from the Reservation to London, where he winds up being exhibited as an ethnological curiosity, evocative of the "human showcases" of World's Fairs that were widespread until the mid-1920s (Greenhalgh 82). Eventually John wearies of his celebrity status as token savage and flees the New World, only to become the ultimate tourist spectacle in the novel's climactic scene.

Beginning with Jerome Meckier's 1969 study, critics who have considered the relationship between these two authors have tended to focus on Huxley's rejection of the Lawrencian primitive—a reading I do not dispute.[6] What has not been adequately appreciated is the shared context for these writings: namely, the interwar mania for Southwest Indians. This essay argues that Lawrence and Huxley were engaged in a parallel project of satirizing what I will call "ethnological tourism": tourism that takes travelers to sites such as the tropics, reservations, and ethnological exhibits, mimicking modern ethnology's goal of observing traditional customs and ceremonies firsthand.[7] In satirizing the way that tourism transforms the reservations and pueblos of the Southwest into ethnological spectacle, Lawrence and Huxley go beyond the modern trope of anti-tourism;[8] they explore the potentially destructive effects of cultural spectatorship on indigenous cultures, and thus implicitly critique the modes of observation and representation that characterize modern ethnography as well. Coming at the vogue of the Indian from two very different perspectives—Lawrence as a primitivist longing to reconnect with lost origins, Huxley as a satirist wishing to expose primitivism as a utopian fantasy—these writers nonetheless provide a similar critique of the way both tourism and ethnography potentially disrupt local traditions, objectifying indigenous people and commodifying their culture. In this way, they are prescient observers of issues that continue to confront indigenous groups, many of whom are reliant on tourist revenue for economic livelihood, as well as ethnographers, who are increasingly self-conscious about their positioning vis-à-vis the cultures they observe.[9] I argue that Lawrence and Huxley expose the practice of turning native cultures into objects of scientific curiosity and spectacles for touristic consumption, yet do not always consider the implications of their own ethnographic gazes.

The following section places Lawrence's essays in the overlapping contexts of pertinent ethnographies, tourist advertisements, and the display practices of the Santa Fe Railway and its affiliate, the Fred Harvey Company—the force behind much Southwest tourism in the period, including the Southwest ethnological exhibitions displayed at the 1915 World's Fair. An examination of this material suggests that though ethnography defined itself against tourism in the interwar period—assuming a specialized and

ostensibly disinterested stance in contrast to a popular and commercial one—
these discourses frequently overlapped and converged in the Southwest.

### "So we've saved the pueblos for Fred Harvey"

A 1928 ad in *Travel* magazine for "Harveycar Motor Cruises" in New
Mexico depicts a Native American couple standing before a quiet pueblo,
edged by vacant desert and hills, with the ironic caption, "Is this really
the New World?" The ad appeals to, and helps construct, the virtual tourist's fantasies of engaging in quasi-ethnological discovery of a people who,
according to the ad copy, continue to live as in pre-Columbian times; by
visiting the Southwest, tourists are invited to step back in history via the
familiar trope of spatial anachronism.[10] The citizens of Huxley's *Brave New
World* are meant to ask the same question ("Is this really the New World?"),
albeit with a different inflection, when they visit the New Mexican Reservation—constructed as an exotic, archaic outpost of "savagery" that is a
mere rocket-ride away from London. (Huxley's more Hobbesian view of the
primitive, contrasting with the Romantic primitivism of the Harvey ad, will
be discussed below.)

In the contemporaneous *Patterns of Culture*, Ruth Benedict seems to
co-opt the language of advertisers by characterizing the Pueblo Indians of
the Southwest as "one of the most widely known primitive peoples in Western civilization, . . . in easy reach of any transcontinental traveler" (57). She
beckons tourists to come see these famed Indians for themselves. Reading
Benedict together with Lawrence's Southwest essays—which are teeming
with tourists he tries to avoid—reminds us that the emerging norms of ethnographic writing called for significant acts of erasure, as Benedict goes on to
efface from her text the numerous travelers alongside whom she conducted
her fieldwork.

It was the Atchison Topeka Santa Fe Railway, together with the affili-
ated Fred Harvey Company, that brought Southwest Indians within (in
Benedict's phrase) "easy reach" of ordinary travelers.[11] Indeed, the Fred Harvey publicity machine was likely behind Lawrence's figure of "the Indian who
sells you baskets on Albuquerque station," insofar as Fred Harvey aggressively employed Native American artisans to market products on railway
platforms, in front of gift shops such as "the Indian Building and Curio Shop"
in Albuquerque. In 1901, Fred Harvey opened its "Indian Department" to
coordinate efforts in marketing the image and artifacts of the Indian, distill-
ing what could be perceived as a comprehensive "Southwest experience" in
the hotel-restaurant-museum complexes known as Harvey Houses, at least
one of which Lawrence visited (Dodge 234). The Harvey Company was "*the
major source for southwest ethnological materials*" for tourists, collectors, and

museums, including the Smithsonian and the Field Museum of Natural History (Weigle and Babcock 67), selling "enough Indian curios to put a touch of Navajo or Hopi in every U.S. home," in the words of one contemporary (Hartwell 31). The head of the Indian Department, Herman Schweitzer, who became known as the principle "Harvey anthropologist," explained in a letter to collector William Randolph Hearst in 1905, that the main objective in promoting "the Indians of the Southwest and their products" was "to furnish an attraction for the Santa Fe"; in other words, Fred Harvey made ethnological tourism big business (Howard 92).

Lawrence and his protagonists repeatedly profess a desire to leave behind the commercial venues for interacting with or observing Indians—the platforms of the Santa Fe Railroad and the populated plazas of Taos—to seek a more intimate cross-cultural encounter.[12] His essays and novella, *St. Mawr*, chart the movement of a self-identified sensitive cultural observer beyond the façade of the Harvey Southwest, and the establishment of a fleeting connection with what is represented as genuine native culture. In following this trajectory, Lawrence's writings emulate the emerging goals of ethnological fieldwork, even as they denounce the mystifications of ethnographic texts.[13]

"The Hopi Snake Dance" (1924) illustrates the ethnological pretensions of Lawrence's writings. With thousands of spectators generally in attendance, the Hopi Snake Dance was the most popular tourist attraction in the Southwest; indeed, it was so popular, and tourists so disruptive that outsiders were eventually prohibited from viewing it (Dilworth 72). In his essay, Lawrence occasionally includes himself among the clamoring crowd, as when he describes being chastened by the Snake Priests' solemnity, which "conquers, for a few seconds, our white-faced flippancy" ("Hopi Snake Dance" 151). For the most part, though, he distances himself from the tourists he stigmatizes—"spectators . . . packed thick . . . greedy with curiosity," regarding the "sacred religious ceremonial" as a "circus-performance" ("Hopi Snake Dance" 145)—fashioning himself as a more culturally sensitive, informed observer, who looks beyond the semblance of crude entertainment to appreciate the indigenous meaning of the ceremony. Lawrence's satire of uncouth tourists finds its counterpart in contemporaneous ethnographic texts: in the introduction to *Argonauts of the Western Pacific*, the manifesto of modern fieldwork methods, Bronislaw Malinowski characterizes the average white resident in the Trobriand Islands as "full of the biased and pre-judged opinions . . . strongly repulsive" to the ethnographic mind (5). Unlike the casual observer, according to Malinowski, the modern fieldworker aims to get inside native culture, "to grasp the native's point of view, his relation to life, to realize *his* vision of *his* world" (25). A copious reader of anthropology, Lawrence seems to co-opt the role of the modern fieldworker by leaving the ignorant tourists behind and entering into imaginative union with the Hopis:

> [The chant] reveals how deep, how deep the men are in the mystery they are practicing, how sunk deep below our world, to the world of snakes, and dark ways in the earth, where are the roots of corn, and where the little rivers of unchannelled, uncreated life-passion run like dark, trickling lightning, to the roots of the corn and to the feet and loins of men, from the earth's innermost dark sun. They are calling in the deep, almost silent snake-language, to the snakes and rays of dark emission from the earth's inward 'Sun'. ("Hopi Snake Dance" 159)

Like a modern anthropologist, Lawrence presumes to have esoteric knowledge of the ceremony, purporting to understand the "deep, almost silent snake-language" of the priests.

When Lawrence rebukes tourists for regarding the sacred religious ceremony of the Hopis as if it were a sensational show, he is criticizing them for misreading the dance in the very way that both contemporary ads and ethnological display practices encouraged. In 1926 Fred Harvey inaugurated Harveycar Indian Detours. These automobile tours, explicated by purportedly expert guides, took tourists "off the beaten track" (Harveycar's slogan) and introduced them to "real" Pueblo Indian home life as well as to native ceremonies like the "weird Hopi Snake Dance" ("Harveycar" 37, photo caption).[14] In this way, the Indian Detours effectively anticipated the response of ethnological tourists like Lawrence, eager to get beyond the commercial façade of Harvey's *other* Southwest, the one that greeted them on the platform at Albuquerque station. Epitomizing Dean MacCannell's idea of the "staged authenticity" of the guided tour (*Tourist* 98), Harveycar did not conceal the staging of the Detours: the couriers were white women costumed in stereotypical native garb and jewelry; the drivers were cowboys, following what was already a cinematic cliché of the Old West.

More importantly, Harveycars promised to choreograph meetings with Indians, entities construed as sights to be seen or as artisans who seemed to be in the business of producing crafts exclusively for touristic consumption. This impression is conveyed by Indian Detour ads that depict Indians with baskets, blankets, or pots, objects that seem metonymically interchangeable with the Indians themselves, inviting the tourist to visually consume artificer as well as artifact. A lone carload of detourists romantically reenact the discovery of indigenous Americans in these images, in a conquest that is commercial rather than military. Meanwhile, Indians stand amicably by in the posture of dutiful servants, as if waiting to be animated by the touristic exchange. The iconography and rhetoric of these ads encourages tourists to regard living people as though they were objects in a museum, as exemplified by a 1928 brochure for Harveycar Indian Detours that invites the tourist to visit "Indian pueblos where one may 'catch archaeology live'" ("Harveycar Motor Cruises" 5).

Echoing the format of the Harvey ads, with their encapsulation of Southwest tourism as a placid encounter with aborigines who court observation, is the cover of February 1926 *Motor Camper and Tourist*, where an Anglo American couple are depicted car camping next to a Native American couple who proffer their wares. The caption "Camping with the Original Americans" seems at first to serve as an invitation to the reader of the magazine to do just that. Yet the cozy preposition "with" belies the oppositional logic of the image, which depicts more of a cross-cultural staring contest than a slumber party. The impression that it is the tourists rather than the "Original Americans" who are on display is conveyed not only by their orientation (facing us rather than turned away), but also by the illusion that the poles supporting the tent's awning demarcate an exhibit space. In inverted fashion, the scene evokes the practice prevailing at World's Fairs of exhibiting various colonized peoples in simulated "natural habitats" for the edification and pleasure of paying visitors. Insofar as this issue of *Motor Camper and Tourist* is meant to promote tourism to the Southwest rather than to encourage tourists to be self-conscious, one can assume that this reversal is not meant to be darkly satirical; nevertheless, the image inadvertently highlights the potential invasiveness of the tourists' gaze, in a way that resonates with Huxley's and Lawrence's satire.

Vacationing in the Southwest and visiting ethnological displays at World's Fairs were not unrelated phenomenon: the elaborate "Painted Desert Exhibition" at the Panama-California Expo in San Diego was sponsored and organized by the Santa Fe Railway and Fred Harvey, and functioned both as a virtual vacation spot in itself and as an ingenuous, and highly effective advertisement for travel to the Southwest.[15] Ten acres of painstakingly simulated Southwest landscape, with imported sandstone, cactus, and sagebrush, as well as plaster and cement made to resemble clay, the Painted Desert was built and inhabited by three hundred Apache, Navajo, and Pueblo Indians. Despite the obvious stagecraft involved in constructing the exhibit, one reporter called it an "open reservation," reinforcing the implied link between the "real" and the virtual Southwest (Kropp 40). Ambiguity about whether fairgoers were to interpret ethnic others as sideshow curiosities or objects of scientific interest was introduced by the spatial logic of the fairgrounds themselves: while the grounds were conventionally divided into an amusement zone ("the Midway" or "Joy Zone") and a zone for education, science, and technology, ethnological exhibits might be placed at either end, and often appeared at both, blurring the distinction between these categories. At the Panama-California Expo, museum organizers doubly cued spectators to read the Hopi Snake Dance as performed for their entertainment, by the placement of the performance in the amusement zone and by its billing as "dramatically sensational" (Dilworth x).[16]

Curtis Hinsley argues that the overriding message of ethnological display was that ethnicity could be consumed, that other cultures, arrayed as so many commodities, were there to be economically colonized and exploited. According to Hinsley the displays transformed living individuals into so many storefront mannequins, like the Indians in the Harvey ads who seem interchangeable with their merchandise: the "observer does not stop to learn; rather, he or she strolls, window-shopping in the department store of exotic cultures" (365). Hinsley goes on to link this practice of "consuming" other cultures to tourism: "public curiosity about other peoples, mediated by the terms of the marketplace, produced an early form of touristic consumption" (363). Indeed, touring the ethnological exhibits and concession stands at World's Fairs was not unlike touring the reservations and pueblos of the Southwest: in the Joy Zone of the Panama-Pacific Expo, fairgoers were transported in little cars to view the sites associated with a replica of "The Grand Canyon of Arizona," including a simulated Indian village; on the way they could stop and purchase a Navajo blanket at a concession stand. In New Mexico or Arizona, conveyed in Harveycars, tourists could likewise watch Indians perform ceremonial dances, buy hand-crafted artifacts, and glimpse some of the quotidian strangeness of Indians constructed as exotic others. Here we have a kind of hall-of-mirrors of staged encounters: the Expo exhibit restages the Harvey Southwest experience, which, as we have seen, is itself already staged. In effect, the human showcases of the Panama-Pacific and Panama-California World's Fairs, of Indian Detours and Harvey Houses, and of myriad advertisements and ethnographic texts, were mutually supporting apparatuses for the display of native people: together, they promoted and normalized the ethnological tourist's gaze.

Lawrence seems to be describing the amusement zone of a World's Fair in "Indians and an Englishman," when he represents himself, a "bewildered straggler out of the far-flung British Empire," stumbling "like a bumpkin in a circus ring, with the horse-lady leaping over my head, the Apache war-whooping in my ear, the Mexican staggering under crosses and bumping me as he goes by, the artist whirling colours across my dazzled vision, the highbrows solemnly disclaiming at me from all the cross-roads" (92–93). The trope of theatricality—signaled by the language of audiences, circus rings, and what he calls "a masquerade of earnestness" (93)—points to the contrivance of a site where cultural others perform their otherness or are perceived as performing it by uncomprehending observers, for whom ordinary customs and dress become the stuff of exotic entertainment.

While the essay depicts Lawrence's attempt to connect with an ostensibly authentic Southwest, behind this staged, touristy façade, at the same time it reproduces key tropes of the tourism literature. Like the Harveycar ad, Lawrence seems to beckon his readers to "catch archaeology live"—to come and stare at exotic Indians before their way of life vanishes—as the essay moves from the circus of the Southwest to a secluded forest setting where the lone Englishman discovers a tribal elder preaching. Though informed that only Apaches are admitted into the circle, Lawrence boasts that he defiantly lurks on the periphery "for hours," wrapped in a Navajo blanket that simultaneously affords him the pleasure of donning an "Indian disguise" (albeit in a garment of the wrong tribe) and feeling "as good as invisible" (96). Rather than openly gawking at native rituals, as he describes the crowds observing the Hopi Snake Dance doing, Lawrence represents himself peering voyeuristically through a "leaf screen" (97)—an idiom of stealth that figures in professional anthropology as well, as evidenced by Malinowski's testosterone-driven characterization of the fieldworker as "an active huntsman" who must outfox "his quarry . . . and follow it up to its most inaccessible lairs" (8). (In *Brave New World*, Huxley seems to parody this scene, illuminating the connections between voyeurism, hunting, and cultural observation, as discussed below.) From this vantage, Lawrence describes a tribal elder as though he were a museum artifact, calling him "an old, mask-like virile figure," " a piece of living red earth," and " a figure of deep pathos" destined to perish (98)—language that resonates with the idiom of ethnographic nostalgia that characterizes the tourist literature. Despite the essay's attempt to conjure a portrait of a more intimate and spontaneous encounter with Indians than that staged for the average tourist, the Englishman of the essay's title emerges as a trespasser and a spy—more furtive than other spectators, but equally riveted by the spectacle of difference.

### Spurious Indians

In the novella *St. Mawr*, the American expatriate, Lou Witt (later Lady Carrington) stands in for Lawrence as a disaffected, alienated modern individual on a spiritual quest that takes her to the Southwest. Lou and her mother Rachel Witt have come to despise the leisure class to which they marginally belong, with its superficial pursuit of vacuous amusements ("so bright and cheerful and *sporting* and brimming with *libido*" [113]). This includes Lou's bohemian husband Rico, who in her view is as superficial (and as insufficiently male) as the rest of the *beau monde*, which is represented as being in a state of "incipient decay" (94). Like Lawrence, Lou seeks a source of vitality to replenish the "rattling nullity" of her existence (87). It is the titular horse, St. Mawr, the "virgin" desert of the Southwest, and the novella's aboriginal characters that embody the vital, primal (and phallic) antidote to the moribund modern condition (78).

While the spiritual poverty of bourgeois European and American culture is certainly a target of critique here, Lawrence is equally concerned with the impoverishment of Indian culture and of once pristine landscapes brought about by processes of modernization, including the tourist industry. En route to America, all the fashionable tourist destinations repulse Lou and her mother: "that post-war Monte Carlo, the Riviera" is characterized as "still more depressing even than Paris" (126) and likewise Texas, with its "Cowboys right out of Zane Grey," disappoints (131). Even the characters' arrival in New Mexico—a site that has been imagined as a pocket of resistance in the sweep of globalization—is surrounded by a sense of anticlimax: "They found the fiesta over in Santa Fe: Indians, Mexicans, artists had finished their great effort to amuse and attract the tourists. *Welcome, Mr. Tourist*, said a great board on one side of the high road. And on the other side, a little nearer to the town: *Thank You, Mr. Tourist*" (132). Their post-fiesta arrival conveys the impression of belatedness that also characterizes Lawrence's essays, the sense that the attempt to escape modern life may be doomed, as these travelers follow the well-trod footsteps of those who have come before them. Looking to escape the contrivance and superficiality of everyday life, Lou and Rachel encounter a Southwest where, in James Buzard's apt description from another context, "all experience is predictable and repetitive, all cultures and objects mere 'touristy' self-parodies" (4). Lawrence's disapprobation of the staging of local culture for the benefit of tourists is here writ large in a comic mode.

Just as in his essays, in *St. Mawr*, Lawrence implies that one must look past the façade presented to the average tourist, past the veneer of modernization, to glimpse the elusive, endangered essence of indigenous culture. In depicting modern civilization as moribund and alienating, and indigenous cultures of the Southwest as vital, Lawrence replicates a distinction made by anthropologist Edward Sapir in *Dial* magazine in 1919, between "genuine" and "spurious" cultures. For Sapir, modern civilization epitomizes "spurious" culture insofar as it is fragmented, overly mechanized, and spiritually sterile, whereas American Indians embody "genuine" culture, which is "inherently harmonious, balanced, [and] self-satisfactory" (90). Lawrence operates within this framework up to a point, but in dwelling on the transformation of native culture into ethnological spectacle as I have been discussing, he presents the threat of a world where modernization is turning all cultures into spurious ones.[17] Unlike Sapir, Lawrence maps the genuine/spurious distinction onto Southwest Indians themselves.

The character Geronimo Trujillo, or Phoenix, functions as a key site in the novella for worrying about the distinction between "genuine" and "spurious" Indians. It is Mrs. Witt who patronizingly renames the Mexican-Indian groom "Phoenix," making the man interchangeable with a place, and reproducing the colonial dynamic of naming that would have been the common practice of Witt's ancestors in the antebellum plantation society of the South. Like the aboriginal Welshman Morgan Lewis, Phoenix is described as barbarically potent and animalistic; aligned with St. Mawr, and so with the primal, natural world, he sits "on a horse as if he grew there" (*St. Mawr* 20). Yet this character's hybridity troubles identity categories: son of a Mexican father and an Indian mother, he is also a shell-shocked veteran of WWI, and one who has cast his lot with American expatriates in Europe. Even before the war, historical circumstances conspired to alienate him from his indigenous past; he was educated in "one of the Indian high schools," such as Carlisle, whose mission was consistent with that of the U.S. government's then recent policy of assimilation (8).[18] Phoenix's modern pedigree thus renders him potentially spurious according to Lawrence's (and Lou's) schema; his education, travel, and fraternization with other expatriates, threaten to "absorb" him "into white civilization" (as Lawrence writes of the "red Indian" in "New Mexico") (144). His given name, Geronimo, invokes the career of the famous Chiricahua Apache prisoner of war who performed at the 1904 St. Louis World's Fair and in Buffalo Bill's Wild West. Geronimo's celebrity status as a Show Indian, and his participation in the ethnographically confused extravaganza, the Wild West, would presumably classify him among the Indians on the platform of the Santa Fe, whom Lawrence regards as disingenuously performing native identity for paying tourists.

Still, beyond the "curious film of civilization" (141), the narrative hints that Phoenix retains a glimmer of genuine Indianness, his eyes serving as the locus of an unchanged essence of indigenous identity: though "he might pass as a sunburnt citizen of any nation, . . . when you knew him, and looked right into his eyes, you saw that unforgettable glint of the Indian" (*St. Mawr* 7). Thus fetishized, Phoenix becomes a symbol of Indian identity that is in danger of being submerged or extinguished by encroachment of the Santa Fe Railway, Fred Harvey, and other manifestations of tourism and modernization.

As in his other Southwest and Mexican fiction, Lawrence envisions bridging what he regards as the "two ends of humanity"—"our own thin end, and the last dark strand from the previous, pre-white era" (qtd. in Rossman 183)—with a sexual union, in which a white woman prostrates herself before an "aboriginal phallic male" (*St. Mawr* 135):[19] Lou is "inclined to humble herself before the furtive assertiveness of this underground, 'knowing' savage" (Phoenix) who she at first imagines is superior to her trivial, spiritually vapid husband, Rico (136). Significantly, however, she vacillates, doubting this character's status as a *genuine Indian*: "In his rootlessness, his drifting, his real meaninglessness, was he different from Rico? And his childish, spellbound absorption in the motor-car, or in the moving pictures, or in an ice-cream soda—was it very different from Rico?" (136–37). That Phoenix would be interested in cars, movies, or ice-cream sodas is presented as a threat to cultural and racial categories—according to this logic, such tastes threaten to displace native ones, such that Phoenix risks losing his real Indian credentials.[20] In Lawrence's imaginary, as in that of many of his contemporaries, it is crucial that Indians stay genuine—that is to say uncorrupted by contact with white Americans and Europeans—because it is only thus that they can revive ailing modern civilization.

Behind this characterization of Phoenix seems to loom Tony Luhan, the Pueblo Indian at the hub of Mabel Dodge's salon, who served as guide on many of Lawrence's Southwest expeditions. Some were reputedly disappointed that Tony seemed so "modern": "knocking on his door in the hopes of receiving the age-old wisdom of the Indians, they were more likely to get an earful about the automobile he loved to drive" (Rudnick 47). Mabel Dodge was partly responsible for these frustrated expectations, for she represented her husband as "seer and sage," and implied that in marrying him, she had effectively gone native: "When I left the white people's world I *really* left it— it was not a mental attitude or superficial sensational gesture" (Smith 195). At the same time, she regretted having seduced Tony away from his "pattern of life," fearing that she had made him a "spoiled Indian" (qtd. in Smith 207). The word "spoiled" simultaneously infantilizes Tony and evokes a discourse of cultural ruination, where assimilation signals the destruction of traditional societies. Privately the erstwhile Greenwich Village socialite worried that by meeting her halfway in her traditions, Tony had left his own, giving up the very thing that had initially attracted her—his "otherness" (her word, qtd. in Smith 207).

Tony Luhan does not figure prominently in Lawrence's Southwest writings, perhaps because, with his expensive riding boots and Cadillac, the Tiwa tribal leader must have appeared inauthentic to Lawrence. Like Phoenix's potential namesake Geronimo, Luhan was reputed to have been a Show Indian, performing in a Wild West show on Coney Island (Rudnick 192). In becoming Americanized or cosmopolitan, Phoenix, Tony, and the Indian on the platform transgress the boundaries of what Lawrence or Mabel Dodge Luhan recognize as "Indianness." Whereas Lawrence imagines that he can pass between worlds, temporarily entering into Indian culture and then pulling back to describe it, oscillating between insider and outsider in ethnological fashion[21]—he implies that Luhan and other Indians jeopardize their identity by crossing over into mainstream American life. Writing her from England, Lawrence scolds Mabel Dodge for taking Tony too far from the pueblo because it "saps his vitality," commenting that "it would be cruel to bring Tony to Europe;" in another letter, he wonders paternalistically "how Tony will stand New York" (Dodge 278, 279, 311). If Lawrence's quest for a genuine alternative to spurious modernity requires Indians to stay put, like Tony, Phoenix functions as an unresolved challenge to such essentialist racial and cultural categories.[22]

By eschewing the commercial side of the tourist–Indian exchange and by distancing himself from other ethnological tourists as well as what he regarded as modernized Indians, Lawrence cast himself as a critical bystander, one who played no part in the process of transforming native cultures into tourist attractions. Not all writers in Taos so comfortably exempted themselves from the phenomenon. As Alice Corbin Henderson wryly noted of the increasing commercialism of the region, the Taos Art Colony seemed to have "saved the pueblos for Fred Harvey" (qtd. in Jacobs 149). In a 1924 "Fiesta edition" of the regional little magazine, *Laughing Horse*, the American writer, Witter Bynner, implicates himself in the lamentable modernizaton of Santa Fe:

> We are all doing it. We cannot help ourselves. We are attracting people here. We are advertising. We are boosting. . . . [O]ur archaeologists, artists and merchants are busily summoning Indians to Santa Fe and to Gallup for a theatrical presentation of the dances and ceremonies which have hitherto been a communal and at their best a spiritual exercise. . . . To "attract and amuse the tourists," to make a show of our town, are we cutting down and withering its beauty? Are we killing and embalming the best qualities of Santa Fe, in order that a long line may come and look? (n.p.)

In Bynner's view, artists and archaeologists join the company of merchants as "boosters" for the region. Lawrence disavows this connection, rhetorically distancing himself from other tourists. Nonetheless, his writings fully participate in the discourse of ethnographic tourism. Even Lawrence's desire to evade other tourists is anticipated by an industry that devises Harvey-car Indian Detours, promising to take tourists "off the beaten track" and provide them "intimate glimpses of Indian life otherwise not attainable" ("Harveycar Motor Cruises" 12). Figuratively donning the persona of tour guide as well as ethnographer in his Southwest writings, Lawrence implies that he, too, can provide a privileged glimpse into native life. At the limit, Lawrence's Southwest writings even function, ironically, as ambivalent advertisements; his raillery against tourists in essays such as "New Mexico," which first appeared in the travel magazine *Survey Graphic* in 1931, is offset by exalted descriptions of the landscape and people that might persuade readers to take their own "Indian Detours," following the cue of Harvey ads that share the magazine's pages.[23]

## The Past as a Compensatory Utopia

Huxley had little patience with contemporaries who sought alternatives to civilized life in what he regarded as fanciful perceptions of primitive societies. In a 1931 essay, he pokes fun at ethnological tourists, remarking that of late "the few remaining primitive peoples of the earth have achieved a prodigious popularity among those with wishes to fulfill" (*Music* 129). Implicating Lawrence's writings in particular, Huxley proclaims that "the past has become a compensatory Utopia. . . . With every advance of industrial civilization the savage past will be more and more appreciated, and the cult of D. H. Lawrence's *Dark God* may be expected to spread through an ever-widening circle of worshippers" (*Music* 128, 131). In contrast to Lawrence, Huxley envisioned primitive societies in largely Hobbesian terms, and declared unambiguously that it was futile to try to go back to what both writers imagined was a prior evolutionary stage. The two writers come at the vogue of the Indian, then, from very different angles: Lawrence, seeking to penetrate the touristy façade to connect with ancient traditions, and Huxley, rejecting the idea of establishing such a connection as mere Romantic idealism.

While debunking the construction of the Southwest as a primitive utopia, *Brave New World* simultaneously debunks a competing model of ideal society endorsed by World's Fairs, which seemed to provide "a map to future perfection" in the shape of a world made safer, easier, more efficient, and more enjoyable by technology and science (Rydell 219). Conjoining these two visions was not unique: at the 1915 Panama-California Expo, organizers situated a model farm, complete with modern farm equipment, a fruit-bearing orchard, and electricity, alongside the Painted Desert exhibit displaying Southwest Indians. The juxtaposition was intended, in the words of one of the fair organizers, to provide "a sermon" on progress: to reinforce the impression of Native Americans as "the vanished although romantic past and Anglo-America as the triumphant future" (Kropp, *Great Southwest* 38). The structure of Huxley's *Brave New World* reproduces the logic of the Panama-California Expo by juxtaposing the Savage Reservation and the Fordian new world. Rather than an idealized, pastoral representation of "vanishing America," however, the Savage Reservation is defined by its harshness, dirt, and supposedly barbaric customs; a vacation there superficially reinforces the desirability of the new world with its hygiene, efficiency, and emphasis on pleasure. If, as with the Panama-Pacific, the ideological message is that Indians are quaint but that progress and conquest are inevitable and good, the shallow character Lenina gets the message: "progress *is* lovely, isn't it?" (77). Huxley ironizes this response, subverting the rosy narrative of progress and cheery futurism of the World's Fairs, by making the hygienic, efficient, hyper-technological new world a nightmare society.

When John the Savage visits Eton on his tour of the New World, he learns that the reservation where he was raised is regarded as "a place which, owing to unfavourable climatic or geological conditions, or poverty of natural resources, has not been worth the expense of civilizing" (124). Given the harsh conditions of the environment and the "civilized" characters' derogatory view of the natives' way of life (the warden tells Lenina and Bernard that the Indians are "absolute savages" who "still preserve their repulsive habits and customs" [79]), the idea of taking a holiday on a New Mexican "Savage Reservation" is made to seem ludicrous in *Brave New World*. By representing the reservation as a popular tourist destination, Huxley mocks the contemporary craze for travel to the Southwest: Lenina eagerly accepts Bernard's invitation to New Mexico, explaining that she "always wanted to see a savage reservation," and the Director of Hatcheries and Conditioning tells Bernard, "I had the same idea as you.... Wanted to have a look at the savages. Got a permit for New Mexico and went there for my summer holiday" (33, 96).

Surrounded by a straight fence that is said to represent "the geometrical symbol of triumphant human purpose," the reservation is constructed as a prison or zoo (80). That the "triumphant purpose" of the fence is forcible containment is made clear by the pilot's sinister pronouncement, "There is no escape from a Savage Reservation," a warning he means to mute by adding that the savages are "perfectly tame.... They've got enough experience of gas bombs to know that they mustn't play any tricks" (78, 81). The fence serves not only to contain its inhabitants, but also to frame them: following Lawrence, Huxley highlights the exploitative dynamics of confining indigenous people to reservations and then exposing them to the inquisitive gaze of the dominant society. As in the Joy Zone of the World's Fair or in Harvey's Southwest, on Huxley's Savage Reservation, native life is viewed as entertainment: "Everything they do is funny," the pilot remarks pointing at "a sullen young savage" whose oppressed demeanor belies this statement (81). Huxley's characters regard the quotidian life of the "savages" as a tableau for their observation: sighting an "almost naked Indian" climbing down a ladder, Lenina grips Bernard's arm and urges him, "Look" (84)—the single word highlighting the principle activity of the ethnological tourist. Whereas the tourists in Lawrence's essays thrill to exotic otherness, Huxley's character recoils in disgust, repulsed by the man's wrinkled face and toothless mouth, an anti-image of new world youthfulness.

Yet if both writers satirize tourists who regard native life as spectacle, Huxley does not share Lawrence's faith that behind the tourist façade lurks a genuine culture worth reclaiming. For Lawrence, fencing in indigenous cultures is a metaphor for civilization's unfortunate repression of its instinctual side: "'Till now, in sheer terror of ourselves, we have turned our backs on the jungle, fenced it in with an enormous entanglement of barbed wire and declared it did not exist ... Yet unless we proceed to connect ourselves up with our own primeval sources, we shall degenerate" ("The Novel and Feelings" 757). In theory, if not in practice, Lawrence believed that tearing down the fence to connect with indigenous cultures was the last hope for a decadent civilization. In *Beyond the Mexique Bay*, Huxley explicitly rejects Lawrence's primitivism: "When man became an intellectual and spiritual being, he paid for his new privileges with a treasure of intuitions, of emotional spontaneity, of sensuality still innocent of all self-consciousness. Lawrence [mistakenly] thought that we should abandon the new privileges in return for the old treasure" (261). In essays such as "Indians and an Englishman," Lawrence hardly seems like one ready to abandon the privileges of his subject position as an Englishman; his fantasy of connection with Indians is wholly reliant on an implied distance between Indians and Englishmen that he carefully enforces. Still, for Lawrence, a rapprochement between "civilized" and "primitive" life is at least desirable, whereas for Huxley, giving up (or fencing in) "primeval sources" is the price of civilization.

From Huxley's largely anti-primitivist and sometimes xenophobic standpoint, there's no compelling reason to want to reconnect with actual primitive cultures, though he felt that certain facets of pretechnological societies could be incorporated into modern life, as discussed further below. In his travel writing, Huxley counteracts rhetoric that idealizes the "savage past" with pejorative characterizations of indigenous people, such as his description of the Mexican village, Miauhuatlán, as "the deep-rooted weed of primitive human life" (*Beyond* 207). Huxley's attitude during this period has been described as "elitist" and "provincial," despite extensive world travel (Holmes 191); a member of the British Eugenic society, he was not particularly interested in transcending cultural barriers.

Huxley invokes and then subverts the Lawrencian idea of connecting with a primitive past ostensibly embodied in Indian cultures, by showing the convergence of the traditions of the new world and those of the Savage Reservation—hence in Huxley's economy, showing that "the civilized" behave like "savages." At the Reservation's summer festival, Lenina at first "abandon[s] herself" to the primal beat of the drums (86), which reminds her of the orgiastic chanting of the new world's Solidarity Service, a ceremony described in similar terms (65). Attraction becomes repulsion when a "ghastly troop" of Indians emerges "[h]ideously masked or painted out of all semblance of humanity," flinging snakes into the middle of the square, while the dancers circle "snakily, with a soft undulating movement" (87). While many details of this scene (and of that of the Solidarity Service) resemble Lawrence's representation of the Hopi Snake Dance, Huxley debunks Lawrencian primitivism by blending the relatively pacifist details of Lawrence's description with a rendition of a seemingly violent flagellation ritual.[24]

The Hopi Snake Dance merges with a Zuñi initiation ritual when a man in a coyote mask begins to flagellate an eighteen-year-old boy. The scene is conjured graphically from Lenina's horrified perspective:

> The coyote-man raised his whip; there was a long moment of expectancy, then a swift movement, the whistle of the lash and its loud flat-sounding impact on the flesh. The boy's body quivered; but he made no sound . . . The coyote struck again, again; and at every blow at first a gasp, and then a deep groan went up from the crowd. . . . The blood was streaming. . . . Suddenly Lenina covered her face with her hands and began to sob. "Oh, stop them, stop them!" she implored. But the whip fell and fell inexorably. (88)

The sanguinary description of the whipping derives not just from Huxley's imagination, but also, in part, from the language of contemporary ethnographic accounts. In the 1929–1930 Smithsonian *Annual Report of the U. S. American Ethnology Bureau* that Huxley is likely to have read, Ruth Bunzel stresses the severity of the two-step initiation into the Zuñi Katcina Cult: "At the first ceremony they are severely whipped by the katcina priests to inspire them with awe for these creatures. There is a second more severe thrashing at the second ceremony" (518). In the same publication, Leslie White describes the priests "brandishing" whips in a "menacing" manner, as another participant exclaims, "Look at the blood, how it's running down!" (73). While these ethnographers record the intensity of the thrashing, they go on to emphasize the cultural purpose behind the practice: Bunzel explains, "The katcinas whip to install awe for the supernatural, but also to remove sickness and contamination. The whipping of katcinas is a blessing. It is administered with the formula, 'May you be blessed with seeds'" (518). If Huxley reproduces these accounts' more violent imagery, he also echoes the ethnographic impulse to offer cultural justification: as John the Savage explains, he wants to participate in the ritual for "the sake of the pueblo—to make the rain come and the corn grow" (89).

The representation of the flagellation ceremony in *Brave New World* cuts in two ways, which illustrate the complicated relationship between Huxley's and Lawrence's overlapping, yet contrasting, views of ethnological tourism. On the one hand, Huxley emulates Lawrence by juxtaposing the misguided response of ethnological tourists who regard native life as spectacular entertainment with what is posited as an insider's voice that explains the indigenous meaning of the ceremony. This point is reinforced during John's new world tour, when, visiting Eton, he stumbles on a slide show about Reservation life: to John's puzzlement and humiliation, students greet images of the flagellation ritual with laughter (124). The students' irreverent response anticipates the novel's climactic scene, where a crowd of English sightseers, carried away by the thrill of the spectacle, goad John into flagellating Lenina to death, crying "Do the whipping stunt!" (196). By showing that the flagellation ceremony has an indigenous meaning that is lost on the observers from the new world, Huxley replays Lawrence's satire of the ignorance of ethnological tourists.

On the other hand, despite the pretense of openness to the indigenous meaning of the ceremony in this scene, the novel is far from pushing the reader to the conclusion that the primitive society offers a viable alternative to the new world. In his 1946 foreword to *Brave New World*, Huxley represents the Savage's self-flagellation in the novel's final pages as a "retreat from sanity" (xiv)—implying that it is an irrational cultural practice indicating recidivism to a prior evolutionary state. In imbuing the scene with gothic overtones and turning flagellation into a narrative motif, Huxley sensationalizes the ceremony, rather than demystifying it as Lawrence does the Snake Dance. Seen in this light, the specter of the whipping ceremony contributes to Huxley's debunking of Lawrence and his followers' supposedly sentimental view of "savages." While the Reservation houses "old world" values of motherhood, monogamy, and reverence for tradition, it is also a locus of squalor, what is represented as superstition, and sanguinary customs. "Queer" is Lenina's word for it, the same word Huxley uses in the 1946 foreword, where he regrets having offered the Savage "only two alternatives, an insane life in Utopia, or the life of a primitive in an Indian village, a life more human in some respects, but in others hardly less queer and abnormal" (xiv). If the new world and the reservation are equally queer it is because they are equally untenable for Huxley: civilization has run amuck, in part, because it has degenerated into a state of savagery. This obviously puts Huxley in a very different camp from Lawrence, who thinks the way forward for civilization is through a detour to the "savage" past.

Like Lawrence, Huxley was fascinated by contemporary ethnographies, though he was less interested finally in the cultures they represented than in the mode of looking at the world that they suggested. In 1929 and 1930 Huxley read Margaret Mead and Bronislaw Malinowski respectively, both of whose texts figure significantly in *Brave New World*. With irony, he characterizes Mead's *Coming of Age in Samoa* as "an account of savages more puritanical than New England Calvinists in the seventeenth century," and jokes that Malinowski's *Sexual Life of Savages* has inspired him "to write a companion treatise on the *Sexual Life of Gentlemen and Ladies*," adding, "There'd be much odder customs to record than among those extraordinarily rational Trobrianders" (*Letters* 343, 314). This insistence on the superior reason and stricter morality of "Neolithic savages" (*Letters* 326) should be read in the voice of a satirist, whose real agenda is to point up the foibles of his own culture rather than to seriously investigate the beliefs of others. In *Beyond the Mexique Bay*, Huxley reiterates the idea of turning an ethnographic eye back on his own culture: having spent numerous days (and pages) observing the curious customs of Central Americans, he imagines the humiliation of having a party of Mexicans look "on in observant silence while I went through the curious old custom, say, of taking tea in Bloomsbury" (144). Huxley recognizes that the cultural voyeur's binoculars may be turned around, such that English cultural practices become a spectacle for foreign eyes.

In *Brave New World*, Huxley finds an opportunity to write his mock ethnography of modern society, with a particular focus on modern sex lives. The Controller Mustapha Mond contrasts the "appalling dangers of [old fashioned] family life," encompassing misery, sadism, and chastity, with the relative ease of the social structures and sexual practices of the new world. In defending new world sexuality, he cites as model societies both "the savages of Samoa," whose children played "promiscuously among the hibiscus blossoms," and the Trobriand Islanders, among whom fatherhood was supposedly unknown (28). The analogy between Samoan and Trobriand "savages" and the characters of the new world is reinforced by the description of "civilized" children, "naked in the warm June sunshine," sexually frolicking next to blooming shrubs and murmuring bees, and, a few pages later, "naked children furtive in the undergrowth" (21, 31). These passages echo Mead's description of "lusty" Samoans engaged in casual romantic "trysts" among palm fronds and hibiscus blossoms, in the opening pages of *Coming of Age in Samoa* (12–13). The tie between the "savages" studied by Mead and Malinowski and the people of the new world is also reinforced by references to climate: in the new world, embryos are "hatched" in a "tropical" environment, and soma offers an escape to what sounds like the "tropical paradise" of modern ads: "the warm, the richly coloured, the infinitely friendly world of a *soma*-holiday" (7, 60). In

*Brave New World*, England has gone tropical and, paradoxically, given the reign of technology and science in the new world, England has gone native.

While the playful analogy turns the English into ethnographic others, enacting Huxley's fantasy of writing a mock ethnography of curious English customs, the point is not finally that all cultures are relative, or that we are "one family of man" with negligible differences among us. Instead, conceived in an increasingly outmoded evolutionary framework, the formulation is meant to broadcast an attitude of irony concerning the new world's dismissal of traditional family values, the abrogation of monogamy and of fatherhood marking the pathetic descent of the citizens of the new world into primitive irresponsibility. Gesturing to the children of the new world naked in the undergrowth and concluding his discourse on the cultures of Samoa and the Trobriand Islands, the Controller declares triumphantly, "Extremes ... meet. For the good reason that they were made to meet" (28). Huxley adopts this idea of wedding the two worlds of primitive and civilized societies from Lawrence—for whom such a union is a fantasy, while for Huxley, it is a misguided quest. Extremes meet most dramatically in the characterization of John the Savage, born ignominiously to a new world mother and raised on the Reservation.

### John the Savage Goes to London

Replaying and in some senses ironically reversing a long tradition of native display in England, which was at the height of its popularity while Huxley was coming of age, John the Savage is brought back to London where he is exhibited as the civilized-man-brought-up-in-savagery. Proposing to bring John back to London, Bernard tells Mustapha Mond, "I ventured to think ... that your fordship might find the matter of sufficient scientific interest" (108). As in the human showcases of the World's Fairs and of Harvey's Southwest, the aims of entertainment overwhelm those of science. John's mother Linda, in self-imposed exile for having committed the obscenity of natural childbirth, is exhibited in a parody of native display that draws attention to its dehumanizing effects: "There was a gasp, a murmur of astonishment and horror, a young woman screamed. . . . Bloated, sagging, and among those firm youthful bodies, those undistorted faces, a strange and terrifying monster of middle-agedness, Linda advanced into the room" (115). While Linda is displayed as a grotesque, John becomes a star, like Geronimo, who purportedly cashed in on his stardom by selling autographed photographs of himself to tourists. Touring the new world, visiting its institutions and inquiring about its customs, John is an ad hoc ethnographer, but soon becomes a traveling tourist site, drawing droves of unwanted observers wherever he goes.

When John becomes fed up with being the object of both popular and scientific interest ("I'm damned if I'll go on being experimented with," 186), he flees to a lighthouse in Surrey, where he briefly—and seemingly incoherently, given my reading of Huxley's view of primitivism developed thus far—returns to some of the ways of the Reservation, enjoying the simple pleasure of making bows and arrows to kill rabbits, for instance. Indeed, John seems to have traded what Sapir would label spurious culture for a way of life that is represented as potentially more genuine. His retreat to nature, prayer, and handcrafts gestures toward a way of life that is integrated and meaningful—an antidote, though an ineffectual one, to the hyper-specialization of the new world. While Huxley explicitly rejects the idea of returning to primitive origins, he allows that it may be possible "to introduce a salutary element of primitivism into our civilized and industrialized way of life"; specifically, to emulate the "wholeness" of primitive societies, while retaining "the material and intellectual advantages resulting from specialization" (*Beyond* 214, 217). Huxley's travel writings and his send-up of Mead's Samoans in *Brave New World* suggest that he wished to divorce this facet of "primitivism" from primitive cultures themselves, which he regarded according to well-worn primitivist clichés as unhygienic, childlike, superstitious, incapable of individuality, and so forth. It is significant that John does not return to the Reservation: it is the idea of a harmonious, integrated existence, not Indian society itself, that Huxley's protagonist fleetingly, and futilely, attempts to recuperate.

Again, this points to an important distinction between Lawrence and Huxley: Lawrence finds intrinsic value in Indian cultures such as the Hopi, whereas for Huxley, they have value only insofar as they can help to reveal or amend the deficiencies of modern life. Huxley explains his limited, theoretical interest in primitive cultures in this way in his travelogue *Beyond Mexique Bay*: "Most of the little we know about the anthropology of civilized peoples is the fruit of inquiries into the nature of primitive societies. Central America, being just Europe in miniature and with the lid off, is the ideal laboratory in which to study the behavior of the Great Powers" (62). Huxley actually borrows the metaphor of the primitive culture as a "laboratory" for studying "ourselves" from anthropology: Mead makes much the same point in her *Coming of Age in Samoa*, from which he repeatedly quotes in his writings of this period. But for Huxley (unlike for Lawrence or Mead), "savages" are not interesting in themselves—only as a means of shedding light on "civilized" problems.

Without any social framework to sustain him, John's attempt to salvage the "salutary elements" of Reservation life fails, and the Savage becomes the ultimate media event. Tourists arrive en masse, wielding cameras like the spectators ridiculed in Lawrence's Southwest essays; insatiable voyeurs, they pursue John like game as he retreats "in the posture of an animal at bay" (195). Huxley's violent metaphor of the hunt is sustained in the characterization of the reporter, Darwin Bonaparte—whose name fuses the persona of naturalist with that of conqueror. The "Feely Corporation's most expert big game photographer," he successfully "tracks" John, hiding in an oak tree to get clandestine footage of the savage's rituals of atonement (194). As if invoking the image of Lawrence behind the leaf-screen, Bonaparte becomes a warped version of the ethnologist, looting cultural secrets. John's appropriated image is turned into a spectacle for mass consumption when the footage is used to create a sensational, comic *feely* called *The Savage of Surrey*. The commodification of John's decontextualized image burlesques the impulse to mass produce and sell images of indigenous people, for example in picture post cards, Westerns, or the merchandise of the Harvey Company.

Much as Lenina and Bernard are encouraged to regard Indians on the reservation as inhuman, these tourists view the Savage as an animal in a zoo, "staring, laughing, clicking their cameras, throwing (as to an ape) peanuts" (195). Huxley pushes the "greedy curiosity" of the thousands of spectators who long to see "*live rattlesnakes*" in Lawrence's essays up a few notches, turning his sightseers into a blood-thirsty mob who cry in unison to see "the whipping stunt"—a de-sacralized ritual, turned into a tourist event. The tourists are shown to be the real savages, according to a prejudicial perspective that considers primitive cultures to be driven by instinct and mindless collectivity rather than intellect and individuality, when they descend into their own rituals, which echo those of the Indian tribe: "Then suddenly somebody started singing 'Orgy-porgy' and, in a moment, they had all caught up the refrain and, singing, had begun to dance. Orgy-porgy, round and round and round, beating one another in six-eighth time. Orgy porgy" (198). The frenzied crowd helps goad the Savage into flagellating Lenina to death, then taking his own life.

While the novel joins Lawrence in savaging ethnological tourists, it rejects Lawrencian primitivism. "The whipping stunt"—shorn of its cultural associations—signifies a descent into irrationality and barbarism, so that the novel ends with a specter of what Jenny Sharpe has called in another context "Eurosavagery," where the grossest acts of savagery are perpetrated by those who are supposedly "civilized" (6). These qualities bleed back into the original cultural practice, such that the customs of the Reservation seem deserving of their name ("savage"). Thus the novel, in a sense, is anti-modern *and* anti-primitive, at once satirizing the Kodak-wielding ethnological tourists of Huxley's and Lawrence's day by literalizing the symbolic violence of cultural voyeurism, and counteracting romantic stereotypes of primitive cultures with equally (and probably more damning) stereotypes of savagery.

## Conclusion

However much the image of the modern fieldworker as lone discoverer of a pristine culture suggests that ethnology and tourism are antithetical, the texts I've discussed suggest that in the Southwest in the 1920s and 1930s, these domains were linked in significant discursive and institutional ways. The Southwest Pueblos were not only a popular tourist destination in this period, but also "the most-visited venue" for ethnographic research in America (Stocking 220). Whether directly employed by the Harvey Company or working under some other institutional or academic auspices, ethnographers must have served as another group of boosters for the region, inadvertently encouraging tourists to come and observe the local people, whose daily lives were deemed as engrossing as their colorful ceremonies. In Southwest ethnographies, as in Harvey ads and ethnological exhibits, Indians are depicted as sights to be seen, like the famed landscape of Taos or the Painted Desert. In Huxley's depiction of John the Savage as a simultaneous object of scientific and popular scrutiny, and in the melding of the personae of tour guide and ethnologist in Lawrence's essays, the lines between ethnology and tourism blur as well. Huxley and Lawrence are joined in their project of debunking ethnological tourists and, to an extent, ethnologists, but whereas Lawrence installs himself and his protagonists as sensitive observers of indigenous cultures in contrast to the entertainment-seeking tourists, Huxley insists that the motives that inform such a quest are misguided—that primitive life is not a utopian state to be recovered.

While both writers were attuned to the dynamics of cultural observation, from our later historical vantage point, it is easy to see the limitations of their perspectives as well. Lawrence could perceive that *other* tourists, brandishing cameras, might be galling to the Indians they observed, but in endeavoring to differentiate his clandestine form of looking from that of the less discrete observers, he impossibly wished away the similarities of his own position and that of the tourists he satirized.[25] Huxley makes no apology for sharing in what he identifies as the modern predilection for observing others, a relationship he characterizes as a "squint through the binoculars and then good-bye" (*Beyond* 142). However, if Huxley labored less strenuously to differentiate himself from the binocular-wielding tourists both writers mock than Lawrence did, perhaps this is because he had less at stake, for he did not seek intimate knowledge of the indigenous cultures he encountered.

As differently motivated as their criticisms of ethnological tourism were, Lawrence and Huxley shared the premise, common to their time, that indigenous cultures were vanishing before their eyes. Under the potentially intrusive gaze of outsiders, is it inevitable that local cultures will be destroyed, turned by the tourist industry into marketable simulacra of themselves? In a 1996 study of the Wild West shows, the historian L. G. Moses counters the impression that commercializing Indian cultures in the Wild West heyday led to the erosion of traditions: given the prevailing governmental policy of assimilation, he maintains, "the performances actually helped to preserve traditional native culture, even while acquiescing in its transformation into a popularization—even parody—of itself" (qtd. in Kasson 164). In another context, Michel Picard has recently shifted the terms of the debate productively. In his study on Balinese culture, Picard's concern is not whether tourism destroys or preserves, but rather, the way it contributes to the reshaping of native culture. Picard concludes that the Balinese have been "active subjects who [creatively] construct representations of their culture to attract tourists," such that tourism in Bali has become *part of* Balinese culture, participating in "an ongoing process of cultural invention" (46, 47).

Similarly, Southwest Indians seem to have self-consciously tailored their identity in the context of tourism, as suggested by the response of a group of Pueblo Indians to a 1976 court case that ultimately hinged on the question of cultural identity. As Deirdre Evans-Pritchard explains, Indians selling their wares along the Portal of the Museum of New Mexico's Palace of Governors in Santa Fe Plaza continue to draw hundreds of thousands of tourists each year, who regard the Indian craftspeople and merchants, as in Lawrence's day, as "a world-famous landmark" (287). The court case ensued when the museum evicted white artists Paul and Sarah Livingston from the Portal, and they in turn sued the museum for discriminating against them on the basis of race (and lost, on the basis that the museum, as a preserver of culture, had the right to discriminate on a *cultural*, rather than racial, basis). To bolster the museum's case, Pueblo Indians collected tourists' signatures to vouch for their unique right to sell wares in the plaza, in a battle that they represented as one to "retain their identity" (289). What is interesting about this case for my discussion is that the basis for authentic Indian identity cited in this case was one forged in the context of touristic encounters. "The Indian who sells you baskets" whom Lawrence derided as a figure of the commercialization of indigenous culture has become, this case suggests, a new standard for what Dean MacCannell would call a "recreated" ethnic identity. In this way, the Portal case suggests that cultural identities may be more responsive, adaptable, and resilient than either Huxley or Lawrence had reason to believe.

## Notes

I wish to acknowledge the valuable input of a number of people at different stages in the evolution of this project: Celia Marshik, Eric Aronoff, Matt Herman, Steven Rubenstein, Marta Weigle, Tomas Jaehn, Art Bachrach; the anonymous reviewers at *MFS*; and my colleagues at Ohio University including Joseph McLaughlin, Jeremy Webster, Johnnie Wilcox, and Andrew Escobedo. I am also grateful to the Ohio University Research Council (OURC) for awarding me a grant for archival research in New Mexico, and to the external reviewers for this grant, Melba Cuddy-Keane, Marc Manganaro, and James Buzard.

1. For example, in "Lawrence in doubt: a theory of the 'other' and its collapse," Howard Booth argues that from 1917 to 1925 Lawrence oscillated between affirming and repudiating American Indians as a source of renewal for moribund civilization, embracing primitive cultures theoretically, but rejecting them in practice, in racist and sometimes imperialist terms. Mariana Torgovnick points out that Lawrence's definition of "the primitive" "furnishes no consistent political or anthropological thematic," but lapses into primitivist caricature in representing groups he credits, at least theoretically, with complexity and nuance (142).

2. In *Routes: Travel and Translation in the Late Twentieth Century*, James Clifford suggests that the circumscribed, pure, authentic, pristine culture that is the object of modern anthropological investigation (as evidenced in the influential ethnographies of Bronislaw Malinowski and Margaret Mead) is largely a mythical construction, obscuring the many links that connect all cultures, including modes of transportation and translation.

3. My use of the term is informed by Guy Debord's definition of the spectacle as "a social relation among people, mediated by images" (4), and in this regard, I am following Leah Dilworth who has discussed the Southwest of the 1920s, as mediated by the Fred Harvey Company, as tourist spectacle (68). I intend the term in a more general sense as well—referring to that which is put on display in a manner that heightens its strangeness. This sense captures the emphasis in both ethnology and tourism on observing the exotic.

4. I am referring to Langston Hughes's "When the Negro was in Vogue." In this well-known retrospective essay about the Harlem Renaissance, Hughes contemplates what it was like to be in the spotlight as white customers poured into places like the Cotton Club and Jungle Alley in Harlem, and "strangers were given the best ringside tables to sit and stare at the Negro customers—like amusing animals in a zoo." He makes the point that the "ordinary Negro" did not profit from the Harlem "vogue"—a point applicable to the vogue of the Southwest Indian as well (152).

5. Lawrence died in March 1930, and Huxley began collecting the letters later that year and continued the project into 1931; they would be published in September of 1932. *Brave New World* was written from May to August of 1931. In addition to Lawrence's writing, in a 1963 interview, Huxley relates, "I had no trouble finding my way around the English part of *Brave New World*, but I had to do an enormous amount of reading up on New Mexico, because I'd never been there. I read all sorts of Smithsonian Reports on the place and then did the best I could to imagine it" ("Interview" 198). Firchow observes that the "Smithsonian Reports" are the *Annual Reports of the US American Ethnology Bureau to the Secretary of the Smithsonian Institute*.

6. Lawrence and Huxley were close friends from 1926 until Lawrence's death in March 1930. In *Aldous Huxley: Satire and Structure*, James Meckier argues that during his "Lawrencian interlude," Huxley based a string of characters on his mentor, Lawrence, including Mark Rampion in *Point Counter Point* (1928) and John the Savage in *Brave New World*. Ultimately, Meckier argues, Huxley repudiates the Lawrencian primitive and its worship of "phallic consciousness"; for Huxley, "intellect and erudition would always take precedence over his emotions and intuition"

(122). Peter Firchow argues that Huxley suggests the impossibility of Lawrence's fantasy of renewing a moribund "civilization" by tapping into "primitive" culture, through the self-immolation of the character, John the Savage, who symbolically represents the union of the two. See also David Bradshaw's introduction to the 1984 Faber and Faber edition of *Brave New World*.

7. Some explanation is required for my use of "ethnological tourism" rather than "cultural" or "ethnic tourism," both commonly employed in tourism studies. "Cultural tourism" construes culture in a broad sense, embracing travel to the Lake District to buy Beatrix Potter paraphernalia as well as travel to Waikiki to watch staged performances of fire ceremonies. (For elaboration of these terms, see Chris Rojek and John Urry.) I use "ethnological" rather than "cultural" to refer more narrowly to tourism that seeks so-called premodern or traditional cultures as its main object, following in the footsteps of modern ethnologists such as Ruth Bunzel and Margaret Mead. "Ethnic tourism"—defined by Van den Berghe and Keyes as that where "the prime attraction is the cultural exoticism of the local population and its artifacts (clothing, architecture, theater, music, dance, plastic arts)"—is closer to the meaning I intend (345). I employ "ethnological" rather than "ethnic," however, to emphasize the potential bond between the ethnologist and the tourist, figures who often work in the same settings and share some of the same objectives, most notably aiming to see "natives as they really live." A final note: Though the terms "ethnology," "ethnography," and "anthropology" acquire different connotations later in the twentieth century, I use "ethnology" to refer to studies of cultures conducted in the field, as opposed to armchair theorizing. This usage is consistent with professional nomenclature of the day, as in the *US American Ethnology Bureau*, and with Lawrence's and Huxley's respective usages of the term.

8. See Dean MacCannell and James Buzard.

9. On postmodern ethnography and self-reflexivity, see George E. Marcus and Michael M. J. Fischer, *Anthropology as Cultural Critique: An Experimental Moment in the Human Sciences*, and James Clifford, *The Predicament of Culture: Twentieth-Century Ethnography, Literature, and Art*.

10. The term "anachronistic space" is Anne McClintock's (40–42). See Dilworth's *Imagining Indians in the Southwest* for an analysis of the Columbian discovery motif in Fred Harvey advertisements (120–24).

11. The Los Angeles–Chicago line of the Atchison Topeka Santa Fe was completed in 1887, and the Santa Fe (together with Fred Harvey) began its advertising blitz around the turn of the century; tourism tapered off during the Depression (Weigle and Fiore 10). My discussion of the ATSF Railway/Fred Harvey Company is greatly indebted to a stimulating, well-researched collection of essays edited by Marta Weigle and Barbara Babcock, called *The Great Southwest of the Fred Harvey Company and the Santa Fe Railway*.

12. In "The Indian-Detour in Willa Cather's Southwestern Novels," Caroline M. Woidat similarly situates Cather's writing in relation to tourist advertisements produced by the Santa Fe Railway and the Fred Harvey Company, making a compelling case that Cather's fiction echoes the conceits of the tourist literature (and specifically, the preference for the "vanished Native Americans [of the Mesa-Verde Cliff Dwellings] to those still living"), even as Cather attempted to distance herself and her characters from tourism per se (30). Whereas Woidat focuses on the discovery motif in the ads and in Cather's fiction, which, she argues, represents Anglo-Americans enacting a pioneer fantasy in "a sanitized version of

American history" (35), I focus here on the intersection of ethnographic and touristic discourses, which collaborate in the transformation of indigenous cultures into objects-to-be-observed.

13. Though Lawrence would insist that he was "no ethnologist" ("Indians and an Englishman" 95), he frequently positions himself in his Southwest essays as an authoritative observer, explicating indigenous customs and ceremonies in ethnographic fashion. Moreover, the disclaimer may imply a critique of ethnographic practice, rather than the false modesty of an amateur. In "Indians and Entertainment" (1924), Lawrence charges ethnologists such as Adolph Bandelier, author of the ethnological romance, *The Delight Makers*, of "sentimentalizing" Indians to the same extent as the general public, and calls for writers to "debunk the Indian" ("Indians and Entertainment" 103). Hence "I am no ethnologist" may imply "I am not one of that sentimentalizing crowd" rather than "I am not a qualified observer."

14. The Hopi Snake Dance frequently gets "top billing" in Harveycar and other tourism brochures for the Southwest.

15. Twenty-one million visitors attended the concurrently running Panama-California Expo in San Diego and Panama-Pacific in San Francisco. One ad for the Santa Fe Railway ran "Plan now to go and visit the *Grand Canyon* of *Arizona* on the way" (qtd. in Kropp 39); conjoining these destinations in this fashion makes the virtual fair locales such as *The Painted Desert* functionally indistinguishable from real Southwest locations such as the Grand Canyon. Not only did the virtual Southwest serve as an advertisement for "real" travel to New Mexico and Arizona, but World's Fairs more generally have been regarded as providing "a seminal force behind the rise of mass tourism" (Rydell and Gwin 1): Greenhalgh asserts that World's Fairs were the "largest gatherings of people—war or peace—of all time" (1).

16. The St. Louis Fair of 1904 scheduled performances of the Hopi Snake Dance in the Midway amusement zone as well, while presenting a model government-run Indian school in the education zone. In the wake of the 1887 Dawes Act, the St. Louis-Expo organizers used the structure of the fair to implicitly endorse the official government policy of assimilation, while undermining the value and seriousness of traditional Hopi culture. See Kasson for a history of governmental policy toward Native Americans.

17. Several of Lawrence's essays discussed here, including "Indians and an Englishman" (1923), were also first published in *Dial* magazine. Whether Lawrence read Sapir or not, the genuine/spurious distinction is one that animates both his and Huxley's Southwest writings. The trivial *beau monde* of England depicted in *St. Mawr* is suggestive of *spurious culture*, whereas the Indians of Lawrence's Southwest essays and fiction, who have stubbornly maintained the ways of their ancient race, in Lawrence's eyes, exhibit the attributes of *genuine culture*.

18. According to Kasson, institutions like the Carlisle Indian Boarding School took Native Americans from their parents to Americanize them, "teaching them trades, deportment, and the English language" (164)—explicitly aiming to eradicate traditional culture. In a letter to Catherine Carswell from New Mexico (18 May 1924), Lawrence makes his anti-assimilationist position clear: "There is something savage, unbreakable in the spirit of the place out here—the Indians drumming and yelling at our camp-fire in the evening—But they'll be wiped out, too, I expect—schools and education will finish them" (*Letters* 602).

19. In *St. Mawr*, not only does Lou Witt fantasize about a union with Phoenix to regenerate her desiccated culture, but also her mother proposes to (and is

rejected by) the Welsh groom, Lewis, another "aboriginal" male in the novella. In *The Plumed Serpent*, Lawrence simultaneously weds the races and denigrates a "cocksure" modern woman by having his protagonist, the Irish woman Kate Leslie, marry a "pure [Mexican] Indian" Cipriano, who ultimately remains inscrutable to her. By marrying him, she is made to bow down before the phallic mystery of the indigenous god Quetzalcoatl with which he has associated himself, to be debased (feeling "condemned to go through these strange ordeals") and, ultimately, to be psychologically annihilated.

20. The assumption that real Indians unswervingly follow traditional customs, eschewing mainstream American professions, education, and culture, is still one being contested, as demonstrated by the campaign launched by the American Indian College Fund in March 2001 to challenge the stereotype of the static, traditional Indian. This campaign features images of American Indians engaged in study or in a range of respected professions (such as medicine or the law) with the caption "Have You Ever Seen a Real Indian?" The campaign is designed to counteract public ignorance about Indian people, who are too often regarded, according to the organization's website, as "extinct" or "museum relics," stereotypes that have their roots in the rhetoric of ethnological salvage this essay explores.

21. James Clifford describes the participant-observation method of fieldwork in these terms in *Predicament of Culture*, 34.

22. In *Our America*, Walter Benn Michaels argues that in a category of fiction he calls "nativist modernism," the refusal to procreate functions as a means of policing racial and cultural identities. However, while the aboriginal males' refusal to couple with white American females in *St. Mawr* does defend the boundary between Indians and whites (in accordance with Michaels' argument about nativist modernism), withdrawing the threat of miscegenation does not clear the muddied cultural waters in the text: because Phoenix is modernized like the Harvey Indians, he remains of dubious cultural authenticity for Lawrence.

23. Woidat has demonstrated that Cather's writings functioned in this way. She notes, "even Cather's archbishop [from *Death Comes for the Archbishop* (1927)] became a kind of advertisement: the Bishop's Lodge Hotel at Santa Fe enjoyed such rich profits from his story that the managers offered her unlimited free accommodations" (note 18, page 47).

24. In his 1946 Preface, Huxley explains that the flagellation ritual is half "fertility cult and half *Penitente* ferocity" (xiv); thus critics have understood Huxley to blend Lawrence's description of the Hopi Snake Dance and ethnographic descriptions from "the Smithsonian reports" (see note 5 above) with depictions of the flagellation rites of the Christian *Penitents* in New Mexico. Though I am indebted to Firchow for identifying Huxley's possible sources, Firchow does not specifically discuss the echoes between this passage and the reports of Ruth Bunzel and Leslie White (see *End of Utopia* 75).

25. Lawrence's desire to differentiate himself from crass observers, evident in all the essays discussed in this article, is made perhaps most overt in his essay "Taos." While the writer helps a group of unidentified Indians to raise a May Pole, a participant-observer of sorts in this borrowed custom, a tourist takes a snapshot and is promptly told to forfeit her camera. Embarrassed by what he represents as the woman's vulgarity, Lawrence boasts, "I have long since passed the stage when I want to crowd up and stare at anybody's spectacle" (102)—a dubious moral given his undeniable position as an observer of native life.

## Works Cited

Benedict, Ruth. *Patterns of Culture*. 1934. Boston: Houghton, 1989.

Booth, Howard. "Lawrence in doubt: a theory of the 'other' and its collapse," in *Modernism and Empire*, eds. Howard J. Booth and Nigel Rigby. Manchester UP, 2000.

Bradshaw, David. Introduction to *Brave New World*. London: Harper, 1994.

Bunzel, Ruth. "An Analysis of the Katcina Cult of Zũni." 47th *Annual Report of the US American Ethnology Bureau to the Secretary of the Smithsonian Institute: 1929–1930*. Washington: United States Government Printing Office, 1932. 843–1087.

Buzard, James. *The Beaten Track: European Tourism, Literature, and the Ways to "Culture" 1800–1918*. Oxford: Oxford UP, 1993.

Bynner, Witter. "A City of Change." *Laughing Horse*: 11 September 1924: n.p.

Clifford, James. *Predicament of Culture: Twentieth-Century Ethnography, Literature, and Art*. Harvard UP, 1988.

———. *Routes: Travel and Translation in the Late Twentieth Century*. Harvard UP, 1997.

Debord, Guy. *Society of the Spectacle*. Detroit: Black and Red, 1983.

Dilworth, Leah. *Imagining Indians in the Southwest: Persistent Visions of a Primitive Past*. Washington: Smithsonian, 1996.

Dodge Luhan, Mabel. *Lorenzo in Taos*. London: Secker, 1933.

Evans-Pritchard, Deirdre. "The Portal Case: Authenticity, Tourism, Traditions, and the Law." *The Journal of American Folklore* 100.397 (1987): 287–96.

Firchow, Peter Edgerly. *The End of Utopia: a Study of Aldous Huxley's* Brave New World. London: Associated UP, 1984.

Greenhalgh, Paul. *Ephemeral Vistas: The Expositions Universelles, Great Exhibitions and World Fairs, 1851–1939*. Manchester UP, 1988.

Hartwell, Dickinson. "Let's Eat with the Harvey Boys." *Colliers* 9 April 1949: 30–34.

"Harveycar Motor Cruises: off the beaten path in the Great Southwest." *Harveycars: 1928*. New Mexico Guide Book Collection (AC 332, Box 1, Folder 13), Fray Angelico Chavez History Library, Santa Fe.

Hinsley, Curtis M. "The World as Marketplace: Commodification of the Exotic at the World's Columbian Exposition, Chicago, 1893." *Exhibiting Cultures: The Poetics and Politics of Museum Display*. Eds. Ivan Karp and Steven D. Lavine. Washington: Smithsonian, 1991.

Holmes, Charles M. "The Sinister Outer World: Aldous Huxley and International Politics." *Literary Companion to British Literature: Readings on Brave New World*. Ed. Katie de Koster. San Diego: Greenhaven, 1999.

Howard, Kathleen L. "'A most remarkable success': Herman Schweizer and the Fred Harvey Indian Department." Weigle and Babcock, 87–101.

Hughes, Langston. "When the Negro was in Vogue." 1940. *The Heath Anthology of American Literature*. Ed. Paul Smith, et.al. Lexington, Mass.: Heath, 1990.

Huxley, Aldous. *Beyond the Mexique Bay*. 1934. NY: Vintage, 1960.

———. "Interview with Aldous Huxley." *Writers at Work: The Paris Interviews, Second Series*. Ed. George Plimpton. NY: Penguin, 1977.

———. *Brave New World and Brave New World Revisited*. NY: Harper, 1965.

———. *Letters of Aldous Huxley*. Ed. Grover Smith. NY: Harper, 1969.

———. *Music at Night and Other Essays*. 1931. NY: Harper, 1970.

———. "To Julian Huxley." 13 July 1929. Letter 290 of *Letters*. 313–14.

———. "To Mrs. Kethevan Roberts." 28 November 1930. Letter 323 of *Letters*. 343–44.

———. "To Norman Douglas." 7 January 1930. Letter 300 of *Letters*. 326–27.

Jacobs, Margaret D. *Engendered Encounters: Feminism and Pueblo Cultures: 1879–1934.* Lincoln: U of Nebraska P, 1999.

Kasson, Joy S. *Buffalo Bill's Wild West: Celebrity, Memory, and Popular History.* New York: Hill, 2000.

Kinkead-Weekes, Mark. "Decolonizing imagination: Lawrence in the 1920s." *The Cambridge Companion to D. H. Lawrence.* Ed. Anne Fernihough. Cambridge UP, 2001.

Kropp, Phoebe. "'There is a little sermon in that': Constructing the Native Southwest at the San Diego Panama-California Exposition of 1915." Weigle and Babcock 36–46.

Lawrence, D. H. "Hopi Snake Dance." Lawrence, *Mornings.* 136–69.

———. "Indians and an Englishman." McDonald 91–99.

———. "Indians and Entertainment." Lawrence, *Mornings.* 100–08.

———. *Letters of D. H. Lawrence.* Ed. Aldous Huxley. London: Heinemann, 1932.

———. *Mornings in Mexico.* London: Secker, 1927.

———. "New Mexico." McDonald 141–45

———. "The Novel and Feelings." McDonald 756–58.

———. *St. Mawr.* 1924. NY: Random, 1953.

———. "To Catherine Carswell." 18 May 1924. *Letters.* 609–10.

———. "To J. M. Murry." 7 February 1924. *Letters.* 601–02.

MacCannell, Dean. *The Tourist: A New Theory of the Leisure Class.* NY: Schocken, 1976.

Malinowski, Bronislaw. *Argonauts of the Western Pacific.* 1922. Prospect Heights, IL: Waveland, 1984.

Marcus, George E. and Michael M. J. Fischer. *Anthropology as Cultural Critique: An Experimental Moment in the Human Sciences.* Chicago: U of Chicago P, 1986.

McClintock, Anne. *Imperial Leather: Race, Gender and Sexuality in the Colonial Contest.* New York: Routledge, 1995.

McDonald, Edward D., ed. *Phoenix: The Posthumous Papers of D. H. Lawrence.* NY: Viking, 1936.

Mead, Margaret. *Coming of Age in Samoa.* 1928. NY: Harper, 2001.

Meckier, Jerome. *Aldous Huxley: Satire and Structure.* London: Chatto, 1969.

Merrild, Knud. *With D. H. Lawrence in New Mexico: A Memoir of D. H. Lawrence.* New York: Barnes, 1965.

Michaels, Walter Benn. *Our America: Nativism, Modernism, and Pluralism.* Durham: Duke UP, 1995.

Picard, Michel. "Cultural Heritage and Tourist Capital: Cultural Tourism in Bali." *International Tourism: Identity and Change.* Eds. Marie-Francoise Lanfant, John B. Allcock and Edward M. Bruner. London: Sage, 1995.

Pratt, Mary Louise. "Fieldwork in Common Places." *Writing Culture: The Poetics and Politics of Ethnography.* Berkeley: U of California P, 1986.

Rojek, Chris and John Urry, eds. *Touring Cultures: Transformations of Travel and Theory.* London: Routledge, 1977.

Rossman, Charles. "D.H. Lawrence and New Mexico." *D. H. Lawrence: A Centenary Consideration.* Eds. Peter Balbert and Phillip L. Marcus. Ithaca: Cornell UP, 1985.

Rudnick, Lois Palken. *Utopian Vistas: The Mabel Dodge Luhan House and the American Counterculture.* Albuquerque: U of New Mexico P, 1996.

Rydell, Robert W. and Nancy Gwinn, eds. *Fair Representations: World's Fair and the Modern World.* Amsterdam: Vrije UP, 1994.

Rydell, Robert W. *All the World's a Fair: Visions of Empire at American International Expositions, 1876–1916.* Chicago: U of Chicago P, 1989.

Sapir, Edward. "Culture, Genuine and Spurious." *Culture, Language and Personality: Selected Essays*. Ed. David Mandelbaum. Berkeley: U of California P, 1970.

Sharpe, Jenny. *Allegories of Empire: The Figure of Woman in the Colonial Text*. Minneapolis: U of Minnesota P, 1993.

Smith, Sheri. *Reimagining Indians: Native Americans through Anglo Eyes, 1880–1940*. Oxford: Oxford UP, 2000.

Stocking, George. "The Ethnographic Sensibility of the 1920s and the Dualism of the Anthropological Tradition." *Romantic Motives: Essays on Anthropological Sensibility*. Ed. George W. Stocking, Jr. *History of Anthropology*, Vol. 6. Madison: U of Wisconsin P: 1989. 208–76.

Storch, Margaret. "'But Not the America of the Whites': Lawrence's Pursuit of the True Primitive." *The D. H. Lawrence Review* 25.1 (1993): 48–62.

Torgovnick, Mariana. *Gone Primitive: Savage Intellects, Modern Lives*. Chicago: U of Chicago P, 1990.

Turner, Louis and John Ash. *The Golden Hordes: International Tourism and The Pleasure Periphery*. New York: St Martin's, 1976.

Van den Berghe, Pierre L. and Charles F. Keyes. "Introduction: Tourism and Re-Created Ethnicity." *Annals of Tourism Research* 11.3 (1984): 343–52.

Weigle, Marta and Kyle Fiore, eds. *Santa Fe and Taos: The Writer's Era 1916–1941*. Santa Fe: Ancient City, 1994.

Weigle, Marta and Barbara Babcock, eds. *The Great Southwest of the Fred Harvey Company and the Santa Fe Railway*. Phoenix: The Heard Museum, 1996.

White, Leslie. "The Acoma Indians: Ceremonies and Ceremonialism." *47th Annual Report of the US American Ethnology Bureau to the Secretary of the Smithsonian Institute: 1929–1930*. Washington: United States Government Printing Office, 1932. 63–125.

Woidat, Caroline M. "The Indian-Detour in Willa Cather's Southwestern Novels." *Twentieth-Century Literature* 48 (2002): 22–49.

# Chronology

| | |
|---|---|
| 1894 | Born on July 26 in Godalming, Surrey, England, to Leonard and Julia Huxley. His grandfather, Thomas Henry Huxley, was an important scientist who developed Darwin's theories on evolution, as well as a thinker who first used the term "agnostic." He also has a distant maternal relation to famed English poet Matthew Arnold. |
| 1908 | Mother dies of cancer. |
| 1910 | Eye illness renders Huxley temporarily blind, foiling plans for medical school, for which he had been preparing. Later, although his vision recovers, Huxley does not gain sufficient sight to fight in World War I. |
| 1916 | Earns BA from Balliol College, Oxford University. While there, makes his first literary friendships, with Lytton Strachey, Bertrand Russell, and D. H. Lawrence. Also publishes first book, a collection of poems entitled *The Burning Wheel*. |
| 1917 | Hired as schoolmaster at Eton College in Eton, England. |
| 1919 | Becomes staff member of *Athanaeum* and *Westminster Gazette*. Marries Maria Nys. |
| 1920 | Huxley's only child, Matthew, is born. In the decade following, the Huxleys travel a great deal, living in London intermittently. They visit Italy, India, and America for more extended visits. |

| | |
|---|---|
| 1921 | *Crome Yellow* published in London; the following year it is published in New York. |
| 1923 | *Antic Hay* published. |
| 1924 | As a result of early novel successes, Huxley is able to leave his editorial jobs to pursue writing full time. |
| 1925 | *Those Barren Leaves* published. Huxleys travel around the world for most of the year. |
| 1928 | *Point Counter Point* published in the United States. |
| 1931 | During a fevered four months, writes *Brave New World*. |
| 1937 | Huxleys move permanently to the United States. By 1938, they are settled in Hollywood, and Huxley begins work as a screenwriter. |
| 1940 | Writes the screenplay for the film adaptation of Jane Austen's *Pride and Prejudice*. |
| 1946 | Following World War II, pens a new introduction to *Brave New World*, recanting his stated idea of the novel, that mass social sanity was impossible in the world of his time. Also publishes *The Perennial Philosophy*, his own collected writings (with others) further defining *social sanity* and musing on means of achieving it. |
| 1954 | Publishes *The Doors of Perception*, a nonfictional account of his experience with hallucinogens and other "mind-expanding" substances, including LSD. The account provided another facet to Huxley's fame, and the book was a counterculture sensation in the years that followed. Huxley's chemical experimentation lasts through the 1950s and into the 1960s. |
| 1955 | Maria Huxley dies. |
| 1956 | Publishes *Heaven and Hell*, another book chronicling drug experiences. Marries Laura Archera. |
| 1958 | Publishes *Brave New World Revisited*, essays that address problems only thematically present in the novel, as well as in a great deal of Huxley's other work. |
| 1959 | American Academy of Arts and Letters awards Huxley the Award of Merit for the Novel. |
| 1962 | Publishes *Island*, considered by some to be the utopian antidote to *Brave New World*'s dystopia. |
| 1963 | Dies November 22. Ashes are returned to England and laid to rest in Huxley's parents' grave. |

# *Contributors*

HAROLD BLOOM is Sterling Professor of the Humanities at Yale University. Educated at Cornell and Yale universities, he is the author of more than 30 books, including *Shelley's Mythmaking* (1959), *Blake's Apocalypse* (1963), *Yeats* (1970), *The Anxiety of Influence* (1973), *A Map of Misreading* (1975), *Kabbalah and Criticism* (1975), *Agon: Toward a Theory of Revisionism* (1982), *The American Religion* (1992), *The Western Canon* (1994), *Omens of Millennium: The Gnosis of Angels, Dreams, and Resurrection* (1996), *Shakespeare: The Invention of the Human* (1998), *How to Read and Why* (2000), *Genius: A Mosaic of One Hundred Exemplary Creative Minds* (2002), *Hamlet: Poem Unlimited* (2003), *Where Shall Wisdom Be Found?* (2004), *Jesus and Yahweh: The Names Divine* (2005), *Till I End My Song: A Gathering of Last Poems* (2010), and *The Anatomy of Influence: Literature as a Way of Life* (2011). In addition, he is the author of hundreds of articles, reviews, and editorial introductions. In 1999, Professor Bloom received the American Academy of Arts and Letters' Gold Medal for Criticism. He has also received the International Prize of Catalonia, the Alfonso Reyes Prize of Mexico, and the Hans Christian Andersen Bicentennial Prize of Denmark.

PHILIP THODY was a professor of French literature at the University of Leeds, where he also for many years was head of the department and served on every university committee. He authored thirty books and many articles.

PETER EDGERLY FIRCHOW was a professor at the University of Minnesota. He published *Reluctant Modernists: Aldous Huxley and Some Contemporaries, Modern Utopian Fictions from H.G. Wells to Iris Murdoch*, and many other writings.

HANS J. RINDISBACHER is a professor of German at Pomona College, where he also is chair of the department of German and Russian. He published *The Smell of Books: A Cultural-Historical Study of Olfactory Perception in Literature* as well as other works.

MARIO VARRICCHIO teaches at the Università di Padova.

BRAD BUCHANAN is an assistant professor who teaches modern British and American literature and creative writing at California State University, Sacramento, where he also is chair of the English department. His writing has appeared in many journals in the United States and Canada.

JEROME MECKIER has been a professor at the University of Kentucky. He is a coeditor of *Aldous Huxley Annual: A Journal of Twentieth-Century Thought and Beyond*, the official organ of the Aldous Huxley Society at the Centre for Aldous Huxley Studies in Münster, Germany. He is the author of *Hidden Rivalries in Victorian Fiction: Dickens, Realism, and Revaluation* and other titles.

LAURA FROST has been an assistant professor at Yale. She has authored *Sex Drives: Fantasies of Fascism in Literary Modernism*.

CAREY SNYDER is an associate professor at Ohio University. She also is director of studies of the Honors Tutorial College. She has published *British Fiction and Cross-Cultural Encounters: Ethnographic Modernism from Wells to Woolf*.

# Bibliography

Aplin, John. "Aldous Huxley's Music Criticism: Some Sources for the Fiction." *English Language Notes* 21 (September 1983): 58–62.

Atkins, John. *Aldous Huxley: A Literary Study*. New York, Orion Press, [1968, c1967].

Baker, Robert S. "Aldous Huxley: History and Science Between the Wars." *Clio* 25 (Spring 1996): 293–300.

———. Brave New World: *History, Science, and Dystopia*. Boston: Twayne Publishers, 1990.

Birnbaum, Milton. *Aldous Huxley's Quest for Values*. Knoxville: University of Tennessee Press, [1971].

Bloom, Harold., ed. *Aldous Huxley*. Philadelphia: Chelsea House, 2003.

———. *Aldous Huxley's* Brave New World. Bloom's Guides series. Philadelphia: Chelsea House, 2004.

Bowering, Peter. *Aldous Huxley: A Study of the Major Novels*. London: Athlone Press, 1968.

Brander, Laurence. *Aldous Huxley: A Critical Study*. Cranbury: Bucknell University Press, 1970.

Calder, Jenni. *Huxley and Orwell,* Brave New World *and* Nineteen Eighty-Four. London: E. Arnold, 1976.

Sisir, Chatterjee. *Aldous Huxley: A Study*. Calcutta: Mukhopadnyay [1966].

Cooksey, Thomas L. *Masterpieces of Philosophical Literature*. Westport, Conn.: Greenwood, 2006.

Dasgupta, Sanjukta. *The Novels of Huxley and Hemingway: A Study in Two Planes of Reality*. New Delhi: Prestige, 1996.

189

Deery, Jane. *Aldous Huxley and the Mysticism of Science*. New York: St. Martin's Press, 1996.

———. "*Brave New World*, the Sequel: Huxley and Contemporary Film." In *The Perennial Satirist: Essays in Honour of Bernfried Nugel*, edited by Peter E. Firchow and Hermann J. Real. Germany: Lit, 2005.

de Koster, Katie, ed. *Readings on* Brave New World. San Diego, Calif: Greenhaven, 1999.

Disch, Thomas M. "*Brave New World* Revisited Once Again." *On SF*. Ann Arbor: University of Michigan Press, 2005.

Ferns, C. S. *Aldous Huxley, Novelist*. London: Athlone Press; Atlantic Highlands, N.J.: Humanities Press, 1980.

Firchow, Peter Edgerly. *Aldous Huxley: A Satirist and Novelist*. Minneapolis: University of Minnesota Press, 1972.

———. *The End of Utopia: A Study of Aldous Huxley's* Brave New World. Lewisburg: Bucknell University Press, 1984.

Gandhi, Kishore. *Aldous Huxley: The Search for Perennial Religion*. New Delhi: Arnold-Heinemann, 1980.

Gottlieb, Erika. *Dystopian Fiction East and West*. Montreal: McGill-Queen's University Press, 2001.

Greenblatt, Stephen J. *Three Modern Satirists: Waugh, Orwell, and Huxley*. New Haven: Yale University Press, 1965.

Higdon, David Leon. "Aldous Huxley and the Hopi Snake Dance." *Aldous Huxley Annual: A Journal of Twentieth-Century Thought and Beyond* 8 (2008): 137–152.

———. "The Provocations of Lenina in Huxley's *Brave New World*." *International Fiction Review* 29, nos. 1–2 (2002): 78–83.

Holmes, Charles M. *Aldous Huxley and the Way to Reality*. Bloomington: Indiana University Press, 1970.

Horan, Thomas. "Revolutions from the Waist Downwards: Desire as Rebellion in Yevgeny Zamyatin's *We*, George Orwell's *1984*, and Aldous Huxley's *Brave New World*." *Extrapolation: A Journal of Science Fiction and Fantasy* 48, no. 2 (Summer 2007): 314–339.

Huxley, Julian. *Aldous Huxley: A Memorial Volume*. New York: Harper, 1965.

Huxley, Laura Archera. *This Timeless Moment: A Personal View of Aldous Huxley*. New York: Farrar, Straus, 1968.

Izzo, David Garrett, and Kim Kirkpatrick, eds. *Huxley's* Brave New World: *Essays*. Jefferson, N.C.: McFarland, 2008.

Krishnan, Bharathi. *Aspects of Structure, Technique and Quest in Aldous Huxley's Major Novels*. Uppsala: Universitetsbiblioteket; Stockholm: Distributor, Almqvist & Wiksell International, 1977.

Kuehn, Robert E., ed. *Aldous Huxley: A Collection of Critical Essays*. Englewood Cliffs, N.J.: Prentice-Hall, 1974.

Madden, Deanna. "Women in Dystopia: Misogyny in *Brave New World*, *1984*, and *A Clockwork Orange*." In *Misogyny in Literature: An Essay Collection*, edited by Katherine Anne Ackley, 289–313. New York: Garland, 1992.

March, Cristie L. "A Dystopic View of Gender in Aldous Huxley's *Brave New World* (1932)." In *Women in Literature: Reading through the Lens of Gender*, edited by Jerilyn Fisher and Ellen S. Silber, 53–55. Westport, Conn.: Greenwood, 2003.

Meckier, Jerome. *Aldous Huxley: Satire and Structure*. New York: Barnes & Noble, 1969.

Meckier, Jerome, ed. *Critical Essays on Aldous Huxley*. Boston: G. K. Hall, 1996.

McQuillan, Gene. "The Politics of Allusion: *Brave New World* and the Debates about Biotechnologies." *Studies in the Humanities* 33, no. 1 (June 2006): 79–100.

Newman, Wayne. "Dystopian Literature: Four Works Considered." *Journal of Kyoritsu Women's Junior College* 34 (February 1991): 57–65.

Nugel, Bernfried. *Now More than Ever: Proceedings of the Aldous Huxley Centenary Symposium, Münster, 1994*. New York: P. Lang, 1996.

Nugel, Bernfried, Uwe Rasch, and Gerhard Wagner, eds. *Aldous Huxley, Man of Letters: Thinker, Critic and Artist: Proceedings of the Third International Aldous Huxley Symposium, Riga 2004*. Berlin, Germany: Lit, 2007.

Ramamurty, K. Bhaskara. *Aldous Huxley: A Study of His Novels*. New York: Asia Pub. House, 1974.

Scales, Derek P. *Aldous Huxley and French Literature*. Sydney: Sydney University Press for Australian Humanities Research Council, [1969].

Thiel, Berthold. *Aldous Huxley's* Brave New World. Amsterdam: B.R. Grüner, 1980.

Vohra, S. K. *Negative Utopian Fiction: Aldous Huxley and George Orwell, Commitment and Fabulation*. Meerut: Shalabh Prakashan, 1987.

Watts, Harold H. *Aldous Huxley*. New York, Twayne Publishers, [1969].

Woodcock, George. *Dawn and the Darkest Hour: A Study of Aldous Huxley*. New York: Viking, 1972.

# Acknowledgments

Philip Thody, *"Brave New World."* From *Aldous Huxley: A Biographical Introduction*. Published by Studio Vista. Copyright © Philip Thody 1973.

Peter Edgerly Firchow, "From Savages to Men Like Gods." From *The End of Utopia: A Study of Aldous Huxley's Brave New World*. Published by Bucknell University Press. Copyright © 1984 by Associated University Presses.

Hans J. Rindisbacher, "Sweet Scents and Stench: Traces of Post/Modernism in Aldous Huxley's *Brave New World.*" From *Now More Than Ever: Proceedings of the Aldous Huxley Centenary Symposium*, edited by Bernfried Nugel. Copyright © 1995 Peter Lang GmbH.

Mario Varricchio, "Power of Images/Images of Power in *Brave New World* and *Nineteen Eighty-Four.*" From *Utopian Studies* 10, no. 1 (1999): 98–114. Copyright © 1999 Society for Utopian Studies.

Brad Buchanan, "Oedipus in Dystopia: Freud and Lawrence in Aldous Huxley's *Brave New World.*" From *Journal of Modern Literature* 25, nos. 3–4 (Summer 2002): 75–89. Copyright © 2002 Indiana University Press.

Jerome Mechier, "Aldous Huxley's Americanization of the *Brave New World* Typescript." From *Twentieth Century Literature* 48, no. 4 (Winter 2002): 427-60. Copyright © 2002 Hofstra University.

Laura Frost, "Huxley's Feelies: The Cinema of Sensation in *Brave New World*." From *Twentieth Century Literature* 52, no. 4 (Winter 2006): 443-73. Copyright © 2006 Hofstra University.

Carey Snyder. "'When the Indian Was in Vogue': D. H. Lawrence, Aldous Huxley, and Ethnological Tourism in the Southwest." From *Modern Fiction Studies* 53, no. 4 (Winter 2007): 662–96. Published by the Department of English, Purdue University, and the Purdue Research Foundation. Copyright © 2007 by the Johns Hopkins University Press.

Every effort has been made to contact the owners of copyrighted material and secure copyright permission. Articles appearing in this volume generally appear much as they did in their original publication with few or no editorial changes. In some cases, foreign language text has been removed from the original essay. Those interested in locating the original source will find the information cited above.

# Index

Characters in literary works are indexed by first name (if any), followed by the name of the work in parentheses

administrators (*Brave New World*), 6, 15

Adorno, Theodor W., 130
  *Dialectic of Enlightenment*, 40

*After Many a Summer Dies the Swan*, 144

Alexandrov, G.V., 133

Altman, Rick, 137

*Antic Hay*, 2
  Shearwater in, 8

*Anticipations* (Wells), 99

*Ape and Essence*, 144
  humankind in, 37–38
  use of smells in, 47

Armytage, W.H.G.
  *Yesterday's Tomorrows*, 13

Arnheim, Rudolf
  "A New Laocoön: Artistic Composites and the Talking Film," 132–133

Arnold, Matthew, 8, 12–13

Arnold, Thomas, 12–13

Astle, Richard
  "Dracula as Totemic Monster: Lacan, Freud, Oedipus and History," 81

Barry, Iris, 127
  *Let's Go to the Pictures*, 126

Baudelaire, Charles, 40, 42

Benedict, Ruth
  *Patterns of Culture*, 153, 156

Benjamin, Walter, 126

Berdyaev, Nikolai
  *The End of Our Time*, 24

Berlin, Isaiah
  *Two Concepts of Liberty*, 14

Bernard Marx (*Brave New World*), 31, 102, 114
  difference, 79, 82
  exile, 79, 96, 103, 106, 113
  fury, 97
  intellectual, 77
  and John, 13, 44, 55, 77, 101, 105, 110–111, 113, 172
  and Lenina, 11, 13, 44, 63, 85, 87, 96–97, 100, 106–108, 111, 167, 174
  loneliness, 12
  physical defect, 12
  and the reservation, 11, 77, 87, 108–109
  sex life, 96

Bernstein, Leonard, 145

Betts, Ernest, 132
  "Ordeal by 'Talkie,'" 125
  "Why 'Talkies' Are Unsound," 125

*Beyond the Mexique Bay*, 28, 168,
    171, 173
Bloom, Harold
    introduction, 1–2
Bow, Clara, 136
*Brothers Karamazov, The*
    (Dostoevsky), 7
Browning, Robert
    *Pippa Passes*, 96
Buchanan, Brad, 187
    on the influences on *Brave New
        World*, 73–93
Bunzel, Ruth, 169
Burnham, James
    *The Managerial Revolution*, 54
Bynner, Witter, 165

*Candide* (Voltaire), 18
Carlyle, Thomas, 28
Chaplin, Charlie, 126–127, 133, 142,
    144–145
*Chemins de la Liberté, Les* (Sarte), 7
Chinitz, David, 130
Churchill, Winston, 22
"Cinema, The" (Woolf), 127
*Civilization and Its Discontents*
    (Freud), 79, 81
Clifford, James, 154
*Coming of Age in Samoa* (Mead), 171,
    173
Corbin, Alain
    *The Foul and the Fragrant*, 40
Crary, Jonathan, 126
Crick, Bernard, 54
*Crome Yellow*, 27
    Mr. Scogan in, 5–6, 24
    personal dilemma in, 7
Cushing, Frank
    *Zuñi Folk Tales*, 30
Cyprus Experiment in *Brave New
    World*, 20

*Dark God* (Lawrence), 30, 166
Darwin, Charles, 18, 25
*Das Parfum* (Süskind), 37

*Day After Tomorrow, The* (Gibbs),
    26
DeMille, Cecil B., 136, 142
"Desert, The" (essay)
    solitude in, 3
*Devils of Loudun, The*, 5
*Dialectic of Enlightenment* (Adorno
    and Horkheimer), 40
Dickinson, Lowes, 30
Diderot, Denis, 13
Disraeli, Benjamin, 17
Donaldson, Leonard, 142
Dostoevsky, Fyodor
    *The Brothers Karamazov*, 7
*Do What You Will*, 84
"Dracula as Totemic Monster:
    Lacan, Freud, Oedipus and
    History" (Astle), 81
Dunaway, David King, 141

Eisenstein, Sergei, 133
Eliot, T.S., 10, 18, 131
    *The Waste Land*, 2
*End of Our Time, The* (Berdyaev),
    24
*Ends and Means*, 10
Evans-Pritchard, Deidre, 176
*Eyeless in Gaza*, 10, 30
    Hollywood in, 129

Fanny Crowne (*Brave New World*),
    54–55, 96–97
*Farcial History of Richard Greenow,
    The*
    free association in, 9
Fay, Eliot, 32
feelies episode in *Brave New World*
    John's distaste for, 54, 56–57, 59,
        62–63, 78, 80, 97, 129–135,
        137–138, 140, 145–146, 174
*Fiction and the Reading Public*
    (Leavis), 136
Firchow, Peter Edgerly, 54, 80, 187
    on Huxley's attack on Wells in
        *Brave New World*, 17–35

*First and Last Freedom, The*
    (Krishnamurti), 6
*First Men in the Moon, The* (Wells),
    23
Flaherty, Robert, 135
"Formulations Regarding the Two
    Principles in Mental Functioning"
    (Freud), 80
*Foul and the Fragrant, The* (Corbin),
    40
Frazer, James
    *Sacrificial God*, 32
Fred Harvey Company, 155–156,
    158–160, 165
French symbolism, 42
Freud, Sigmund, 9–11
    *Civilization and Its Discontents*,
        79, 81
    Eros and Thanatos concept,
        39–40, 46
    "Formulations Regarding the
        Two Principles in Mental
        Functioning," 80
    *Group Psychology and the Analysis
        of the Ego*, 81
    human nature, 73, 83
    influence on *Brave New World*,
        73–76, 82
    Oedipus complex, 74–78, 80–81,
        84, 88
    pleasure principle, 83
    sex theories, 73–75, 78, 80, 85,
        88
    *Totem and Taboo*, 75
Frost, Laura, 188
    on the cinema of sensation in
        *Brave New World*, 125–152
*Future as Nightmare, The* (Hillegas),
    18

Gaines, Jane, 139
Gibbs, Philip
    *The Day After Tomorrow*, 26
Girard, René
    *Violence and the Sacred*, 78

Glyn, Elinor, 137, 140, 145
    *It*, 136
Graves, Robert, 136
*Grey Eminence*, 5
Grishkin, Eliot, 134
*Group Psychology and the Analysis of
    the Ego* (Freud), 81
Gunning, Tom, 126, 138

Haeberlin, H.K., 31
Haldane, Charlotte
    *Nature*, 7–8
Haldane, J.B.S., 18, 23
*Hamlet* (Shakespeare), 6, 76–77
Hansen, Miriam, 126, 139
Heard, Gerald, 24, 85
Hearst, William Randolph, 157
*Heaven and Hell*, 2
Hegel, Georg Wilhelm Friedrich,
    40, 49
Helmholtz Watson (*Brave New
    World*), 108
    artistic difficulties, 81, 112
    difference, 79, 81
    exile, 79, 87, 103, 113
    lectures, 12
    removal from society, 14
Henderson, Alice Corbin, 165
Henry Ford in the *Brave New World*,
    75, 98, 108
    factories, 101
    guidelines, 104
    insults to, 95–96, 99–100, 102,
        113–115, 142
Henry Foster (*Brave New World*), 1,
    7, 54, 106, 131
    and Bernard, 97
Hillegas, Mark, 23
    *The Future as Nightmare*, 18
Hinsley, Curtis, 160
Hodge, Alan, 136
Holmes, Charles, 73
"Hopi Snake Dance, The"
    (Lawrence), 154, 157–158, 160–
    161, 169

Horkheimer, Max
    *Dialectic of Enlightenment*, 40
Hughes, Langston, 154
human fertility, 3
"Human Potentialities" (essay), 9
Huxley, Julian, 6, 14, 33, 141
    *Memories*, 27
Huxley, Thomas Henry, 3, 11–12,
    14, 18, 88
Huysmans, J.K., 40, 42
    *À Rebours*, 132

"If My Library Burned Tonight"
    (essay), 26
images of power
    in *Brave New World*, 53–72
    in *Nineteen Eighty-Four*, 53–72
"Indians and an Englishman"
    (Lawrence), 168
*Invisible Man, The* (Wells), 19
*Island* (Huxley)
    humankind in, 37–38
    smells in, 47–48
*Island of Dr. Moreau, The* (Wells), 19
*It* (Glyn), 136

*Jazz Singer, The* (film), 125–126,
    129, 139, 143
*Jesting Pilate*
    monogamy in, 11
John "Savage" (*Brave New World*),
    28, 30
    and authority, 22–23
    behavior, 13, 88
    choices, 1–2
    and the cinema, 55–58, 63, 129–
        131, 134–135, 137–138, 140,
        174
    emotions, 21
    and Lenina, 43–46, 55, 57,
        77–78, 80, 106–107, 111, 115,
        131, 134, 138, 170
    libido, 77
    memories, 13, 77, 79, 105–106,
        108–109, 111

morality, 79, 85
Oedipus complex, 76–78, 81
passion for Shakespeare, 2, 6, 13,
    45–46, 57, 76, 78, 81, 87, 137–
    138, 140, 145
personality, 23
refuge, 13
rescue, 13, 44
rights, 7
scent, 44
search for purity, 14
self-importance, 77
solitary condition, 22
soma rations, 43, 86, 113–115
spirit of, 31
suicide, 1–2, 80, 85, 97–98, 103,
    109, 112, 114–115, 135
torment, 102, 104, 142, 169
tours, 101, 108–111, 155, 167,
    170, 172–173, 175
victim, 2
vision of reality, 81, 86
whipping, 1, 13–14, 33, 57, 97, 170
"Just Back from the Snake-Dance—
    Tired Out" (Lawrence), 153

Kant, Immanuel, 40
Kemal, Mustafa, 98
Keynes, John Maynard, 25
*King Lear* (Shakespeare), 57
Knickerbocker, Kenneth L., 96
Kracauer, Siegfried, 126–127
Krishnamurti, Jiddu
    *The First and Last Freedom*, 6

*Last Exit to Brooklyn* (Selby), 7
Lawrence, D.H.
    *Dark God*, 30, 166
    death, 84
    "The Hopi Snake Dance," 154,
        157–158, 160–161, 169
    "Indians and an Englishman," 168
    influence of, 24–33, 74, 83–88,
        103–105, 111, 113, 115, 137,
        155–156

"Just Back from the Snake-Dance—Tired Out," 153
letters of, 17, 83–85, 154, 157
*Mornings in Mexico*, 105, 115
"New Mexico," 166
"The Novel and Feelings," 168
*Pansies*, 26
*The Plumed Serpent*, 98, 103, 105, 115
*The Rainbow*, 136
*Sons and Lovers*, 84–85
Southwest writings, 154, 157–158, 160–170, 172–176
*St. Mawr*, 154, 157, 161–163
Leavis, F.R.
*Scrutiny*, 7–9
Leavis, Q.D., 127
*Fiction and the Reading Public*, 136
Leibniz, Gottfried, 18
Lenina Crowne (*Brave New World*), 54, 144
and Bernard, 11, 13, 44, 63, 85, 87, 96–97, 100, 106–108, 111, 167, 174
charms, 14, 97, 130
dance, 33
death, 174
distaste, 76
and John, 13, 43–46, 55, 57, 78, 80, 106–107, 111, 115, 131–132, 138, 140, 145, 170
perfume, 45
and the reservation, 11, 32, 47, 87, 167, 169
soma pills, 44
*Sons and Lovers*, 84
*Let's Go to the Pictures* (Barry), 126
Linda (*Brave New World*), 102, 107
chemicals, 12–13
death, 44, 78, 86, 112–114
excursion, 11
and Popé, 77, 109
scent, 47
and soma, 63, 86

son, 13, 44, 76–77, 85, 87, 105–106, 109, 172
Livingston, Paul, 176
Livingston, Sarah, 176
Loos, Anita, 144
Low, Rachel, 141
Luhan, Mabel Dodge, 164–165

MacCannell, Dean, 158, 176
Macpherson, Kenneth, 139
Malinowski, Bronislaw, 157, 161
*Sexual Life of Savages*, 171
*Managerial Revolution, The* (Burnham), 54
Mann, Klaus, 19
Mann, Thomas, 42
Marcuse, Herbert, 5
Mead, Margaret
*Coming of Age in Samoa*, 171, 173
Meckier, Jerome, 145, 155, 187–188
on the Americanization of *Brave New World*, 95–123
*Memories* (Huxley, J.), 27
*Men Like Gods* (Wells), 18–21, 26, 100, 103, 108–111, 116
Rupert Catskill in, 22
Merrild, Knud
*A Poet and Two Painters*, 28
Micheaux, Oscar, 140
*Modern Utopia, A* (Wells), 19–21, 23, 98–99, 101
Mond, Alfred, 25–28, 98, 100, 102, 104, 109
*Mornings in Mexico* (Lawrence), 105, 115
Morrell, Ottoline, 85
Moses, L.G., 176
"Movies Commit Suicide, The" (Seldes), 126
Murry, John Middleton, 88
*Son of Woman*, 84–85
*Music at Night*, 24, 30, 84
Mustapha Mond (*Brave New World*), 2, 6, 46, 98
and the cinema, 57

on civilization, 37, 86, 95, 96,
    100, 103, 171–172
consciousness, 79
disciple, 102
experiment, 33
and happiness, 80, 138
John's confrontation with, 111,
    113–115, 130, 137
and soma, 32, 129
speeches, 96–97, 115

*Nature* (Haldane), 7–8
Needham, Joseph, 7, 9
"New Laocoön: Artistic Composites
    and the Talking Film, A"
    (Arnheim), 132–133
"New Mexico" (Lawrence), 166
*Nineteen Eighty-Four* (Orwell)
    Big Brother in, 60, 64, 69, 71
    dreams in, 67–68
    Emmanuel Goldstein in, 60–61
    images of power in, 53–72
    Julia in, 65, 68, 70
    O'Brien in, 61–62, 64–67, 70
    Oceania in, 59–61, 67–71
    propaganda in, 58
    telescreen, 54, 58, 60, 62, 64, 68
    totalitarianism in,61
    Winston in, 59, 61–62, 64–70
Nordau, Max, 132
North, Michael, 130
"Novel and Feelings, The"
    (Lawrence), 168

"Ordeal by 'Talkie'" (Betts), 125
Orwell, George
    *Nineteen Eighty-Four*, 53–72
*Othello* (Shakespeare), 6, 46, 78, 80,
    137–138, 140, 145
*Outline of History* (Wells), 25–26
"Outlook for American Culture:
    Some Reflections in a Machine
    Age, The" (essay), 128

*Pansies* (Lawrence), 26

Parsons, Elsie Clewes, 31
*Patterns of Culture* (Benedict), 153,
    156
*Perennial Philosophy, The*, 1–2
    society in, 14–15
Picard, Michel, 176
*Pippa Passes* (Browning), 96
Plank, William, 59
"Pleasures" (essay), 128–129, 135,
    138
*Plumed Serpent, The* (Lawrence), 98,
    103, 105, 115
*Poet and Two Painters, A* (Merrild),
    28
*Point Counter Point*, 2, 26, 84
    happiness in, 7
    Lord Edward Tantamount in, 3
    Mark Rampion in, 24, 102
    Philip Quarles in, 12, 86
    society in, 3–4, 8
Popé (*Brave New World*), 109
    John's hatred for, 76–78, 85
    and Linda, 77–78
*Proper Studies*, 20, 27, 83–84
Pudovkin, W.I., 133

Rabinovitch, Reuben, 142–143
*Rainbow, The* (Lawrence), 136
*Rebours, À* (Huysman), 132
religious ceremonies in *Brave New
    World*, 81–82, 96
"Revolutions" (essay), 24
Richards, Audrey, 83
Rilke, Rainer Maria, 42
Rindisbacher, Hans J., 187
    on sense of smell in *Brave New
    World*, 37–51
Roberts, Kethevan, 111
Rolland, Romain, 82
Rousseau, Jean-Jacques, 29
Ruskin, John, 28
Russell, Bertrand, 23, 30, 85
    *The Scientific Outlook*, 6

*Sacrificial God* (Frazer), 32

Sapir, Edward, 162, 173
Sartre, Jean-Paul
    Les Chemins de la Liberté, 7
Schiff, Sidney, 112
science in Brave New World, 4, 21,
    27
    applied, 5, 9
    destruction of, 11
    inquiry, 7–8, 11
    intolerance, 8
    knowledge of, 6, 87–88
Scientific Outlook, The (Russell), 6
Scrutiny (Leavis), 7–9
Selby, Hubert Jr.
    Last Exit to Brooklyn, 7
Seldes, Gilbert
    "The Movies Commit Suicide,"
    126
sense of smell
    in Brave New World, 37–51
sexuality in Brave New World, 9, 14,
    73
    aromas, 41
    contraceptives, 10
    desires, 54–55
    eroticism, 42
    incestuous, 76–78, 88
    meaning, 32
    perversion, 75, 80
    and pleasure, 23
    promiscuity, 27, 30, 45, 79, 83,
        85, 87, 96, 134
    regulation, 39
Sexual Life of Savages (Malinowski),
    171
Shakespeare, William
    in Brave New World, 2, 6, 13,
        45–46, 57, 78, 81, 87, 137–
        138, 145
    Hamlet, 6, 76–77
    King Lear, 57
    Othello, 6, 46, 78, 80, 137–138,
        140, 145
    The Tempest, 108, 145
Sharpe, Jenny, 174

Shaw, George Bernard, 126, 141–143
"Silence Is Golden" (essay), 125–126,
    128, 139
Singer, Ben, 126
Smith, Elliot, 30
Smith, Grover, 111
Smith, Percy, 141
snake dance in Brave New World,
    31–32
Snyder, Carey
    on tourism in Brave New World,
    153–183
society in Brave New World
    education, 21
    freedom and equality in, 5, 11,
        20
    future, 37, 53, 64, 76, 129
    inhuman situations in, 5, 14, 28,
        38
    knowledge, 11
    members, 21
    organized, 6, 43
    and politics, 15, 46–47, 53,
        70–71, 88
    rational, 95
    and science, 5, 8
    solidarity, 76
    standardized, 53–54, 57, 79, 88,
        96
    transformation in, 3–4
Son of Woman (Murry), 84–85
Sons and Lovers (Lawrence), 84–85
Sperber, Dan, 38–39
Stamp, Shelley, 140
St. Mawr (Lawrence), 154, 157, 161–
    163
Story of Days to Come, A (Wells), 19
Strousse, Flora, 108
Süskind, Patrick
    Das Parfum, 37
Swift, Jonathan
    Gulliver's Travels, 24

Tempest, The (Shakespeare), 108, 145
Thody, Philip, 3–16, 187

on *Brave New World*, 3–16,
        73–74, 80
*Those Barren Leaves*, 10
    Francis Chellifer in, 5, 8
    nature in, 11
    society in, 5
*Three Weeks in a Helicopter*
    power of cinema in, 131–132,
        134–140, 144
*Time Machine, The* (Wells), 19
*Tono-Bungay* (Wells), 25–26
*Totem and Taboo* (Freud), 75
*Tractatus Logico-Philosophicus*
    (Wittgenstein), 8
"Tragedy and the Whole Truth"
    (essay), 80–81
*Two Concepts of Liberty* (Berlin), 14

Varricchio, Mario, 187
    on images of power in *Brave New
        World* and *Nineteen Eighty-
        Four*, 53–72
Verne, Jules, 18
*Violence and the Sacred* (Girard), 78
Voltaire, 13
    *Candide*, 18

Walkowitz, Judith, 140
*Waste Land, The* (Eliot), 2
water imagery in *Brave New World*, 82
Waters, John, 146
Waugh, Evelyn, 144
*We* (Zamyatin), 103, 111, 115
Wells, H.G.
    *Anticipations*, 99
    in *Brave New World*, 19–20, 27
    *The First Men in the Moon*, 23

future, 17–20, 95, 101–102, 104,
        109, 112, 115
    Huxley's attack on, 17–35
    *The Invisible Man*, 19
    *The Island of Dr. Moreau*, 19
    *Men Like Gods*, 18–22, 26, 100,
        103, 108–111, 116
    *A Modern Utopia*, 19–21, 23,
        98–99, 101
    *Outline of History*, 25–26
    *A Story of Days to Come*, 19
    *The Time Machine*, 19
    *Tono-Bungay*, 25–26
    *When the Sleeper Wakes*, 19, 22–23
    *William Clissold*, 25–26
West, Rebecca, 136
*When the Sleeper Wakes* (Wells), 19,
        22–23
"Where Are the Movies Moving?"
    (essay), 127, 133
Whistler, James McNeill, 133
White, Leslie, 169
"Why 'Talkies' Are Unsound"
    (Betts), 125
Wilde, Oscar, 40, 42
*William Clissold* (Wells), 25–26
Wittgenstein, Ludwig
    *Tractatus Logico-Philosophicus*, 8
Woolf, Virginia
    "The Cinema," 127
World War II, 1, 53–54

*Yesterday's Tomorrows* (Armytage), 13

Zamyatin, Yevgeny
    *We*, 103, 111, 115
Zola, Émile, 40
*Zuñi Folk Tales* (Cushing), 30